MNEMONIC ECOLOGIES

MNEMONIC ECOLOGIES

Memory and Nature Conservation along the Former Iron Curtain

SONJA K. PIECK

The MIT Press
Cambridge, Massachusetts
London, England

The MIT Press would like to thank the anonymous peer reviewers who provided comments on drafts of this book. The generous work of academic experts is essential for establishing the authority and quality of our publications. We acknowledge with gratitude the contributions of these otherwise uncredited readers.

This book was set in Adobe Garamond and Berthold Akzidenz Grotesk by Jen Jackowitz. Printed and bound in the United States of America.

Library of Congress Cataloging-in-Publication Data

Names: Pieck, Sonja K., author.
Title: Mnemonic ecologies : memory and nature conservation along the former
   Iron Curtain / Sonja K. Pieck.
Description: Cambridge, Massachusetts : The MIT Press, [2023] | Includes
   bibliographical references and index.
Identifiers: LCCN 2022038607 (print) | LCCN 2022038608 (ebook) | ISBN
   9780262546164 (paperback) | ISBN 9780262375252 (epub) | ISBN
   9780262375245 (pdf)
Subjects: LCSH: Nature conservation—Germany—History—20th century. |
   Environmental protection—Germany—History—20th century. | Greenbelts—
   Germany—History—20th century.
Classification: LCC QH77.G3 P49 2023 (print) | LCC QH77.G3 (ebook) |
   DDC 333.720943—dc23/eng/20230405
LC record available at https://lccn.loc.gov/2022038607
LC ebook record available at https://lccn.loc.gov/2022038608

10 9 8 7 6 5 4 3 2 1

For Sophia Irene

You have to have such faith
to be able to sit in the shade of a tree
that has not yet been born.

—Ricardo Esquivia Ballestas, SembrandoPaz.org

CONTENTS

INTRODUCTION   *1*

1 ESTABLISHING MNEMONIC ECOLOGIES   *15*

2 DEATH STRIP, LIFELINE, MEMORIAL: THE MAKING OF THE
   GREEN BELT   *35*

3 ROMANCING HEIMAT: THE ROOTS OF GREEN BELT
   CONSERVATION   *67*

4 MNEMONIC ECOLOGIES IN THE MATERIAL AND STORIED
   BORDERLANDS   *85*

5 MNEMONIC ECOLOGIES IN THE MANAGED AND WILD
   BORDERLANDS   *121*

6 GLOBAL MNEMONIC ECOLOGIES   *153*

CONCLUSION   *183*

Acknowledgments   *193*
Notes   *197*
Bibliography   *235*
Index   *265*

INTRODUCTION

Grief sits in places. This much was clear as I stood in the former inter-German borderlands on a scorching hot day in July 2018. It was my fifth trip here as I sought to better understand a colossal conservation project that was transforming the former border between East and West Germany. Here the Allies had split the country in half after the Second World War. This line through the middle of Germany became ground zero of the Cold War, a thin ribbon that divided two economic and political systems from each other. With Soviet help, socialist East Germany—also known as the German Democratic Republic (GDR)—built up the most militarized border infrastructure the world had seen at the time. Dozens of East German villages were razed to make way for the border's construction; locals lost their land, property, communities, and in many cases, family members or even their own lives. Much of this restricted zone itself was deforested, flattened, and mowed regularly to improve border surveillance. At the same time as this militarization depopulated central Germany, the vacuum it left behind attracted hundreds of endangered plant and animal species that found refuge from increased agricultural and urban development elsewhere. Over four decades, these changes in the landscape along with its floral and faunal inhabitants created new, emergent ecologies in the borderlands.[1] Since the end of the Cold War in 1989 and dissolution of the inter-German border, West and East German conservationists have been transforming this space into a protected area called the "Green Belt," or Grünes Band in German.

Today, the Green Belt covers an area of 17,712 hectares, and consists of 146 different types of habitats, many endangered, that offer a home to over 1,200 plant and animal species on Germany's Red List.[2]

Conservation, then, is occurring on scarred and troubled lands. The place where I stood that summer was a long band—about 30 meters wide—of relatively open, shrubby space, framed to the left and right by forest. This area in southern Thuringia, within sight of the Bavarian border (figure 0.1), would have been strictly off-limits to any East or West German civilian during the Cold War.

There would have been guard towers and floodlights, and maybe attack dogs and spring guns, and the ground underneath me would have been mined too. That day, there was hardly any trace left of those lethal structures, just some concrete slabs of the old patrol road that heavily armed East German border guards would have driven along during their rounds. The antivehicular ditch was still there, but overgrown as it was, it remained more suggestion than fact. The same went for an old GDR border marker, once painted in the German black, red, and gold, now broken into several pieces with its cracked concrete and rebar claimed by nettles and brambles. Other than that, it was me, the cicadas, the birds, the shrubs, the trees, the warm breeze, and the memory of the dead.

As I stood in the heat, squinting in the sunlight and wiping my sweaty palms on my shorts, my eye caught sight of a group of wooden crosses under a tree nearby. I walked over slowly, conscious of how loudly my steps sounded, and realized that this was an ad hoc memorial site; I had seen several on my trips over the years. There were three crosses, huddled in the shade of a lone young oak, and the group was framed to the left and right by two markers (figure 0.2). On the left, a carved wooden sign, put up in 2015, said, "Nie vergessen! Die Nacht der Todesschüsse" (Never forget! The night of the fatal shots). It was here, on December 19, 1970, that a GDR soldier shot two of his comrades in the back as he fled across the frozen minefield to West Germany. The sign commemorating this had been put up by other former GDR soldiers who, as the sentence carved into the wooden board indicated, "had been there" that night. To the right of the crosses, somebody—in a ritual of mourning—had put up another sign, this one a letter-sized sheet

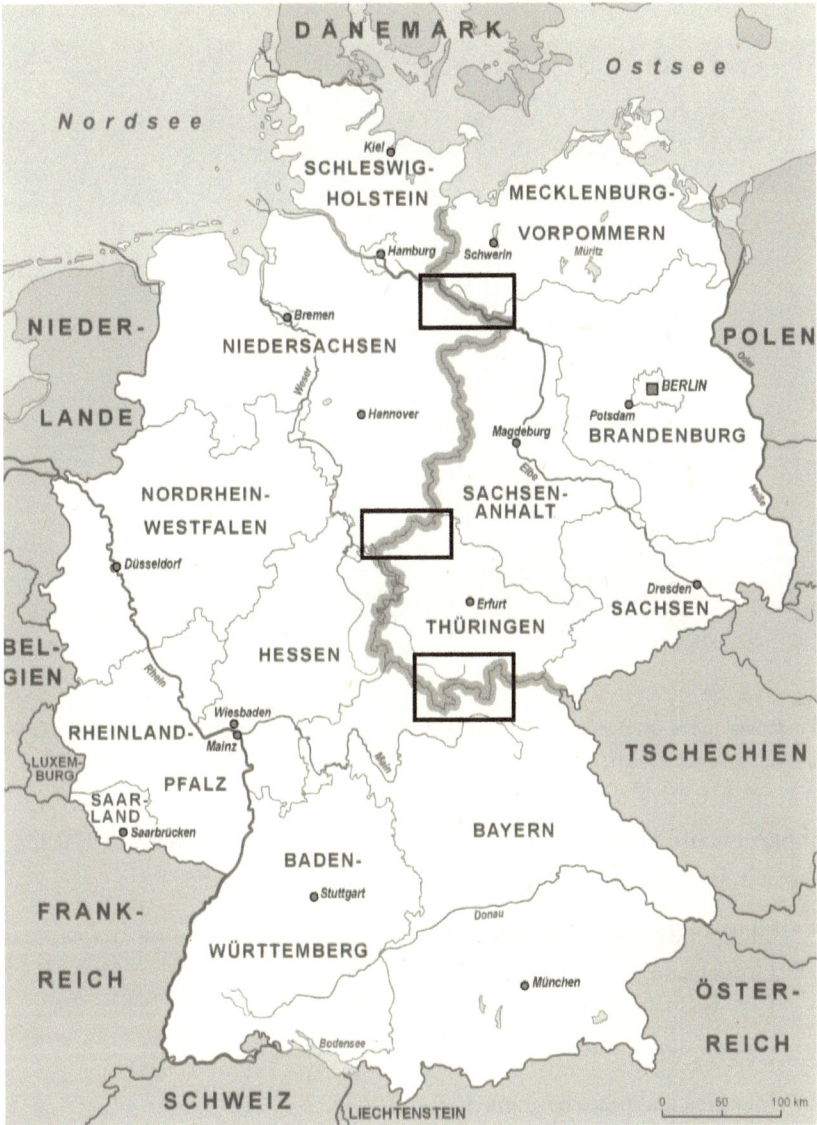

Figure 0.1
The general location of the Green Belt along the former border between West and East Germany. The highlighted regions are discussed in greater detail in the book: the Elbe River in the north, the Eichsfeld in the center, and the border between northern Bavaria and Thuringia in the south. *Author*: NordNordWest, September 15, 2014, with modifications by Lencer. *Source*: Wikimedia Commons, https://commons.wikimedia.org/wiki/User:NordNordWest/Gallery /Location_maps#/media/File:Germany_adm_location_map.svg, Creative Commons License CC-BY-SA 3.0. Reprinted by permission, with author's edits.

Figure 0.2
A memorial to the dead in the landscape of the former border. In the background is a strip of open land, punctuated by trees, and behind that, the edge of the forest. *Source*: Sonja Pieck.

of paper behind glass. At the bottom was a photo of the border in 1970 and above it, by old-fashioned typewriter, the following lines:

> Glück und Frieden sei beschieden
> Deutschland, unserm Vaterland!
> Laßt das Licht des Friedens scheinen
> Daß nie eine Mutter mehr ihren Sohn beweint!

> May bliss and peace be granted
> To Germany, our fatherland!
> Let the light of peace shine
> So that no mother ever again weeps for her son!

I was struck by the uneasy juxtaposition of hope for the future and the weight of the past, and pondered the invocation of fatherland and motherhood in the name of peace. Underneath the framed text and photo, there was a curious and symbolically intricate arrangement: nailed to the wooden post was a piece of the former border fence—unmistakable with its distinctive, diamond-shaped metal grille. Fastened to that were several loops of barbed wire, arranged to look like a wreath. And indeed, someone had carefully attached plastic roses to it with fabric ribbons, both now bleached by sunlight. It was unclear to me whether a single person or group had created this memorial, or whether it had gradually developed from successive but different acts and with different intentions.

Beyond my personal emotional response to this place, the memorial is noteworthy for another reason: this small spot is an example of a vernacular form of commemoration. It is in the many small places where tragedy occurred, where lives were lost or forever altered, that much of the borderlands' inherent complexity is found. These three crosses are not the product of a governmental decision; there was no pomp and circumstance in their creation or placement, no politicized national agenda in their message, and no museum or other lasting stone-and-mortar claim to the past. Instead, the wooden crosses mark a local event that remains meaningful to local people. I looked again at the crosses and tried to imagine that December night: the shots, scuffle, and yells, the desperate flight, and the dark and wintry silence.

How strange to be standing here finally, I thought. I am German—born in the capital of West Germany, Bonn, in the 1970s and raised in a diplomatic family. I could hardly have grown up farther from the border. My ties to Germany, however, were always there. It is a place of roots and origin, home to family and cherished friends, and an anchor of my identity. I lived there when the Berlin Wall fell and the divided country tumbled into reunification, and I witnessed some of the rapid West German takeover of the East. Yet the border long remained a vexingly fuzzy space in my mind. Eight years of research for this book have allowed me to discover my country anew and prompted me to ask questions of it—and myself—that I had not had the chance to do until I encountered the borderlands for the first time.

That July, I was visiting this part of the Green Belt with Dr. Dieter Franz, an ornithologist and one of the longtime architects of the Green Belt conservation project. Still deep in my own thoughts, I turned away from the shady spot beneath the oak, and our conversation returned to the ecological aspects of the former borderlands. Franz explained to me that the challenge was to keep this long strip of land open: if conservationists did nothing, forest succession would simply swallow up this middle section. In fact, to the left and right of where we were standing the trees were dense and dark. When conservation first started along this portion of the border, this actually *was* woodland that had sprung up quickly after the last of the GDR border-clearing measures had ended. In the beginning it was hard, manual labor that cut down some of the biggest trees, enough for smaller machines to come in and do the rest. In a matter of years, the border strip had been cleared once again, the patrol road (known in German as the *Kolonnenweg*) had reappeared, and more important, so had several rare bird species that require open land (*Offenland*) habitat, like the northern shrike (*Lanius excubitor*). Franz had to raise his voice at this point; a tractor driven by a local farmer contracted to mow the grasses along the Kolonnenweg threatened to drown him out. I waited for the machine to roar past, and through a cloud of dust I asked another question: Why were the forests not left to simply fill the spaces cleared by the GDR border police all of those years ago? Why not allow succession to reclaim that land, to "let nature be nature," as some German wilderness advocates would say? Franz explained that in the decades of division, from the 1940s to the 1980s, this open border space had become home to many different species, more than were present before. In other words, merely "rewilding" this space—allowing age-old ecological processes to return—would not maximize biodiversity. Nature alone was not enough here. Rather, careful human management was required to increase the conservation value of this land. As we walked back to the car, another thing occurred to me: if not for the Green Belt's management approach that kept the forest back, the grieving comrades and family members of those border guards would never have been able to put their memorial here, in the place where their loved ones had died.

Twenty minutes later, after driving in Franz's Opel station wagon along too many small gravel roads for me to maintain my bearings, we arrived at another part of the Green Belt, and the contrast could not have been starker. Again we were surrounded by agricultural land, again I could make out the Kolonnenweg. But this time, as we walked on the concrete slabs, we soon had to duck in between reeds that crowded our path. In less than a minute, we were standing in the middle of a wetland. This was a part of the Rodach, the river that gave this valley its name and had acted as a border stream during the decades of partition. Not long ago, parts of the Rodach had been *renaturiert*, a German word that literally means "renatured." The restoration project removed the stream's concrete banks and re-created the more softly meandering patterns characteristic of undisturbed flowing water. Shortly after the project was completed, beavers (*Castor fiber*) settled in this part of the Rodach, and their dams backed up the river's flow, creating the ponds, and with them, the heavy curtain of reeds. The beavers themselves had been driven to near extinction in the 1860s, but were reintroduced into Bavaria a century later, from where they have successfully recolonized many of Germany's waterways. In contrast to the earlier site, this was a place of spontaneous rewilding. In the quarter hour that we stood there looking over the water, we saw coots (*Fulica atra*), a marsh harrier (*Circus aeruginosus*), red kite (*Milvus milvus*), and gray heron (*Ardea cinereal*). A large and noisy flock of common starlings (*Sturnus vulgaris*) wove in and out of the reeds, and as we walked back, we could hear the distinctive reeling song of a Savi's warbler (*Locustella luscinioides*). We got in the car again, and as the Opel crested the next hill and I caught a view of the surrounding expanse of monocropped agricultural fields, I felt my grief over the border's many fatalities mix with joy and hope over its ecological revival.

This, then, is the strange contradiction of the Green Belt. How can these elements—concrete and water, death and life, remembrance and hope, past and future, the managed and the wild—possibly coexist in the same space? How is this landscape signified, and how can or should it be read? By whom? How should this place be curated and managed, and who should do so? The border that divided Germany for forty years and led to the death of nearly four hundred people has, over the past decades, become the country's largest conservation project. Nongovernmental organizations (NGOs), federal and state agencies, and local municipalities are working together to craft a continuous ecological network from the border's imprint. It will become a corridor that binds together over a hundred different kinds of habitats into one long protected area running through the center of Germany, from the Czech Republic to the Baltic Sea.

As my July trip showed, though, the borderlands are deep, complex, and layered landscapes, and because of their troubled histories make for a complicated conservation target.[3] The transformation of these lands has not occurred without struggle, including opposition from landowners and farmers who feel once again threatened in their rights and access to land, and are worried that an all-powerful state (represented, justifiably or not, by the career conservationist) will once more force them into decisions not of their own making. Others who suffered directly from the border's construction want all traces of it gone. Meanwhile, Green Belt supporters argue that there is no better way to honor the traumatic and lethal past than by creating a living, flourishing memorial to it, but border victims associations warn that the Green Belt's celebration of biodiversity thus far has had a way of erasing—or even greenwashing—a painful past.

The Bund für Umwelt und Naturschutz Deutschland (BUND, Federation for Environment and Nature Conservation Germany), the German NGO spearheading this project, has a bold ecological vision that it underscores with powerful slogans: "Borders separate, nature connects!"—the clarion call for conservation to heal the rifts of world war and nearly half a century of partition. The Green Belt is presented thus as a timeless, borderless nature that can suture the wounds of violent division and ensure that "what belongs together will grow together"—former chancellor Willy Brandt's as yet unrealized vision of German reunification. To make this happen, German conservationists are engaged in a series of ecological experiments that on the one hand, turn classical conservation paradigms on their head, and on the other, aim to make manifest the stories of grief and loss, joy and love, that undergird this landscape.

* * *

This book attempts to do two things: it aims to delineate a field of inquiry that merges ecology with a consideration of memory, and does so by offering an in-depth case study of the Green Belt, drawing from it both practical and ethical considerations for Germany and far beyond it. I understand the

Green Belt as an expression of a socioecological hybrid, a conservation space in a human-made landscape, a closely managed wilderness, an unnatural nature. The example of the Green Belt illuminates how the traces of war and memory left in this border landscape are entwined with contemporary conservation politics. I investigate the nexus of land care and curation, of ecological principles and historical memorialization, and of expertise and community participation. Central to my argument is the notion of *mnemonic ecologies* as a way of conceptualizing the complex and mutual entanglements of emergent ecosystems and historical memory. *Mnemonic* means "of or relating to memory" and provides the broadest possible framing for the work this book does. The roots of the word can be traced to the ancient Greek *mnēmē* (meaning "remembrance" or "memory"), something even reflected in Greek mythology: Mnemosyne was the goddess of memory and daughter of Gaia—*Earth*. Through the lens of mnemonic ecologies, then, I make long-overdue linkages between memory and the natural world. The framework of mnemonic ecologies can help develop a new conservation ethos and practice that is sensitive to the landscape's past while being collaborative, empathetic, and more deeply acknowledging of the interlacing between humans and the places they inhabit.

The German case serves as a success story and cautionary tale. Germany is one of Europe's most densely settled and industrialized countries. German conservationists have had to contend with the fact that, as a staff member of Germany's Federal Nature Agency stated so starkly to me, "space is our scarcest resource."[4] While both the United States and Germany share romantic traditions that shaped their respective environmental movements, white US conservationists, influenced by the country's westward expansion, celebrated the wilderness "frontier" and made it the main interest of conservation for over a century. In Germany, however, writers, artists, and government officials highlighted the pastoral ideal, the rural idyll. From its infancy, German conservation has treated landscape as profoundly cultural.

The Green Belt is anchored in this tradition and yet it is a different creature. A cultural landscape it is, though one marked not simply by small towns and traditional agriculture but instead by war, violence, and division. We are not only talking about hedgerows but also about high-voltage fences, not just about cover crops but minefields too. The borderlands are cultural landscapes because they were crafted from previously inhabited or working landscapes; in fact, much of the former borderlands were cultivated fields expropriated from farmers.[5] They are also cultural because war and militarization themselves have left an imprint that conservationists today are deciding to erase or maintain and memorialize. The way German conservationists contend with this double history is illustrative. I believe that the Green Belt has much to offer US audiences, and global conservation may still have something to learn from its German counterpart.

To make this broader argument, the book is structured as follows. The first chapter introduces the central concept, mnemonic ecologies, to outline this interdisciplinary field. I discuss the field of ecological restoration, and explain the emergence of *novel ecosystems* as a new and consequential idea that shifts ecology toward a more flexible understanding of what nature is as well as what kinds of biodiversity can be considered valuable. The chapter then moves on to bring in the other major component of my argument: memory studies. Here individual, collective, and cultural memory are highlighted, and brought to bear on place and landscape, especially formerly militarized landscapes like the Green Belt. I end this chapter by tying the pieces together and offering five core considerations of mnemonic ecologies, circumscribing this new field of inquiry.

Chapter 2 takes a deeper dive into the history of the Green Belt project. I situate its beginnings in the partition after the Second World War and look at the gradual hardening of the GDR border over the ensuing decades. My focus here is, first, on the ecological implications of the developing military infrastructure, and second, its dissolution. Even before the fateful year 1989, German conservationists on both sides of the border were aware of the ecological resurgence occurring in this space. I explain how the Green Belt functions as a novel ecosystem and chart the activism of German conservationists, particularly the BUND, through the present. I end this section by explaining the BUND's vision of the Green Belt and its guiding principles for its ecological management. In order to understand the value of the Green Belt as articulated by its advocates, this chapter places the project within Germany's ongoing biodiversity crisis.

The third chapter examines the current Green Belt project as part of a much longer tradition of German conservationism reaching back to the early nineteenth century and centered on the defense of *Heimat*, a cultural landscape codified as homeland, and through it, national heritage. Since the 1970s, the newer, more radical environmental movement, galvanized by the ruptures of 1968, has chafed against the more conservative, place-bound conservationism of earlier decades. This chapter shows how the Green Belt is an outgrowth of these two major traditions and as such is built from the tensions between them—it is both about a specific vision of home and history, and a call for an environmental awakening and radical consciousness shift in Germany today.

The fourth chapter explores how memory and ecology connect in material and narrative ways along the Green Belt. Can conservation aid in healing both social and ecological wounds, and if so, how? The book travels to two sites of landscape art and another marked by the ruins of a village razed by GDR government in 1970 to build the border. I bring in a third element of memory work through a closer look at the role of storytelling, using a recently published book and multimedia traveling show called the *Green Belt Adventure* (*Abenteuer Grünes Band*). Such forms of commemoration—both curated and not—offer different and uneven possibilities for conserving wounded land. This is made clear by the vociferous debates over the Green Belt's designation as a national nature monument, which demonstrate how the country's partition along with people's memories of expropriation and state control continue to haunt the present.

Chapter 5 offers a different angle on the ecology-memory nexus by exploring how ecologies are made to enact memory, and how individual plant and animal organisms in their very bodies anchor remembrance and the memory of a seemingly idyllic past. By looking at ostensibly contrasting projects, I examine how particular human notions of the past come to matter in embodied, material ways in Green Belt conservation. River restoration and rewilding activities along the Elbe in northern Germany aim at erasing more recent human pasts in favor of rehabilitating ancient ecological processes. Meanwhile, in other parts of the Green Belt, the emphasis is the opposite: managing against natural dynamics in the interest of maintaining open land and a carefully tended cultural landscape of the German Heimat, populated with rare plant and animal species that act as genetic holograms of a lost age.

Chapter 6 identifies global lessons from the German Green Belt by tracing concentric circles outward from the book's central case study. I begin by discussing the emergence of the European Green Belt, the BUND-led attempt to replicate its conservation project across the entire former Iron Curtain corridor. I then move on to a case striking in its basic resemblance to the German one: the partition of Korea and ecological revival of its famous demilitarized zone. From there I move out further to include other well-known cases of postviolent landscapes that also happen to be havens for biodiversity: Cambodia and Colombia. Across all of these countries, while memorialization is in process, it remains often state centered and punctuated, and tends to ignore the vernacular landscapes of trauma and the ways local people try to make sense of their pasts by drawing on and from the places they call home. Because the most biodiverse regions in the world tend to be inhabited—and in too many cases have been the sites of significant armed conflict—conservation and restoration must find ways to think mnemonically, reckoning with ecological memories (e.g., the legacy effects of war on ecological processes) as well as social ones. There are both practical and ethical reasons for this that I outline in this chapter.

In the book's conclusion, I offer more concrete recommendations for conservationists and restorationists to enrich and sensibilize their work through a multidisciplinary approach that weaves together ecological principles and memorialization. Grief and pain graft onto landscapes, loss and bitterness can linger between people, and absent life remains present for those who survived. Places as well as plant and animal bodies can be scarred, and the living, still breathing creatures of today may still be haunted by those who passed before them. Paying attention to local landscapes of memory, however, will remain an important part of conservation and restoration practice here as well.

* * *

Ultimately this book is about wounded places and their complicated recovery and transformation, about acts of violence and their ecological redemption, and about how memory is ecological and political at once. It is a meditation on trauma, loss, and return. It is about how we heal the lands we love and thereby heal ourselves.

1 ESTABLISHING MNEMONIC ECOLOGIES

Mnemonic Ecologies queries the intersection between memory, memorialization, ecological restoration, and conservation. In broad terms, ecological communities have memorial qualities for the human beings who use and reside in, manage, and ultimately coconstitute them. Landscapes often reveal the traces of past human lives in the ways the trees grow, in the species settled there, in the slope of the hills, or in the toxicants in the water. Human beings may also actively cultivate memories through particular ecological choices by planting memorial groves, celebrating and performing rituals in significant places, harvesting and eating certain foods, or burying the dead near important natural features.

This book looks closely at one such intersection of ecology and memory: the former inter-German borderlands that are being slowly transformed into a protected ecological corridor called the Green Belt. In this chapter, I review the history of major ecological concepts that inform my analysis. I outline the already existing connections between ecology and memory studies as well as the growing interest in "layered landscapes," and comment on the increasingly pressing need to enact restoration and conservation in more sensitive ways in landscapes marked by violence and pain. I end by offering several key considerations on mnemonic ecologies.

The borderlands are layered landscapes, but as I will explain in the next chapter, they were not fully perceived as such by conservationists for the first two decades of the Green Belt's existence. Before efforts were made to convert the former inter-German borderlands into a memorial landscape, these lands were a conservation and restoration project. I will refer frequently to these terms, even though conservation and restoration have distinct histories, lineages, and assumptions. The Green Belt, however, as the introduction indicates and subsequent chapters will show, is a hybrid space where classical preservation approaches that seek to protect existing systems from further deterioration sit closely alongside those that attempt to nurture emergent ecological assemblages or rehabilitate ancient ecological dynamics.

In general, conservation aspires to safeguard against the loss of habitat and species, whereas restoration is focused on their recovery. Conservation has been mostly confined to the life sciences and shaped by new paradigms in ecology, especially by the nonequilibrium thinking that has replaced the balance-of-nature idea with notions of disturbance and flux. With this shift, conservation has begun to change from an emphasis on small islands of protected areas that are to be left undisturbed so they can remain in balance for all time to an approach that recognizes instability as the prime mover.[1] If stasis is assumed to be true and desirable, then one of the most sensible ways to safeguard biodiversity is to establish protected areas by identifying species to be preserved, controlling tracts of land, and isolating them from the surrounding landscape. This also means keeping people out of designated areas including, controversially, removing local residents by force. But once the openness and inconstancy of natural systems is recognized, it is a short and logical conclusion that human beings must be understood as part of a disturbance regime that shapes a landscape. If we further assume that rather than stable, somewhat self-contained units, ecosystems are heterogeneous and permeable systems that interact with many other variables at the land-scape and regional levels, then arguably conservation must become flexible in terms of scale as well. From this realization, new conservation geographies based on a landscape-level approach have emerged or expanded: biosphere reserves, transboundary parks, and ecological corridors and networks have now entered the picture.[2] Taking a landscape view broadens conservation sensibilities because it avoids dichotomizing environments as natural/unnatural or intact/degraded, and instead sees a "complex mosaic of ecosystems or 'patches' in varying states of modification, each of which delivers various combinations of services and presents assorted management challenges and opportunities."[3] The Green Belt in Germany is an example of this larger-scale, networked thinking.

ECOLOGICAL RESTORATION

Restoration borrows much from conservation, though it is more concerned with recovery rather than protection, and contrary to conservation, puts humans squarely in the picture, not just as a cause of environmental destruction, but as keys to environmental healing. First formulated in the late 1980s (around the same time that conservation biology emerged), restoration tries to understand how ecosystems have changed from their previous state (usually due to human disturbances) and then project how to move those systems back to a less disturbed state.[4] For generations, environmentalism's main plotline has been that the loss of areas described as "natural" is permanent and irreversible. Yet restoration's best work shows that this need not be true, that it is possible for us to re-create reasonably accurate, functional versions of some ecosystems and landscapes.[5] To do so, restoration draws on all branches of ecological science, considers all levels of biodiversity (from genes to landscapes), and pulls from related sciences including hydrology and geomorphology. Increasingly, restoration practitioners are in communication with the social sciences as well, including geography, anthropology, and economics, recognizing that many ecosystems are inhabited, and many provide essential services to local communities.[6]

Restoration is specifically premised on the idea of disturbance, flux, and instability in ecosystems. In the view of its organizing body, ecological restoration is

> an intentional activity that initiates or accelerates the recovery of an ecosystem with respect to its health, integrity and sustainability. Frequently, the ecosystem that requires restoration has been degraded, damaged, transformed or entirely destroyed as the direct or indirect result of human activities. In some cases, these impacts to ecosystems have been caused or aggravated by natural agencies such as wildfire, floods, storms, or volcanic eruption, to the point at which the ecosystem cannot recover its predisturbance state or its historic developmental trajectory.

The Society for Ecological Restoration further defines an ecosystem as "restored" when "it contains sufficient biotic and abiotic resources to continue its development without further assistance or subsidy. It will sustain itself structurally and functionally. It will demonstrate resilience to normal ranges of environmental stress and disturbance. It will interact with contiguous ecosystems in terms of biotic and abiotic flows and cultural interactions."[7]

A more recent effort by the Society for Ecological Restoration seeks to establish a series of standards for restoration activities, imagining these in the form of a "five-star system" that ranks recovery outcomes in terms of a handful of thresholds.[8] Yet the insistence on certain conditions across such indicators as "species composition" or "external exchanges" appears somewhat rigid and restrictive given the scale and scope of ecosystemic changes. In contrast to the Society for Ecological Restoration, the International Union for Conservation of Nature (IUCN) together with the World Commission on Protected Areas offers guidance for restoration practitioners through a principles-first approach. To them, ecological restoration can be "confined to reducing pressures and allowing natural recovery, or involve significant interventions." But above all, restoration ought to be effective ("re-establishing and maintaining protected area values"), efficient ("maximizing beneficial outcomes while minimizing costs in time, resources and effort"), and engaging ("collaborating with partners and stakeholders, promoting participation and enhancing visitor experience").[9] Guidelines for best practices, in turn, give each of these broad principles greater specificity, but with enough room for innovation and context-specific adaptation and interpretation.[10]

Two key points are evident in these definitions. First, ecological restoration is an intentional activity that involves human measurements and judgments on ecosystem health, resilience, and integrity. Second, ecological restoration is not just about improving ecosystem function, nor is it about strict preservation; it is about creating an ecosystem that may well resemble the one prior to being damaged or degraded, but it also means that restoration should create ecosystems that can evolve on their own even after the human work of restoration has ceased.

In Germany, *restoration* is usually translated as "renaturing" (*Renaturierung*). Its semantics imply a dualistic understanding of nature-society relationships, as if human beings can strip "nature" out of its context and—with some effort, time, and care—put it back in. Formal restoration in Germany has been around for at least two hundred years, if one includes the broad-scale reforestation projects in Prussia and elsewhere. Since the beginning of the twentieth century, restoration activities have included stream rehabilitation, reversing the drainage of bogs and wetlands, and restoring habitat in old lignite coal mining regions. Much of German thinking on restoration has been influenced by US-based scholarship, including the many English-language specialty journals or Society for Ecological Restoration, which inspired the German counterpart, the Gesellschaft für Ökologie (Society for Ecology), created in 1997.[11] But while US scientists often still insist on a clear distinction between conservation and restoration, the practitioners I spoke with in Germany simply conceived of themselves as conservationists (*Naturschützer*, literally "nature protectors") and folded restoration (*Renaturierung*) into a broadly understood project of safeguarding species, ecosystems, and ecological processes. The book will thus follow their cue and speak of the two alongside each other.

Novel Ecosystems

With the shifts in ecological thinking, from stasis to disturbance and flux, from isolated protected areas to regions and landscape approaches, and from islands to corridors, some restoration ecologists introduced a concept that has since received quite a bit of scrutiny: novel ecosystems. A *novel ecosystem* is

> a system of abiotic, biotic and social components (and their interactions) that, by virtue of human influence, differ from those that prevailed historically, having a tendency to self-organize and manifest novel qualities without intensive human management. Novel ecosystems are distinguished from hybrid ecosystems by practical limitations (a combination of ecological, environmental and social thresholds) on the recovery of historical qualities.[12]

In other words, novelty and human influence are the crucial elements here.

German restorationists have been using this idea as well, but they modify this US-centric definition by pointing to differences in approaches across the two countries. Unlike commonly assumed in Europe, in the United States, "areas continuously used for agriculture or forestry are not included . . . as novel ecosystems; rather, the acceptance of unsteered or unexpected ecosystem development is an essential basis of [the US] concept." Further, German restorationists point out that "novelty is a question of temporal perspective. For restoration ecology in North and South America, pre-Columbian (supposedly) untouched nature is often still used as the reference state."[13] In the German context, however, restoration receives a different cast. It aims at the restoration of ecosystems and natural landscapes (*Naturlandschaft*); the restoration of mostly traditional land uses of the historical, cultural landscape; and the creation of new ecological or land use systems (novel ecosystems) in strongly disturbed landscapes.[14] Cultural landscapes, as they developed historically (and continuously) in central Europe after the end of the Ice Age, are valued here to an extent rarely seen in US restoration practice.

Whether in the United States or Germany, though, human agency is the operating factor in these systems. Because change is assumed to be normal, many ecosystems can be considered "novel" at one point or another due to human influences (e.g., early hunting or fires).[15] Yet in the new millennium, the scale, scope, and rate of change have increased, and along with them the appearance of novel environments, species assemblages, and alterations in ecosystem functions. How much change is needed to produce a novel ecosystem? Some suggest that "novelty" presumes a system so far outside the historical range of variability that it has crossed a point of no return—for instance, it might exhibit new traits (in hydrology or nutrient cycling) and be composed of species not formerly native to the area. This distinguishes a novel system from a "hybrid" one, which may still retain predisturbance characteristics. Whereas the latter could practically still be reversed, novel ecosystems have crossed certain biotic and abiotic thresholds that make this impossible. To work around this ambiguity, one could frame a definition in terms of what a novel ecosystem is *not*. It is not "(1) a system that would have occupied that space in the past (i.e., part of a historical range of variability);

(2) managed intensively for specific production or built over; or (3) managed with the purpose of reproducing the historical ecosystem (i.e., classic restoration)."[16]

By postulating that certain ecosystems can reach a point of no return, the notion of novelty raises questions about historical reference conditions while at the same time offering up conservation opportunities arising from human-induced changes.[17] Indeed, one of the most vexing questions for restoration ecologists concerns authenticity or historical fidelity. To what extent is it possible (or desirable) to re-create a "predisturbance state" or an ecosystem's "historic developmental trajectory," as the Society for Ecological Restoration suggests? Is any restoration simply human artifice and hubris, as some would have it?[18] And if we assume that ecological change is ongoing and disturbance is normal, how do we decide on a desirable ecological state in the first place? For some, historical authenticity is too restrictive a notion in ecological restoration and should be replaced by a broadened conception that includes "any endpoint that is expressed, or that could be reasonably expressed, within the entire ecoregion for the kind of ecosystem being restored."[19] By loosening our framework somewhat, restoration could be about re-creating a healthy, functioning ecosystem where one has been degraded or destroyed, even if that was not necessarily the original one. An ecosystem's resilience would in this case be as or more important than literal authenticity.

While historical fidelity has received its share of criticism, scholars and practitioners insist that an attachment to history should remain relevant for restorationists.[20] Knowledge of past environments can reveal ecological patterns and hence provide indispensable reference points for future planning (e.g., what the historical range of ecological variability has been, and what past events still have legacy effects into the present and future). But history plays into restoration in other forms as well: past and current human practices and beliefs can also be integrated into restoration planning, especially if they function to redress earlier damages to traditional livelihoods. Finally, an awareness of history, specifically of historicity (the quality of being historical), can itself "become a virtue alongside humility, self-restraint, and care for non-humans. . . . [R]espect for historical fidelity highlights the limits of our ecological knowledge."[21]

The discussions around history in ecological restoration, then, begin to point us toward places like the Green Belt. Ecologies have pasts, and pasts are crafted through ecologies. To understand this more deeply, ecological work—whether understood as conservation or restoration—must be a multidisciplinary pursuit. It occurs in particular places, and many of those places were or currently are either inhabited or used by human communities. The human dimension of restoration is at least threefold. First, it is human activities that have pushed many systems outside the range of historical variability and into hybrid or novel states. Second, because most landscapes are either inhabited or used in certain ways by human communities, almost any kind of restoration practice must take human needs into consideration. Third, restoration, like its close relative conservation, necessarily carries a moral burden and is based on a host of human value judgments about what is desirable, how an ecosystem should be changed, and ultimately, what is worth saving and why.

For some, the moral character of restoration is its greatest strength.[22] Engaging in restoration forces its practitioners to ask the hard questions: Why are we doing this? What kind of ecosystem are we aiming for, and why this one and not another? How will we know we have succeeded? What does restoration say about our relationship to nature? And if an ecological community can only come to be due to human intervention, can it be considered "natural"? What does such a descriptor even mean in a world where restoration will become more and more common? There is a sense that "we either intentionally modify or intentionally don't modify, but we make an intentional decision to create a landscape that *means something to us*."[23] Restoration can thus realize a positive, reconciliatory relationship with the more-than-human, which asks morally much more of us. Instead of demanding that we withdraw from nature, restoration forces us to engage ourselves—our bodies, labor, care, time, and money—in actively saving what is left to us and rebuilding spaces for other life-forms.[24] And lastly, we engage memory—individual and collective, ecological and social—as an important, if altogether underrecognized, element.

HUMAN MEMORY AND PLACE

When we speak of memory, we need to distinguish between its cognitive, social, and cultural dimensions, and between individual and collective, or cultural, memory. Reading across various disciplines, memory emerges as a quality that structures not just individual identity but interhuman relationships, our sense of place, and our understandings of the past, present, and future. A mnemonic approach to ecological restoration in layered landscapes must take seriously such a foundational part of the human experience.

Individual memory is the foundation of our identities, the way we make sense of our lives. Being able to remember where one is from and who one's family members or ancestors are, or recalling one's childhood or adolescence, for instance, are crucial elements of our self-definition and give us roots in this world.[25] Individual memories can be latent as much as they can be conscious, and may require a trigger (a visit to a place from one's past or bumping into a forgotten acquaintance) to evoke them.[26] More problematic memories, including old traumas and repressed feelings, can also erupt suddenly and violently into our everyday lives.[27]

Individual memories have several features in common.[28] They are unique to each individual, or in other words, perspectival. Individual memories are often also fragmentary, unstable, and fleeting. They do not acquire coherence and structure until they are arranged to form a narrative or story. And lastly, individual memories do not exist in isolation but rather in connection with the memories of others: they are interlinked, and can confirm and strengthen one another. This latter quality already points to the fact that individual memories are networked with others, giving memory not merely an individual but a collective and even cultural quality too.

The core argument of collective memory is that because human beings are social creatures, memories are socially mediated and anchored: they rely on narration, materialization, and ritualization to endure and remain relevant to people. Collective and individual memory are mutually dependent: "One may say that the individual remembers by placing himself in the perspective of the group, but one may also affirm that the memory of the group realizes and manifests itself in individual memories."[29] Mnemonic communities texture memory in identity-producing ways. Groups ensure that new members are socialized into that community's past and that their identities align with that of the larger collective. One such group might be the family, where members jointly produce and maintain memories (e.g., by talking about old photographs together), crafting narratives that can be shared across generations, thereby giving the family cohesion and continuity.[30] In the context of social tension, militarization, and even war, group identities of all kinds become activated, putting distinct mnemonic socializations into clear relief and frequently with dire consequences.

Generations are also mnemonic communities of sorts. As anyone who has tried (and failed) to understand their own grandparents or children will know, every generation crafts its own ways of accessing and relating to the past, deriving from it new values and sensitivities. Therefore generational shifts shape a larger society's memory, and memorialization—in the Green Belt and elsewhere—will need to respond to the changing demands this entails. Generational divides become particularly important in addressing memories that are too intense or uncomfortable to process immediately, and it has been noted that it can take a generation to overcome "memory paralysis" and collectively deal with adverse experiences.[31]

While the collective memory tradition draws our attention to the social milieu, there is still the question of the larger culture. In response, historians have more recently proposed a theory of cultural memory that foregrounds cultural events and rituals, and helps explain how memory could be transmitted across generations and space. *Cultural memory* is "human memory embedded in cultural frames, such as the landscape or townscape in which people grew up, the texts they learned, the feasts they celebrated, the churches or synagogues they frequented, the music they listened to, and especially the stories they were told and by and in which they live."[32] Cultural memory relies on durable carriers (monuments, texts, and images, but also rituals, festivals, and anniversaries) and exists somewhat separate from the many individuals who hold much more limited memories. Of course the meanings of these carriers are never fixed; they have to be constantly reexamined, discussed, and renewed as each succeeding generation must on its own appropriate and then transmit them, always with reference to changing circumstances.[33] Cultural memory conditions and frames smaller-scale individual and group memories, but these also, in turn, reverberate upward to slowly modify larger-scale and longer-term memory traditions.

WEAVING TOGETHER ECOLOGY AND MEMORY

So far we have traveled across a range of disciplines and ideas that shape the argument for mnemonic ecologies. Restoration ecology allows us to think of reversing negative human influences and reestablishing earlier ecological relationships as we try to heal the damages humans have wrought. The recent introduction of novel ecosystems pushes this one step further by signaling that some changes inflicted by human action need not be entirely negative or destructive. At the very least, even if some changes are irreversible, there is still conservation potential to be realized in these spaces. Novel ecosystems take the role of human actors seriously, and rather than classical conservation's insistence on clear boundaries between human and nonhuman life, this newer form of restoration ecology insists on our engagement with the natural world.

Meanwhile, the foundational tenets of memory studies teach us that memory can be considered along cognitive, social, and cultural dimensions. While individual memories anchor human identities, they are set in a social milieu, and in turn are activated by and communicated to others, whether in the family or within a generation. Moreover, social groups constitute and are shaped by culture, and so memories can also be carried by texts, images, monuments, rituals, and festivals, transcending individual lifetimes. Importantly, however, even if cultural memory carriers seem durable, their meanings are never fixed. Memory is mutable and contested, but no less crucial to human life.

How do ecology and memory come together? One place to begin our consideration of mnemonic ecologies is to investigate how mutable memories adhere to places. We can then consider one particular set of landscapes where the prevalence of memory is unavoidable: those marked by violence and militarization.

Landscape and Memory

Nature is loaded with meaning, creating landscapes that have informed individual and collective identities for generations and continue to do so today. The connection between landscape and memory—and through memory, with identity—can be so close that the two practically merge, making it hard to separate out where beliefs, fantasies, and myths about certain places begin and end: "landscapes are culture before they are nature; constructs of the imagination projected onto wood and water and rock."[34] Nature and landscape become foils for cultural identities, a way for certain groups to make political claims, and reference to landscape becomes one of the key components of a national narrative.

Equally inescapable is the fact that memory, and more specifically the act of memorialization, is shot through with power: dominant individuals and groups insist on the commemoration of particular people, places, and events while silencing or simply overwriting other kinds of memories. What and who should be remembered, who remembers, and how one remembers are all questions that the study of memory and memorialization bring to the fore.

Given the spatial elements of memory, another important question is, of course, *where* one remembers. Spatiality is a fluctuating, contingent, and multivalent thing that cannot be assumed to be fixed across time nor stable in its meaning. Places are made rather than given; they are assigned meaning through the attachment of memories, identities, and emotions. In the process of placemaking, landscapes can "simultaneously embody presences and absences, voids and ruins, intentional forgetting and painful remembering."[35] Buildings and monuments often far outlast human lifetimes and thus act as visible remnants of the past. How such structures are used, narrated, and remembered, whether they are destroyed or carefully tended, can illuminate deeply held and otherwise-hidden collective identities and memories. Species extinctions, meanwhile, leave behind voids that modern genomics promises to fill with engineered organisms, generating new and puzzling "spectral ecologies."[36] Scholars frequently use the language of "hauntings" and "ghosts" to convey this ambiguous quality of the past-in-place. Hauntings happen "when the over-and-done-with comes alive, when what's been in your blind spot comes into view." We are troubled and changed by these hauntings and forced to confront our relation to that place. In the process, our positions can be altered: "Being haunted draws us affectively, sometimes against our will and always a bit magically, into the structure of feeling of a reality we come to experience, not as cold knowledge, but as a transformative recognition."[37]

If a place was the site of a violent event—a civil war, natural hazard, terrorist bombing, or state-sanctioned killing along a militarized border—it can produce a particular kind of haunting, namely trauma. *Trauma* is the Greek word for "wound." The American Psychological Association defines it as "an emotional response to a terrible event. . . . Immediately after the event, shock and denial are typical. Longer term reactions include unpredictable emotions, flashbacks, strained relationships and even physical symptoms like headaches or nausea."[38] I use a less clinical definition in this book, following the lead of historians and scholars of memory for whom trauma is a psychic wound "that can be traced back to life-threatening and deeply injurious experiences of extreme violence," and therefore may "have strange and identity-threatening qualities."[39] Taking a broader view, I assume that trauma can be held not simply by individuals but also by groups. In this case, we speak of collective or cultural trauma that occurs when groups have experienced an extreme or deeply painful event that forever shapes their consciousness as members of that group, indelibly marking their memories and forever shaping their identities.[40] Violence is enacted in particular locations, wounding places along with the people in them. Any kind of intervention there, including ecological restoration and conservation, may stir up this emotional sediment.

Place-based interventions could, however, offer opportunities for resolution too. For historians of trauma, living fully "does not mean avoidance, harmonization, simply forgetting the past, or submerging oneself within the present. It means coming to terms with the trauma, including its details, and critically engaging the tendency to act out the past and even to recognize why it may be necessary and even in certain respects desirable or at least compelling."[41] In other words, trauma will be resolved *through* memory, not in its absence.

Core to this task is memorialization, or the act of preserving remembrance, which can take social, relational, and material forms. Memorials and monuments are material mnemonic devices that interrupt the quotidian and attempt to force a reflection not simply on individual but also group or collective history. Ecological elements—from sacred groves to animal bodies—have long been harnessed for that purpose. Monuments exist "in the tension between the presence of the past and the presence of the future, between memory and history, between testimony and archive, between one and another, between nature and built environment." They are a way of "giving image or shape to something that frequently cannot be thought or remembered otherwise, and in making that memory available to the community as a whole. They serve as living reminders that appeal to others to remember."[42] The act of designing and erecting monuments forms part of a politics of memory. Participating in memorialization, on the one hand, and experiencing memorial sites and monuments, on the other, are part of a politics of healing as well. Trauma does not just attach to the past; it often attaches to places.

Layered Landscapes

Ecology and memory come together in the restoration of so-called layered landscapes—that is, spaces that have accumulated layers of biological and geological as well as social and cultural history.[43] The landscape is constituted as "an enduring record of—and testimony to—the lives and works of past generations who have dwelt within it, and in so doing, have left there something of themselves."[44] Spaces regarded as "natural" (as in nonhuman) raise a host of questions when seen in this more complex light: How should we understand the traces of past human lives in places that seem wild today?[45] Whose memories are going to be honored, and who will narrate them? In more populated rural places, similar questions emerge once conservation, restoration, or rewilding projects seek to remake the landscape. Once land use is set to change, the place that anchors human memories and identities is threatened, and locals react. Along with historians, geographers, and environmental philosophers, I argue that we can view the landscape as a palimpsest built from layers of meaning and memory. Questions around which layers are considered more valuable, which are made visible, and which are hidden thus become political considerations. In landscapes marred by war, violence, and death this becomes especially poignant.

Militarized landscapes are "simultaneously material and cultural sites that have been partially or fully mobilized to achieve military aims."[46] As one can imagine, these lands are ambiguous ones. Militarization can scar a place, quite literally etching itself into soil and trees, permanently transforming the land. It may also leave behind traumatized beings. After the military ceases operations and leaves the area, its presence lingers in the buildings, demolished or not, in infrastructure no longer used, in the toxicants saturating the ground, and even in human remains, unclaimed or unburied. Both in Germany and the United States, former military lands are already being converted into so-called wildlands: places where human intervention has ceased, and where nonhuman life is allowed to flourish amid the decommissioned weapons arsenals and toxic waste dumps.[47] Such a conversion may make sense from an ecological standpoint: because militarized land is emptied of civilian presence it often becomes attractive to nonhuman species. It can also be a cost-effective and beneficial way to deal with the long-term contamination of military lands. But the transformation of blighted land into something other—wilder—can obscure the huge environmental toll that military activity takes on ecosystems worldwide and tends to erase the human histories beneath. This further muddies the meaning of militarized spaces. What does (or should) the conversion from battlefield to wildlife preserve signify? For whom? And who gets to tell that story? What if "our judgments on benignity and ruthlessness, on depredation and development, are easily reversed from an ecological perspective"?[48] And in landscapes that witnessed battles, massacres, and killings, how should the dead—whose bones may still litter the ground and whose ghosts trouble the living—be remembered when those spaces are transformed into ecological refuges? Can ecological resurgence undo or mask the death and destruction that preceded it? Should it? In many cases, restoration and conservation are moving ahead with little attention to these complicated questions.

MNEMONIC ECOLOGIES

Using the case of the Green Belt along Germany's former inner border, this book shows how ecological communities—and the human ambitions to restore, conserve, use, or change them—intersect with memory. The inter-German borderlands are an excellent place to explore this nexus given its troubled history and the ways in which conservationists are slowly learning to contend with it. The German case also provides an anchor point for an entire field of inquiry that seeks to trace and build connections between ecological and mnemonic considerations. Mnemonic ecologies can take a range of forms that together create a larger framework for conceptualizing the connections between memory, landscape, ecosystems, and human and other-than-human life. For greater analytic clarity, I outline them separately here, but the book's—and framework's—empirical richness ultimately derives from the ways in which these considerations intertwine on the ground.

Mnemonic Ecologies Are the Result of Explicit Commemorative Practices

Spaces of heritage and remembrance use a variety of devices to anchor memory in a landscape and prompt people to remember past events or values: artifacts, installations, exhibits, monuments, inscriptions, and other signifiers. Nature is often appropriated as such a device. For millennia, human beings have attached their memories to particular nonhuman forms, and tended them with purpose and care. The degree of ecological agency varies, from ecologies that preexisted human presence and still survive because they are protected by individuals and communities from destruction and disturbance, to those ecological relationships that have been specifically crafted for memorial purposes.

Aside from marking death, mnemonic ecologies may mark life, such as by trees that are planted after the birth of a child or around a homestead to grow with, and beyond, a human lifetime. Memories can equally attach to the bodies of animals as well as other more-than-human entities like rivers, rocks, and soils. In some cases, ecologies are enrolled as monuments to past events, but with the passage of time and generational forgetting, memorial markers can literally outgrow their original intention and become detached from their original referents. Their meanings may collapse, disappear, or become reinterpreted in new and different ways.

Mnemonic Ecologies Are the Accidental or Collateral Effects of Prior Human Lives

Mnemonic ecologies are frequently coincidental, emergent, and unsteered. Past human activities may have changed landscapes in such a way to produce lasting yet unintended ecological effects. Ecological arrangements may therefore mark the presence of absence: overgrazing during the Middle Ages created the dry grasslands so prized by European conservationists today; a nuclear explosion decades ago has allowed earlier ecosystems to regenerate, however radioactive they might be; and old apple trees in the middle of a purported wilderness might make us pause to consider who planted and cared for them so long ago.

Ruination and decay create unruly mnemonic ecologies. They can establish and disrupt our sense of the past, grow over its traces, hide or change it, and create hybrid formations that provoke new meanings for present and future generations. Through ruination, "cultural remembering proceeds not through reflection on a static memorial remnant but through a process that slowly pulls the remnant into other ecologies and expressions of value, accommodating simultaneous resonances of death and rebirth, loss and renewal."[49] Rich ruderal natures spontaneously emerge from industrial ruins, on brownfields, along old roads, or in the urban interstices. Decay and emergence produce forgetting, but forgetting one version of the past opens up new possibilities for recollection and explanation.

Mnemonic Ecologies Are Long-Term Legacies of Past Land Use or Disturbance Made Relevant Today

Drawing on landscape and historical ecology, we can include here the legacy effects of past human land use and anthropogenic disturbances that force consideration of previous generations. This means taking the long view of human history and landscapes.[50] Past human land uses including grazing and fire—may have so significantly changed the flow of water, structure of the soils, or composition of plant communities that their lingering effects continue to shape landscapes and human habitation patterns and cultures today. Bringing this past into the present raises questions not simply related to ecological management (e.g., to what extent should fire be part of forestry?) but also the value of nondominant cultures. If Native peoples have helped generate landscapes regarded as quintessentially "American" (e.g., the prairies), or if forest gardens several thousands of years old help explain concentrated biodiversity in the Amazon rain forest today, what sorts of politics, if any, flow from these realizations? To what extent do present-day landscapes ask us to create new kinds of cultural memories that establish the validity of peoples often unseen? To the degree that cultural memories help define generations, a related question then is whether a reckoning with the past can prod us to think of ourselves in new ways, an especially high-stakes consideration with respect to our use and abuse of the earth.

Mnemonic Ecologies May Be Other-than-Human

Psychologists know that human beings are not the only creatures who remember. The capacity to recall the past exists in most nonhuman animals, including invertebrates, and fulfills a range of functions that generally enhance the survival chances of the individual. Beings as diverse as elephants and bees, pigeons and dogs, octopuses and primates, are able to remember past experiences and log observations that can aid them in avoiding conflict and predators, and with finding food, mates, or hiding places. It is less well-known that plants, too, may have the capacity to "remember."[51] Can we imagine mnemonic ecologies that are the expression of more-than-human bodies and relationships? Red deer migration patterns in central Europe are shown to have changed due to the decades-long presence of the Iron Curtain. Even after their disappearance around 1990, today's does and their young— generations removed from the animals alive during the partition—still refuse to cross from the forests in the Czech Republic to the German side.[52] Meanwhile, scientists use concepts like *ecological memory* to describe the ways in which ecosystems have adapted to repeated disturbance, creating both resilience and flexibility to change. Do the memories of animals and plants, even if they might be qualitatively different than that of humans, create new ecologies? And to what extent is it possible (or indeed unavoidable) to grant landscape itself an active role in memorial processes?[53]

Mnemonic Ecologies Are Patterned by Emotions

Memories are a way of relating to the world, and they elicit particular emotions, from joy to fear to grief, and emotions in turn can elicit, strengthen, weaken, and skew memories.[54] In fact, emotions carry memory, and it has been shown that memories that do not provoke emotion are more readily forgotten than those that do.[55] Memorial actions that produce emotional responses can be more effective in conveying their message and more lasting across time.

Care is at the center of most environmental work (both care for and about), and in this age of loss, grief is unavoidable. Many feel that grief even more keenly because Western culture has no rituals to help process the loss of species or ecosystems that so many care about.[56] In the new millennium, new words have emerged to describe this complex of emotions. The term *solastalgia* describes "the distress that is produced by environmental change impacting on people while they are directly connected to their home environment."[57] Close in meaning, *ecological grief* is "the grief felt in relation to experienced or anticipated ecological losses, including the loss of species, ecosystems and meaningful landscapes due to acute or chronic environmental change."[58] *Eco-nostalgia* names the regret and longing for past environments, often perceived to be more whole and healthy.[59]

Yet memory is prismatic: mnemonic ecologies are arguably undergirded by affection, love, and joy as much as they are by sorrow. *Biophilia* for psychologist Erich Fromm was "the passionate love of life and of all that is alive"—a term later elaborated by biologist Edward O. Wilson.[60] Ecological restoration for many practitioners is hope enacted in the landscape. By attempting to re-create older ecologies based on the (cultural) remembrance of things past and the grief for things gone, restoration promises to alleviate sorrow and the pain of living with constant loss. Meanwhile, positive emotional attachments to place crucially shape landscapes and their uses. Conflicts over conservation and restoration, along the Green Belt as elsewhere, are more often than not also struggles over different visions and understandings of a place, of what it means to care for or about it, of human identities attached to the past, and of embodied and felt connections to previous generations that remain relevant to local people in the places they inhabit.

* * *

As we now turn our attention to the German borderlands, we should see them as densely layered landscapes with evocative, mnemonic qualities. Their celebrated ecological resurgence is an accident of history that happened as much because of the border as it did in spite of it. To understand this, we must take a closer look at the border's beginnings and then metamorphosis over the past half century. The Green Belt constitutes in many ways a novel ecosystem—one that could not have emerged without human intervention, though which now has acquired its own logic and dynamism. But it is much more than that: a place where the wounds of the Cold War lie more exposed than elsewhere, a killing field, and ultimately a palimpsest, a many-layered thing, whose restoration and maintenance will require careful, empathetic, and multidisciplinary practices that attend to both ecological principles and human needs.

The Green Belt, the largest conservation and restoration project in Germany's history, thus becomes a way for us to see landscape through the lens of mnemonic ecologies. The book shows how such an approach can help craft a new conservation ethos and practice for both Germany and elsewhere: present to both ecological and human history, sensitive to the emotional geographies that connect people to place, and honoring the memorial qualities of nature. Conservationists in Germany have already learned from past experience to be creative and flexible, but conflicts all along the layered landscapes of the former borderlands have also demonstrated that more questions must yet be answered. It is an exciting time for the Green Belt, a place where ecology and memory meet.

2 DEATH STRIP, LIFELINE, MEMORIAL: THE MAKING OF THE GREEN BELT

The GDR was founded on October 7, 1949, as the new border separating it from its West German counterpart slowly solidified. Within days, on October 16, the first lethal shots were fired across that boundary, killing Karl Sommer, a civilian from southern Thuringia who had passed across the demarcation line to northern Bavaria to buy food for his family and was on his way home. He died of his wounds while still on the Bavarian side. His story is one of 327 in a recently published accounting of border-related fatalities.[1]

In its development from a porous demarcation line to the world's most heavily fortified border, the boundary separating West and East Germany led to killing, maiming, displacement, persecution, and immiseration; in the border's forty-year existence, in addition to those who died at or near the border, about 75,000 people were arrested and imprisoned for attempting or planning to escape across the border, and thousands lost their property and homelands.[2] Hundreds of thousands more were incarcerated for political reasons, or had to suffer surveillance, repeated and invasive controls, and discrimination and repression all along the border and beyond.[3] The borderlands are wounded terrain, etched with grief, anger, and despair. A strange irony of history produced a mnemonic ecological condition: a damned place that has become a thing of beauty and refuge. These dense layers of past and present must be treated with care, and conservationists must tend to local people, local knowledges, and local natures to understand how the borderlands have been both made and experienced.

Replacing the postwar demarcation line, the GDR (under Soviet influence) announced the beginning of a formal border regime, manifesting most immediately in the demarcation of a five-hundred-meter-wide security strip and five-kilometer-wide prohibited zone (*Sperrgebiet*). To forcibly impose its vision on an inhabited landscape, in 1952 and again in 1961, the GDR relocated thousands of residents from their homes and farms near the border into the East German hinterlands.[4] Centuries-old villages were razed to the ground, and ancestral land belonging to the residents was expropriated and made state property or resold to the East German farmers who remained nearby. The deportations came as a shock. In the case of Sonneberg in southern Thuringia near the border of Bavaria, for instance, paramilitary units arrived before dawn, pounded on doors, and told residents they had twenty-four hours to pack their belongings and leave. The frail, elderly, injured, and pregnant were evacuated without exception, their trucks loaded at gunpoint. With brutal swiftness, residents lost their homes, property, jobs, land, and community. The deportations felt "terrifyingly random" since "many upstanding citizens were targeted, even as known troublemakers were spared. . . . Maybe neighbors had denounced them."[5] Residents were also often mobilized or forced to build fences and clear forests to expand the border fortifications.[6]

By the mid-1960s, ever more modern barrier systems were built. The accelerated construction was an immediate response to the division of Berlin. Until then, the city had acted as an escape valve for desperate East Germans, who could travel there and board a flight to the west. With the sudden erection of the formidable Berlin Wall, potential escapees would now need to breach the inter-German border, something the GDR government was keen to prevent. The 1960s thus saw the greatest construction boom in the borderlands.[7] A patrol road (Kolonnenweg) was added to allow for year-round surveillance by armored vehicles. Spring guns, antivehicular ditches, floodlights, guard dogs, and steel-reinforced fences covered with electric trip wires were added incrementally. By the 1970s, the GDR border forces were building fences farther back from the actual demarcation line, leaving a five-hundred-meter-wide cleared strip on which any escapee could be easily seen and shot. The deadliest addition were land mines. No longer encased in wood that would rot away over time, the new and improved weapons were now plastic, hidden in a thirty-meter-wide strip (though minefields did not exist continuously along the border due to their high cost). Behind the patrol roads, ditches and spring guns, guard dogs, and minefields existed a hundred-meter-wide "no-man's-land" before the actual borderline to West Germany would be crossed (figure 2.1).

The imposition of the border in rural areas wreaked havoc on agriculture and existing land tenure regimes. Frontier farmers felt the impact of the demarcation lines the moment they were drawn in 1945 as access to their fields was made difficult or denied entirely. In some places, the border solidified quite suddenly in late May 1952 when the GDR decided

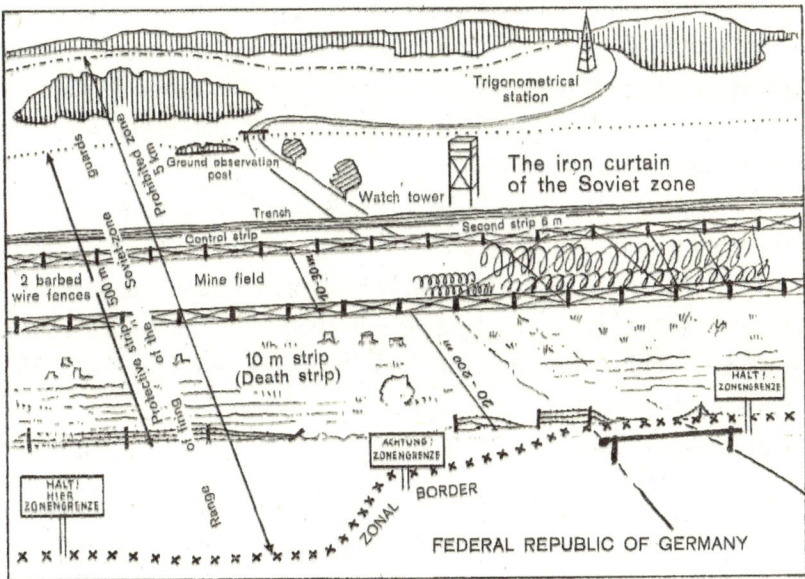

Figure 2.1

A generalized diagram of the inter-German border, showing the inner death strip and wider protective strip as well as a number of military elements including minefields, observation towers, and barbed wire fence. *Source*: Ministerium für Bundesangelegenheiten, Vertriebene und Flüchtlinge.

to formally seal the boundary. In Eichsfeld, a rural region in central Germany, about 330 people were deported from the border areas to the GDR hinterland, while over 700 farmers managed to flee to West Germany, frequently taking farm equipment and livestock with them, thereby making it harder for those left behind to get by. The massive buildup of military border infrastructure in the 1950s transformed the landscape of central Germany. According to traditional land inheritance customs, for centuries land had been apportioned among a farmer's surviving children, creating by the 1950s a patchwork of small subsistence farms. The GDR's push to close the border cut right through it, threatening the property rights and land access of dozens of farming families. The border's expansion swallowed up much agricultural land in the East, and the GDR police imposed significant restrictions, such as by demanding that farmwork only happen during daylight hours and prohibiting the planting of taller crops like corn lest they provide hiding places for possible escapees. In the West, the border made cultivation more challenging due to East German surveillance and significant herbicide drift.[8] Physical distance between people in East and West Germany increased as a result, entrenching the border yet also giving new, emergent ecosystems a berth.

Starting in the late 1950s and early 1960s, East German farmers also had to contend with the upheavals of Soviet-induced agrarian reform that eliminated their ancestral property rights. Farmers often resisted this wrenching change, but as a result they and their families frequently suffered harassment by the GDR police and authorities.[9] A contemporary *London Times* correspondent reported on the state's collectivization drive and final dissolution of small farms in East Germany:

> They start by describing the bright prospects of a Socialist future, continue with threats, and end with accusations. Loud-speaker vehicles are stationed outside [the farmer's] house, and for hours on end deafening appeals are made to him to hand his land over to the cooperative, and if he displays reluctance he is denounced as an enemy of the State, a criminal enemy of the new Socialist order, a saboteur of peace. During the night floodlights are directed at his windows. The "persuader teams" work on him in shifts and do not hesitate to move into his bedroom and prevent him from sleeping: and the "brainwashing" process continues until it finally leads to the required result. . . .

Refugees describe many tragedies among farmers—suicides and imprisonment of those caught while trying to escape. Much land in east Germany has been worked by the same family for generations.[10]

In the 1960s, whether in the East German Eichsfeld or beyond, many who disagreed with collectivization ended up fleeing or at least tried. In spring 1960, the GDR's Volkspolizei (VoPos, or national police) "ran dragnets through Berlin's trains, arresting and taking hundreds of refugees off to prison and forced labor camps for 'reeducation.' Almost 200,000 escaped in 1960 despite the intensified watch on them, and another 207,026 fled in the first seven months of 1961."[11] Even postreunification, land—who owns it, who can use it to what purpose, and who should narrate its past and how—continues to be one of the most heated arenas of conflict in the borderlands, with immediate and urgent consequences for Green Belt conservation.

The border's construction and maintenance, and all-pervasive presence of the East German state that helped support it, have left indelible marks on multiple generations of East Germans. The Federal Foundation for the Study of the Communist Dictatorship in Eastern Germany (Bundesstiftung zur Aufarbeitung der SED-Diktatur), was established by the reunified German government in 1998 to assess the activities and impacts of the GDR government between 1949–1990.[12] Its newest report summarizes the consequences of political persecution in the GDR:

> Many people were subjected to long-term traumas that resulted from several individual events and that persist to this day. . . . The persecution measures could be very different. They included personal controls (for example, spying into the private/professional sphere, house searches, provocations) for the purpose of wearing down a person's psyche and reputation, various phases of detention with physical and, above all, psychological torture, further reprisals after detention, negative experiences with officials (such as the police, courts, authorities), suspensions from educational institutions, and the loss of social status, of jobs or of familiar environments. . . . The forced relocations from the border areas were also associated with dramatic burdens, the loss of property, a decline in social standing, and often housing in unacceptable conditions.[13]

In the context of GDR history, psychic scars from state-sponsored repression continue to manifest in a variety of ways, including feelings of fear, shame, anger, and distrust. There may be phobias of enclosed spaces, either from the forced relocations in cramped train cars or jails and interrogation cells, and there are persistent feelings of "complete helplessness and a high degree of distrust towards the state, all authorities or even persons of authority. There is often a pronounced need for justice."[14]

THE ECOLOGICAL IMPACT OF THE BORDER

While the border's consequences for the human population are generally thought to be overwhelmingly negative, that same militarized boundary had, by today's standards, much more ambiguous ecological effects. We can safely say that the impact of the border on the German landscape, including flora and fauna, was immense. All along the demarcation line, woods were cleared, undergrowth was destroyed, and earth was flattened. The border zone was continuously mowed and blanketed with herbicides to keep the area as open and bare as possible, so that escapee footsteps could be visible in the landscape. In some cases, spraying was so intense that the chemical clouds would drift over to West German farmers' fields and cover their crops.[15] Two herbicides were dominant along the border: SYS 67 Omnidel, consisting of 2,2-Dichloropropionic acid, and Azaplant Combi, which relies on Amitrol and Simazin, chemicals that have been banned in the European Union by now.[16] As funding for the border declined, even diesel fuel was applied to kill the last bit of vegetation.

Meanwhile, the land mines that had been placed along sections of the border led to massive deaths among forest animals that tripped the mines as they followed their old paths through woods and meadows, prompting one local hunter to refer to some of these stretches of borderlands as "cadaver fields."[17] Over time, the GDR border regime added heavy fencing to either side of the minefields, and animal deaths declined. But border fences have significant impacts for biodiversity, mainly in terms of cutting seasonal migration and disrupting genetic exchange.[18]

It was with some surprise, then, that starting in the 1970s, more and more evidence pointed the other way: that numerous plant and animal species, becoming rare elsewhere, were finding new homes along the border in the novel ecosystems coincidentally emerging from this militarized landscape. As the Cold War and with it the border fortifications proceeded, the region around it became quieter. In part this was due of course to the deportations in East Germany. But more generally, what had been the middle of Germany had become, rather suddenly, its periphery. Centuries-old trade networks and transportation routes were cut, and factories were closed. People to the east and west began reorienting themselves away from the border and toward their new centers.[19]

While the GDR continued to heavily spray some parts of the border, others were only cleared or mowed occasionally. This was true especially for the swath of land on the western side of the border fence, which was kept clear of major vegetation but otherwise saw no significant intervention. This used to be the original control strip and had been harrowed back in 1952, but since then the GDR had moved the fortifications back, thus creating an area of open land as the final obstacle for anyone daring or desperate enough to escape East Germany.[20] Unlike the surrounding farmlands, this part of the border remained free of herbicides or fertilizers, and allowed the development of extensive meadows and grasslands. Rich in seeds, insects, and small vertebrates, these spaces in turn attracted larger animals, most pronounced among them bird species that had become increasingly rare in other parts of Germany. Unlike mammals, birds were less troubled by minefields and fences, and instead found ample nesting and foraging sites. Later studies focusing on the increasing populations of the whinchat (*Saxicola rubetra*) and its close relatives, the bluethroat (*Luscinia svecica*) and stonechat (*Saxicola rubicola*), found that the border fortifications *themselves* were the cause, replacing habitat that was fast being lost elsewhere. The border installations offered microstructures that were attractive in multiple ways: metal fences functioned as singing or hunting perches, antivehicular ditches offered cover from predators or functioned as nesting sites, and the fallow land of the death strip increased access to insect food sources.[21] In other words, technology meant to intimidate, maim, and kill had received an entirely different interpretation, and was repurposed in the interests of the living. The novel ecosystem emerging in the shadow of the wall, while displacing some species (like beeches, firs, and other trees along with forest-dwelling animals), generated new spaces and hence gave rise to new species arrangements, which in turn were rendered valuable in human eyes due to the rarity of those species elsewhere. This reversal becomes the central pillar of a narrative of resurgence, expressed perhaps most eloquently in the image below, widely broadcast in the early years of Green Belt advocacy (figure 2.2).

Another major impact of the border concerned the recovery of freshwater bodies. The Drömling wetland in Saxony-Anhalt, for instance, had been drained and rendered moderately arable starting in the eighteenth century. The construction of the border, however, made further maintenance of the drainage ditches impossible, and within years, the Drömling flooded the fields and pastures once more. Reeds started expanding again, along with stands of spruces and gray alders. Animals followed, including storks and lapwings, creating the conditions for a reemerging community of water-dependent animals. Decades before the border fell, the Drömling was a focus of conservation efforts in both West and East Germany.[22] The old

Figure 2.2
The whinchat (*Saxicola rubetra*) singing from its perch, a former GDR border post. This photograph, taken shortly after reunification, became the emblem of the early Green Belt effort, representing nature's conquest over the Cold War. *Source*: Thomas Stephan, used with permission.

demarcation line on which much of the 1949 partition was based often used rivers or creeks as natural divisions between aristocratic houses and later states. Beginning in the late 19th nineteenth century and especially in the twentieth century, German engineers straightened rivers to rationalize the flow of water and therefore reduce the risk of disastrous flooding.[23] Where the GDR border coincided with streams, though, these kinds of interventions were impossible. One illustrative example here is the Föritz, a small border river in northern Franconia, Bavaria. Prior to the German postwar partition, the Föritz meandered in a classical pattern. Yet by 1988, the river had been significantly modified and straightened; gone were the loops and secondary arms of the river. The only place where the Föritz retained its old pattern was where it overlapped with the GDR fortifications and any intervention in the streambed was curtailed for decades.[24] Not surprisingly, it is precisely here along the Föritz that some of the last thick-shelled river mussels (*Unio crassus*) can be found in Germany.[25] Today, the rest of the Föritz is undergoing significant restoration, modeled on the borderlands portions that had escaped German water engineering in the twentieth century.

THE ESTABLISHMENT OF THE GREEN BELT

The person most intimately identified with the German Green Belt is geo-ecologist Kai Frobel, who came of age at a time when the modern German environmental movement emerged. The "father of the Green Belt" grew up in the village of Hassenberg, Bavaria, spitting distance from the border wall. Throughout high school and then university, Frobel studied bird distributions along the western edge of the border, noting the concentrations of rare species alongside it. Together with other interested youths and conservationists, he founded the Ecological Working Group Coburg (Arbeitskreis Ökologie Coburg) in the late 1970s, and began surveying flora and fauna in the entire region of Coburg. Among the most important maps the group produced is one bolstering Frobel's earlier findings: the whinchat, a songbird fast vanishing from Germany's agricultural landscape, was breeding right along the border: the small, black squares were arranged in a near-perfect imitation of the border line (figure 2.3). According to Frobel, the publication

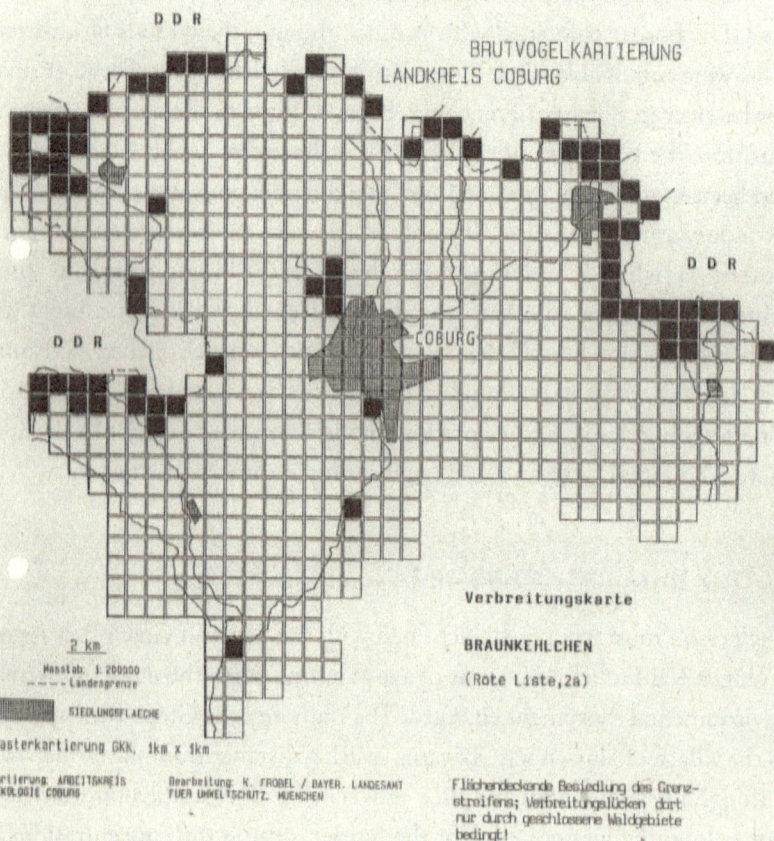

Figure 2.3

An early map of the distribution of the whinchat in northern Bavaria. The top edge marks the border to East Germany, and the blacked-out squares are the locations where breeding populations were located. *Source*: BUND Fachbereich Grünes Band, used with permission.

of these results was a way to shame the West German public, especially its state institutions. Nature conservation was really *so* bad that of all places, it was the former GDR death strip that offered refuge for so many species that only twenty years earlier had been common in Bavaria: "The survey was really a way for us to illustrate how pathetic conservation was in the West."[26] After his university days, in 1987, Frobel became the acting director of the BUND's Nuremberg office, where he still works today and that he has helped transform into the Green Belt project office.

Meanwhile, another scientist, documentary filmmaker Heinz Sielmann, had had the same insight. In a now-famous episode of his popular weekly television show *Expeditionen ins Tierreich* (Expeditions into the animal kingdom) in fall 1988, Sielmann stood within sight of the GDR wall and explained to his viewers,

> The fence is 1,393 kilometers long, built by the other German state and arbitrarily cutting through nature and landscape. Nature, my dear viewers, knows no bounds, "it is based on freedom, and it is rich through freedom." Friedrich Schiller said these beautiful words almost 200 years ago. Walls, fences, barbed wire are *un*natural. And this inner-German border is also unnatural, because it cuts the connectedness of neighbors and the naturally grown nature and cultural areas. But in the shadow of the border, where the no-man's-land becomes hostile and inhospitable to humans, an interesting flora and fauna has survived and developed.

In what now seem like prophetic terms, Sielmann ended his film thus:

> If you think of the history of this border in the middle of Germany, then you can hardly find in it anything positive. But maybe it still offers us conservationists a chance. As we have seen, there are still intact habitats in the shadow of the border, refuges of nature with a rich flora and fauna, a tempting goal for a joint conservation project of East and West. In any case, my dear viewers, I cannot imagine a better monument for a vanquished inner-German border than a large national park from the Baltic Sea to the Thuringian Forest.[27]

While Sielmann spoke in these terms, the idea of a singular corridor was for Frobel not yet part of the vision. In scientific circles, corridor thinking was not widespread at the time. Frobel first encountered it in a US publication, the *Audubon Wildlife Report 1989/1990*, which gave him a glimpse of how the German borderlands, once preserved as a singular protected area, could act as a "highway for nature" at the very same time as it could become part of the project of German reunification.[28]

An ambitious, symbolically laden conservation vision had been born. The fall of the Berlin Wall on November 9, 1989, and with it the functional end of the GDR, caught most people in the two Germanies by complete surprise. When Frobel arrived at work the following Monday morning, his boss, Hubert Weiger, called him into his office. Weiger had long been deeply involved in the West German environmental movement and also had connections to East German environmentalists, as did Frobel. The two of them decided to seize the opportunity (figure 2.4). In a letter from November 11, 1989, that the BUND sent to a network of West and East German conservationists, Weiger called for a meeting on December 9 at the Eisteich (ice pond) Restaurant in Hof, a small Bavarian town near the GDR.[29] The letter stated that the opening of the border "finally allowed a long overdue exchange of information and experiences among conservationist on both sides. Given the many common problems such as air and water pollution or conservation, there is an urgent need that we work together. . . . Because we wish to arrange for this meeting to be as open as possible, we ask our friends in the GDR to distribute the included copies of this invitation to others."[30]

Weiger followed up his call with a lengthy press release on November 30, 1989, that underscored the importance of the borderlands for species conservation: "The opening of the borders between the Federal Republic and the GDR also open up entirely new opportunities and perspectives for environmentalism and conservation on both sides of the border," he stated. The press release explained that the "habitat and structural diversity, as well as the enormous spatial extent of the border strip and the absence of fertilization and herbicide application, had made the 'death strip' into the largest contiguous biotope in Germany." Not only this, but because of intensive agriculture on both sides of the border, "entire species populations are dependent on this border strip," such as the whinchat, shrike, and other now-iconic animals. This extraordinary community was being endangered by "untrammeled" road construction crisscrossing the border and threatening to carve up remaining precious habitat. Weiger concluded by restating the organization's belief that only a close collaboration between West and East German conservationists could combat these threats: "Our environmental movement has received renewed energy from the successes of citizen

Figure 2.4

Hubert Weiger (*left*) and Kai Frobel (*right*), key figures in the creation of the Green Belt. *Source*: BUND Fachbereich Grünes Band, used with permission.

protests in the GDR" that could help West Germans demand fundamental ecological reforms as well.[31]

On December 9, 1989, a month after the fall of the wall, when Frobel and Weiger arrived in the town of Hof they found travel chaotic, with cross-border traffic disrupting any semblance of vehicular order. When they pulled into the overfilled parking lot of the restaurant where the meeting was supposed to take place, Frobel recalled that "we were very upset to see all these cars. We thought they stopped there to park and then go shopping in the inner city. Then, we realized they were our guests."[32] In fact, four hundred environmentalists had made it to the meeting. The restaurant could not hold the crowd, and people stood in hallways and spilled out into the street. Frobel got over his astonishment, and at the meeting, in a stuffy, overcrowded room, he called for the development of a "green belt" to safeguard the precious ecological diversity that had emerged in the border's shadow. It was the ecological backbone of central Europe and had to be secured immediately. Attendees enthusiastically and unanimously supported the resolution to create this protected area:

- The border strip between the Federal Republic [FRG] and the German Democratic Republic is to be safeguarded as an ecological backbone of central Europe, that is, an immediate protection of these areas must occur in the GDR and the FRG.
- Beyond this, extensive, transboundary protected areas shall be created or connected to each other.
- The detailed planning should be carried out by the Institute for Landscape Research and Conservation (ILN) and the Federal Research Agency for Conservation and Landscape Ecology (BFANL).
- During the detailed planning, the needs of local residents must be given adequate consideration.
- This demand is not a retroactive justification for the border.[33]

With the resolution in place, the next step was to get the word out—and fast. While conservationists were getting organized, so were other interest groups, including large civil engineering companies working to reestablish a highway network in the border area. The Bavarian Association for Nature Conservation's (Bund Naturschutz Bayern, or BN) newsletter of February 15, 1990, identified three acute needs:

- Heightened vigilance towards projects in the border region.
- A rapid mapping and representation of the most important biotopes in the border region to prevent interventions in these spaces.
- A detailed biotope- and species-survey in the area near the border within the next two years.

By request of the Bavarian Environmental Ministry and under the guidance of Frobel and Dieter Franz, Frank Reissenweber, a biologist then working for the Bavarian Association for the Protection of Birds (Landesverband für Vogelschutz) oversaw and helped carry out the ambitious study that eventually produced a five-hundred-page report. Across Franconia in northern Bavaria as well as in Saxony and Thuringia, Frobel's original study from the 1970s was confirmed again and again. In the area around Coburg, 167 different bird species were recorded, 122 of them residents rather than merely migrating through. Of those 122 species, 46 were on the Red List for Bavaria or the FRG.[34] For dragonflies, another indicator, the numbers suggested a similar picture: of the 32 documented species in the region, 18 were likely entries to the Red List. In a written update to a colleague in August 1990, Frobel explained that the greatest emerging threat to these species in the region was agriculture, specifically the land claims of West German farmers, alongside a boom in road construction seeking to reconnect all the places the border had severed from each other.

Meanwhile, the BUND worked hard to attract media attention, and indeed newspapers, magazines, and television began investigating and ultimately celebrating this "lifeline" that had sprung from the GDR "death strip." The same year in November, just one year after the fall of the wall, environmental minister Klaus Töpfer (who would later lead the United Nations Environment Programme from 1998 to 2006) officially voiced his support for the nascent Green Belt.[35]

All in all, conservationists were now in a better position to make their case for protecting the borderlands, but they were tested almost immediately. The diverse habitats that had emerged in the borderlands were already under siege from many sides; in the chaotic years following the end of the GDR, the property relations along the border—land expropriated by the GDR to build its wall—were thrown into utter confusion. When the border regime dissolved practically overnight, this previous no-man's-land turned into anything and everything, all cataloged in the 1990 ecological survey: the borderlands became a waste dump for some, a quarry for others, an improvised motorcycle track, and a newly farmed field. After reunification, many nearby residents were keen to make the border disappear by cultivating every inch of land (often illegally), including areas in the former GDR minefield. Other parts of the border, previously mowed and now left without further intervention, had already started overgrowing in the months since the fall of the GDR, threatening to destroy the habitats of the whinchat and shrike, species dependent on open, shrubby spaces.

The real test, however, came in the form of the 1996 Wall Property Law, an attempt by the newly unified German government (though of course a government dominated by former West Germany) to impose order on the unruly borderlands. In essence, the law (known in Germany as the Mauergrundstückgesetz, or MauerG for short) allowed formerly expropriated landowners to purchase back their family lands at 25 percent of the current market rate. The law had been conceived with Berlin properties in mind. Yet the fact that it would have consequences far beyond the metropolis was not seriously considered. There were outcries from various sides: property owners were indignant that they were charged anything at all for land that had been theirs before the war while conservationists were appalled that these precious habitats—in such dire need of state protection—were being turned over into private hands. The roughly eighteen hundred reclamations (repurchases) under the Wall Property Law totaled two thousand hectares of borderlands. In rare cases, the BUND was able to intervene and negotiate a settlement by paying the government 25 percent and the current property owner 75 percent of the market value, with the parcel then becoming the property of the NGO. Similar strategies were, though, also practiced by the large agrarian collectives in the former East Germany that wanted land back for farming. The BUND meanwhile, having founded a Green Belt project office in 1998 under Frobel's leadership, lobbied hard for a moratorium on property sales, which it eventually achieved that same year. At that point, about 10 percent of the Green Belt had fallen into private ownership during the first few years of the Wall Property Law. Another 55 percent still belonged to the federal government, which intended to sell the parcels on the open market, with only the remaining 35 percent held by conservationists.[36]

While at the local level property relations were still in limbo along the border, at the national level, things were not much clearer. Where did the decision-making capacity for conservation rest? Was it the federal government's responsibility or rather more local bodies? And given the collapse of East Germany, and acute need to rebuild a shockingly derelict economy and infrastructure there, where did the environment fall in the list of priorities? The BUND argued that the federal government should make exceptions for areas with conservation value and either donate those parcels or sell them for a symbolically modest amount to the federal state governments or conservation organizations. The federal government shot back that conservation was the matter of the states, not central government. This wrangling finally reached a temporary halt when the finance ministry agreed to stop the sale of parcels that conservationists had identified as valuable.[37] Still, in practice, it often simply meant that conservation organizations were offered those lands for sale first—and at their full market value. In many cases, the NGOs had to forego purchase and the parcels fell to affluent private individuals after all.

In order to raise the required funds, the BUND became creative: in 2002, the NGO started selling Green Belt "shares" at sixty-five euros a piece. Most of the money thus raised was invested in land acquisition; by 2015, nearly 700 hectares were safeguarded this way.[38] Conservationists landed a media coup in June 2002 when Mikhail Gorbachev purchased a share in the Green Belt—a symbolically deep act of restitution and reconciliation.

By 2005, after intense lobbying by the conservation community, the federal government decided that rather than sell off the borderland properties in its control (11,500 hectares) to private buyers, it would delegate authority over them to the federal states with the mandate to earmark them for conservation.[39] Some federal states were not particularly keen on having land uses so restricted by conservation requirements as to make their sale (and hence revenue) impossible. Thuringia, however, led the way by accepting the land transfer and setting the parcels aside for their protection. Because Thuringia has the highest proportion of borderlands of any German state, the Green Belt had thereby achieved significant expansion and greater legal certainty. The land transfer was finally cemented by written agreement in 2008, and shortly thereafter 3,800 hectares were granted to the Thuringian conservation foundation (Stiftung Naturschutz Thüringen), which continues to be the most significant property owner of border parcels in Germany.

Things also shifted at the national level. In the early 2000s, the Federal Agency for Nature Conservation (Bundesamt für Naturschutz, or BfN), began supporting the effort as well with some of the first grants funding a biological assessment that would become the basis for Green Belt conservation work in the coming decade. In addition to financial support, key people in local government helped the effort along, with the state of Thuringia—because it has the highest proportion of Green Belt lands among all federal states—being the most prominent, even when it was under conservative Christian Democratic Union leadership. Even today, the Green Belt project is anchored by staff across the environmental ministries in former East German states. By 2007, as the German national government (a Left-Green coalition) devised its national biodiversity strategy, the Green Belt was identified as a vanguard or "beacon" project. And in 2009, the federal government renewed the Federal Conservation Law (Bundesnaturschutzgesetz, or BNatSchG for short) and included a demand in paragraph 21 for ecological networks and corridors to occupy at least 10 percent of the national territory. The Green Belt is clearly in many regions the primary axis for this.[40]

"The Green Belt Experience"

After decades of uncertainty, the federal decisions renewed the momentum around the Green Belt. As the anxiety lessened, the BUND felt free to think in new ways about the project. To increase its appeal, raise public awareness of the borderlands transformation, and heighten local people's acceptance for conservation in their midst, the BUND (with 3.6 million euros in financing from the BfN) launched a nature tourism initiative along the Green Belt. Between 2007 and 2011, under the running head "The Green Belt Experience" (Erlebnis Grünes Band), the BUND developed touristic potential in three selected locations: the Elbe/Altmark region in northern Germany, the Harz mountains and national park in the center of the country, and the Thuringian/Franconian forests in the southern part of the Green Belt.[41] The locations were chosen because they "mirror the variability in landscape as much as the different degrees of touristic development and the status of regional and interdisciplinary cooperation." Collaborating with tourist agencies, the BUND developed travel packages that emphasized the motto "Nature, Culture, History," an early attempt to think much more broadly and creatively about the layers in this landscape as well as the Green Belt's possible economic ripple effects in the impoverished regions through which it runs. The BUND worked at better marketing, creating a logo and consistent design for Green Belt–related signage and other informational materials. A look at the tourist brochures from these sites shows the richness of the Green Belt marketing discourse. Besides the fundamentals of how to get there along with some basic facts about the Green Belt, the pamphlets range widely. Maps of local hiking and bicycle trails are shown next to snippets of local history (medieval to twentieth century) and information on local sites of interest (towns, monuments, and natural features). Flip a page and the tourist learns about some of the most charismatic species in the area or finds out about successful restoration projects nearby. Particular care has been taken to make room for "borderland fates" (*Grenzschiksale*), stories of how the military infrastructure affected the lives of local people and shaped the landscape. Two decades after the start of the Green Belt project, the BUND thus attempted to make legible these three regions in a particular way through a nature-culture-history nexus that highlighted particular story lines in an effort to market the Green Belt. The hope was that stronger interest in and support for the project among locals and people elsewhere in Germany would create the political and economic networks to sustain it.[42]

All in all, the Green Belt experience has produced 695 kilometers of marked hiking trails, 440 kilometers of bicycle trails, 5 kilometers of canoeing circuits, 129 informational signs, 71 guided tours, and 22 detailed portable maps.[43] The closing survey that the BUND administered also suggested that awareness of the Green Belt had increased both locally and nationally.[44] Years on from the project, even a cursory look at the three sites shows that the initiative spawned a more solid tourist infrastructure. Hotels and inns have latched on as have other small businesses from farm stores to bike rental shops. National parks and other protected areas feature the Green Belt experience prominently on their websites.[45] A study conducted by the University of Göttingen in 2010 argued that the activities had in fact laid the foundation for sustainable economic development in the border regions, but that their future would be more determined by the attitudes and policies of national-level and local actors, from funders to politicians.[46]

"Closing the Gaps": Projekt Lückenschluss

Despite these expansions and the best efforts of the BUND, the Green Belt is still not the continuous corridor envisioned by its champions. Today, over 10 percent of it remains disrupted by roads, residential development, or agriculture, and as of 2019, there were still dozens of large gaps separating the habitats and disrupting migration routes of plants and animals—some of them over twenty kilometers long.[47] To address this, the BfN funded the BUND's "Closing the Gaps" project proposal with 5.1 million euros (the amount is about 16 percent of the 30 million euro fund that Frobel had requested to purchase back the remaining parcels).[48] The project—which ran from 2012 to 2020—sought to not simply establish baseline data on fragmentation but also develop best practices for mitigation, and then pilot those in several different locations in Thuringia and Saxony-Anhalt.[49] By 2020, the BUND had been able to acquire 310 hectares in and alongside the Green Belt, the spatial equivalent to about 430 soccer fields. In some regions, the gaps were made to disappear entirely, finally closing in on the original vision to create an uninterrupted corridor. The BUND noted that the impact was already visible: while the breeding populations of the whinchat are declining across Germany and will likely disappear entirely, they remained steady or were even growing in the Green Belt.[50]

There are, however, gaps that cannot be closed, such as highways that cut through the corridor now that cannot easily be unbuilt. The hope here is that in exceptional cases, highway overpasses can be developed, and in most other instances, additional land purchases could make it possible to maintain uninterrupted corridors even if they depart somewhat from the borderlands.[51] On the ground, the work to close the gaps is legalistic and time intensive. BUND staff quickly learned that to actually purchase parcels or subdivide them is difficult and bureaucratically complex. Instead, the BUND began negotiating with property owners and farmers about exchanging parcels—their borderland properties for some others nearby. If that was not possible, another option was to create contractual agreements with landowners that they would manage their borderland parcel in the interest of conservation and the BUND would purchase nearby land that would be treated according to the wishes of the property owner. Yet forty years of division continue to reverberate here: some property owners simply do not want to sell their land, come what may. It was expropriated once; it will not be taken again.[52]

The Green Belt: Ecological Vision

According to the logic of its advocates, the Green Belt has ecological value for a number of reasons. First, it has become a refuge for over a thousand animal and plant species that given Germany's industrialized agricultural landscapes, have become rare elsewhere. In many cases, these are species that require a middle ground between forests and fields. Second, the Green Belt's value lies in the stark contrast it offers: a structurally complex mosaic against the monotony of corn or wheat monoculture that surrounds it (figure 2.5). Third, due to its length and location, the Green Belt represents a cross-section of central Europe's terrestrial habitats. In fact, a recent ecological

Figure 2.5
The Green Belt is clearly visible here as a starkly different ecological community from the mono-crop fields on either side. Also note the remnants of the old patrol road on the Green Belt's right edge. *Source*: Klaus Leidorf, used with permission.

survey cataloged no less than 109 different habitat types, ranging from forests to sand dunes, wetlands, bogs, and grassland.[53] Fourth, in the context of accelerated habitat destruction and fragmentation, the Green Belt is seen to be a crucial connector between islands of biodiversity, linking already existing protected areas with each other and thus allowing for gene flow between populations.[54] Finally, the Green Belt is a north-south axis. With increased climatic changes, especially the anticipated warming of central Europe, the Green Belt is said to act as an ecological corridor along which northward species migration can happen, thereby extending the life chances of vulnerable species.[55]

There is more here, though. In the context of a fractured, postreunification Germany, the appeal of ecological connection is obvious. The metaphors of habitat "fragmentation" and its purported opposites—"corridors" and "networks"—do important work. For policy makers, talk of ecological connectors like these can help compel coordination and teamwork across interest groups and geographic areas, all in the name of science, which is posited as neutral, authoritative knowledge beyond interest group politics.[56] These terms can help communicate and justify environmental agendas and encourage compliance. Talk of networking nature also legitimizes greater spatial claims making since the term is predicated on protecting habitat rather than species or populations. While some have voiced concerns that an insistence on corridors—like smaller-scale hedgerows or meadow strips—signals a retreat of the environmental movement, in the context of the Green Belt the term has been used to extend conservation's reach and situate the project not just scientifically but morally as well between memory and ecology, experts and the public, and West and East Germany.[57]

In the Green Belt ecological corridor, the BUND has outlined its ecological management guidelines via specific examples of "landscape care" (*Landschaftspflege*). While the former borderlands are ecologically complex and management recommendations vary, in general three different restoration approaches can be distinguished: hands-off, passive management that allows "natural processes" to unfold with little to no human intervention; hands-on, active, and consistent management that works against such processes and instead maintains habitats that would otherwise disappear in these locations;

and a more classical form of restoration that seeks to create what is assumed to be the original structure of an ecosystem or ecological process in hopes of generating a self-sustaining dynamic in the near future.

In one publication after another, however, the characteristic considered most unique and significant about the Green Belt is its open land. In basic terms, open land (*Offenland*) describes habitats that are neither woods or water, nor asphalted or developed spaces. For the BUND, it includes land that has mostly disappeared elsewhere in Germany: wet and dry meadows, heaths, low-standing shrubs, coppices, and other kinds of ruderal compositions.[58] This is the landscape that the border regime created: most of today's open lands along the Green Belt used to be the no-man's-land between the border fence and the actual borderline between East and West Germany. Ecologically, the open land emphasis of the Green Belt is a pragmatic compromise since it seems to offer at least something to most species. Because these partly open corridors provide a combination of grasslands, shrubs, and trees, the hope is that they will "simultaneously connect patches of both open habitats and woodlands and promote the dispersal of species from both types of habitat."[59]

Maintaining open land also allows the BUND to preserve traces of the former border (figure 2.6). It is the space that the border has *left behind* after its removal and disappearance that is now being managed for ecological and memorial purposes; in a way, ecological emergence and management make present the border's material absence. The concrete slabs of the patrol road or a few border posts may be the only reminder that the border was here, and even they have been removed in many places. What is left is open space, rendered valuable for conservationists through a strange and unanticipated ecological reversal. The border here exists as a suggestion, an allusion (if not illusion) through the bands of open land or concentrations of species otherwise unusual in the region. This predilection toward the recent past is apparent in the BUND's articulation of the overarching goal of the Green Belt's management:

> For the care of the habitat of the terrestrial spaces in the Green Belt, the fundamental goal is to achieve a half-open state with a mosaic-like change between grassland, fallow land, partly vegetation-free areas, and succession

Figure 2.6
The Green Belt, seen here as a cleared band through the forest, represents important open land habitats. It is also a visible reminder of the border, traces of which some Germans would like to see disappear. *Source*: Klaus Leidorf, used with permission.

with shrubs. This would not only provide the most immediate function as habitat, but also offer suitable structures for species with diverse ecological needs. The Green Belt should ideally be recognizable in the landscape throughout its entire length.[60]

So open land is one of the core arguments for the Green Belt's management approach. In addition, the last line is notable in that the Green Belt follows not simply an ecological imperative. As will be discussed later, the BUND has a two-pronged approach. The preeminent and more immediate goal is the conservation and maintenance of particular endangered habitat types, and with them the plant and animal communities that have found a home in them. Yet there is a crucial, secondary component: that the Green Belt should also preserve the imprint of the border. The latter thus forces new dimensions into this ecological project, asking conservationists to also think hard about how to account for a troubled past in this space. As we will see, these two goals at certain times exist in deep conflict with each other and at others emerge as mutually constitutive.

From Ecology to Memory

In the Green Belt's early years, all eyes were on simply protecting as much of the borderlands as possible and with them the many species that had found a refuge there. As described, threats to the land were numerous and pressing, and conservationists remember this time as intensely stressful—a time of damage control and triage. While an early brochure from the mid-1990s briefly describes the Green Belt's potential as a "special kind of open air museum," Frobel admits that in this initial period no one was really thinking about the borderlands in any deeper way other than their ecological importance.[61] It only became apparent over time, and with mounting criticism from residents, politicians, and historians, that the dense layers of this terrain needed attending, that they needed to be honored and rendered visible and narratable in some way.[62] Even then, it was a task for which the BUND was not well prepared.

The remnants of the former military installations are few and far between in today's Green Belt landscape. In the heady early years of Germany's reunification, there was a demand from both sides of the Berlin Wall that the traces of partition be removed and demolished as quickly as possible. Most of the fencing and border posts were pulled down immediately and enthusiastically. It took considerably longer for the minefields to be dug up—in fact, there are stretches of borderland that have not been fully cleared of mines and never will be—and for control towers, bunkers, phone lines, and other components of the border to be destroyed. In many instances, private individuals salvaged border elements for personal use or organized them for preservation. In some cases, their efforts led to the creation of borderlands museums as well as ad hoc, private collections presented in the garages, basements, and attics of local homes. In still other cases, pieces of the border were simply repurposed quietly, pragmatically, and without much to-do; the fencing material, for example, continues to show up around people's homes and backyards, where it helps protect fruit trees from hungry deer or holds together a compost heap or two.

In general terms, the most prominent elements of the border that still dot the Green Belt include the concrete slabs of the patrol road, a number of East German watchtowers, segments of steel fence, and alongside the roads that bisect the Green Belt, remainders of former checkpoints with gates and office buildings. Beyond that, the antivehicular ditches are often still visible alongside the patrol road, and here and there one can still find parts of Stasi tunnels, sniper hideouts, and several former GDR boundary posts, faded, toppled, or in pieces.[63]

Given these scattered remains, and the fact that younger Germans have little to no personal connection to the GDR past, the Green Belt as memorial landscape must be curated to be understood. The Green Belt experience initiative from 2007–2011, mentioned already, tried to make history more visible. Critics had already begun pointing out that conservation could easily lead to a de-historicization of the landscape, greenwashing of a traumatic past, and facile escape from Germans' collective burden to remember.[64] In response, the BUND surveyed the borderlands for opportunities to intensify engagement with history and memory. They were plentiful if one looked for them: in just one of the three model regions, the survey identified thirty-nine relics of the former border that could be made accessible to visitors in different ways.[65] In my own travels along the Green Belt, which began several years after the conclusion of the initiative, I have encountered frequent signage that helps explain and render visible some of the landscape's layers, telling stories both ecological and historical. Brochures aimed at visitors and tourists similarly highlight environmental successes and tragic "border tales" that the BUND considers worthy of attention.

In cooperation with the Union of Victims' Associations of Communist Tyranny (Union der Opferverbände kommunistischer Gewaltherrschaft), the BUND then established several memorials for those who were killed trying to escape the GDR.[66] At the same time, the BUND changed the way it manages its youth volunteers. For years it had organized international youth camps that focused on "landscape care" (Landschaftspflege), such as curtailing forest succession in open land by cutting back tree seedlings. More recently, these youth camps have been infused with history lessons, raising not just young people's ecological awareness but educating them about the border and Germany's partition as well. Part of their activities involves hearing from survivors and witnesses of the border regime.[67]

A new phase in the development of the Green Belt was launched in 2019 with the Lenzen Declaration.[68] In response to continuing concerns that the Green Belt ecologizes decades of Sozialistische Einheitspartei Deutschland (SED) rule and the Cold War, the BUND has committed itself to a much more thorough and careful approach to history.[69] More specifically, the Lenzen Declaration calls for the creation of "model projects between conservationists and historians to explore the basis and potentials for a particular culture of remembrance [*Erinnerungskultur*] along the Green Belt."[70] Further, borderland museums with direct connections to Green Belt lands should receive increased funding and staffing as well as offer improved educational materials. The model projects should use historical analysis and discussion to determine whether to add more elements to the memorial landscape, including possibly linkages to online information or installation of the well-known *Stolpersteine*.[71] In the coming decades, the Green Belt advocates are thus seeking to deepen their historical work and memorial considerations.

CURRENT ENVIRONMENTAL SITUATION IN GERMANY

That historical and memorial work has come relatively late for the BUND, because its focus for the first decade and beyond was simply to secure precious borderland and save its plant and animals species. Of all the countries in western Europe, Germany's landscapes can seem to the observer among the most domesticated, most harnessed to human needs, and most manufactured. It is also a country with one of the strongest and most celebrated environmental movements.

Environmentalism in Germany today is rarely politically contested. In fact, being green is for many Germans not just a source of pride but a source of national identity too, and "what it mean[s] to be green, in a particular place and time, says a lot about what it mean[s] to be German."[72] Recent surveys regarding environmental awareness and attitudes toward conservation show a population generally supportive, with some interesting caveats.

While over three-quarters of the German population is aware of and concerned about biodiversity decline, many locate that diversity outside Germany, presumably in places like sub-Saharan Africa or the Amazon rain forest.[73] To the extent that the Green Belt responds to larger-scale issues around biodiversity loss, this might be good news. But the fact that the Green Belt is deeply embedded in local and regional conservation concerns might leave its advocates on the defensive. This is worrisome for many since species decline in Germany shows no sign of stopping.

Today's threats to biodiversity (at the genetic, species, and ecosystem levels) are multiple, and because they are often entwined with each other, almost intractable. All factors are anthropogenic and have histories. At the top of the list in Germany is habitat fragmentation and degradation, which is in turn driven by agricultural intensification, pollution, urban development, road and railway construction, and the more and more frequent arrival of invasive species. A recent governmental study found that favorable conditions exist only for 29 percent of the surveyed species and 28 percent of Germany's habitats.[74] Altogether, the conservation outlook in Germany is not rosy. In the context of the Green Belt, agriculture, urbanization, and roads are the most pronounced challenges.

As elsewhere in the Global North, agricultural intensification in the twentieth century has utterly changed the German landscape. In the GDR, this took the form of collectivization, transforming a patchworked, small-parceled landscape into massive fields that belonged to agricultural production cooperatives (Landwirtschafliche Produktionsgenossenschaften), averaging roughly five thousand hectares each. Large fields were planted with a single crop, and the gigantic monocultures resulted in a marked decline in other forms of life in the fields.[75] Meanwhile, across the border in West Germany, agricultural modernization consolidated tiny family parcels into machine-friendly long rectangles with straight edges and paved access roads. In the process, in both Germanys, agricultural landscapes were essentially cleansed of hedges and tree groves, furrows and ditches were flattened, and boggy, soft land was drained while heavy fertilizer and pesticide use polluted the air and water.[76]

The long-term costs of this ecological simplification can be measured in many troubling ways today, including the plummeting numbers of insects and birds. Researchers measured the total aerial insect biomass between 1989 and 2016 across almost a hundred different locations in Germany. Their result: flying insects had declined a shocking 76 percent in twenty-seven years. The study's authors suggest that agricultural intensification is the plausible cause of this loss.[77] Birds are hardly faring any better, and those in agricultural regions are hardest hit. In roughly the same period, the lapwing (*Vanellus vanellus*) declined 75 percent, the whinchat—the Green Belt's unofficial emblem—dropped by 80 percent, and the gray partridge (*Perdix perdix*) almost disappeared, losing 94 percent of its numbers.[78] While some bird populations are indeed growing—such as the white-tailed eagle (*Haliaeetus albicilla*) and Eurasian crane (*Grus grus*)—it is the unspectacular, "common" birds like starlings, larks, and sparrows whose numbers are in precipitous decline, down 57 percent since 1980 all across Europe.[79] The data from the Pan-European Common Bird Monitoring Scheme are striking, not just in that they show a significant loss of birds, but that they show it for farmland species specifically. In other words, these are not birds that need pristine or isolated habitats but rather ones that have long lived with humans and had adapted well to human activity. Agricultural intensification has made life hard for even these creatures: too few crop varieties that are too densely planted, too many chemicals, too frequent mowing, too much land drained, and too little land left fallow.

As harmful as intensive agriculture is, it is being squeezed by competing land use demands. Alongside land consolidation and a shrinking farm population, the growth of urban areas and traffic networks impinge directly on formerly cultivated fields, further shrinking any surviving open and fallow land.[80] In fact, the increase in urban and transportation infrastructure between 2009 and 2012 swallowed up seventy-four hectares per day, clearly outpacing the thirty hectares per day maximum proposed in the national biodiversity strategy.[81] While urban development destroys habitat through conversion, road construction fragments it, making migrations impossible for many species, killing those animals that try, and inhibiting healthy gene flow between populations on either side of a road.[82] In the immediate postreunification years, road construction accelerated massively as communities euphorically reconnected long-severed relations and happily built new ones in an effort to stitch the two Germanies back together. By 2005, 450 roads cut through the Green Belt, and in Coburg, a town so significant in the Green Belt's history, the local highway ramp was built directly into the former border strip.[83] According to Frobel, since 1989, 14,000 kilometers of new roads have been built between the two Germanies.[84] Because of increased traffic demands, many highways are now being expanded to three or even four lanes in each direction. To address this worsening situation, a federal program launched in 2012 called Wiedervernetzung (reconnectivity) is trying to reduce road-related habitat fragmentation while increasing the linkages between existing habitats. The program seeks to inform planners of less disruptive alternatives, and where roads are already in use, provides funding for tunnels and overpasses that allow animals to safely cross.[85] Whether the program will meet its goals is not yet clear, but what *is* clear is that the Green Belt meets the requirements for an ecological connector, so much so that it was mentioned by name in the 2009 federal conservation law. The Green Belt must be understood in the context of these ecological challenges, especially since it is repeatedly presented as the solution to them.

RESURGENT ECOLOGIES, COMPLICATED HISTORIES

The militarizing of the border landscape in the decades after the Second World War and construction of ever more sophisticated barriers to escape—including fences, spring guns, and minefields—had ambiguous ecological effects. On the one hand, the border wreaked havoc for some species, but on the other hand, it became a safe space for others. And beyond the minefields, the border forced an end to most human management. Wetlands and streams, for instance, were left to their own devices, offering habitat to otherwise-endangered flora and fauna.

By the 1960s, the effects of these novel ecosystems were becoming clearer to observers, and by the 1970s, buoyed by a newly emergent environmental movement, the borderlands were revealed through empirical studies as an ecological refuge. Under the leadership of the BUND, especially Frobel, the borderlands became the focus of intense activism—something that only accelerated with the sudden collapse of the GDR and end of the forty-year-old partition in 1989. Despite a number of obstacles, including the legal limbo of the early reunification years, the BUND has managed to put the majority of the former borderlands under some form of protection. For the remaining parcels, the work to add them to the Green Belt and thus create one of the continent's largest contiguous ecological corridors is ongoing. The ecological vision for the Green Belt is, thanks to the borderlands' ecological diversity, also varied. In some places, the BUND suggests passive conservation, while in others it is either classical restoration or active management. Ecological interventions here seek to preserve the border's imprint to arrest forest succession, thereby re-creating (or maintaining) the ecological regime of the Cold War.

Yet memorial and historical considerations were a distant second to the ecological ones during the first two decades of the Green Belt's growth. Increasingly, the BUND has acknowledged this oversight and begun delving more deeply into the nexus of ecology and memory. Later chapters explore in much greater detail how this is being accomplished, what explicit and implicit politics of such an approach contains, and what the strengths and limitations of a mnemonic ecological perspective are in the borderlands. Before doing so, however, we must go back in time to better understand the Green Belt as an outgrowth of Germany's conservation tradition and as a project that exists in tension with that history. Tracing these roots allows for greater insight into how the past continues to be created and re-created in the manifold projects along the former inter-German border, and how these represent both strengths and limitations for conservation.

3 ROMANCING HEIMAT: THE ROOTS OF GREEN BELT CONSERVATION

The Green Belt is tightly connected to the German history of postwar division and the Cold War. As will be shown later, it also strongly reverberates with the ongoing project of reunification and remaining schisms between the two Germanys. But the Green Belt's roots into the past reach deeper than that. This chapter offers a selective reading of the German conservation movement, highlighting elements from the eighteenth, nineteenth, and early twentieth centuries that remain relevant to the Green Belt today. While conservation in the borderlands appears to be a recent ecological innovation, it is clearly heir to these older traditions, and shaped by their strengths and limitations. Within the framework of mnemonic ecologies, however, it also becomes apparent that German conservation is shaped by a complex emotional charge inherent to those pasts: a nostalgic attachment to place, love for an idealized homeland, and fear of loss of specific natures and the certainty they seemed to offer.

PROTECTING THE CULTURAL LANDSCAPE

As in the United States, German conservation emerged through the experience of industrialization in the eighteenth and nineteenth centuries. By the latter half of the nineteenth century, urban areas were expanding, railway and road networks were being built, and rural communities were increasingly uprooted from traditional, agricultural lifeways in Germany's transition to an industrializing country. In response, the romantic movement advocated for a return to nature and ostensibly more innocent time. The romantics' aesthetic sensibility was transferred to the working landscape of small farms, fields, hedgerows, and forest. Yet it was indeed primarily an aesthetic interest: in their pursuit of the sublime, industrialization's purported opposite, romantics favored an idealizing, abstract, and distant gaze rather than a close study of rural life's material reality.[1] As opposed to untouched wilderness, the cultural landscape therefore emerged as the focal point of attention for the educated middle class, an "ideal [that] emphasized regional diversity and vernacular landscapes as the foundations of German culture and formed the basis of German land use planning and environmental stewardship well into the twentieth century."[2] This pastoral imaginary informed the conservation movements of the late nineteenth and early twentieth centuries, including the drive to safeguard (natural) monuments (*Denkmalschutz*), protect the homeland (*Heimatschutz*), and preserve nature (*Naturschutz*).

Given their appreciation for the working landscape, one might assume that conservationists in the nineteenth and early twentieth centuries would have had a particular interest in and knowledge of agriculture—the element that had been historically (and continues to be) one of the prime shapers of that landscape. Yet from the beginning of the conservation movement, its mostly urban and middle-class supporters held onto a notion of the rural idyll that barely resembled reality. This attitude is of course only possible with distance: basking in the beauty of an agricultural landscape is much easier when one is not required to perform backbreaking labor and worry about one's physical survival from one season to the next. So while agricultural policy over the past several centuries has been aimed at modernizing the sector (which necessitates profound changes to land use), the rising conservation movement was guided by a static vision of an 1850s–1870s' working landscape that it considered aesthetically pleasing and wished to preserve—an attitude that informs much conservation work to this day and helps explain some of the conflicts in the making of the Green Belt.[3]

The nineteenth century also birthed the concept of the natural monument. Propelled by the romantic imperative, some sites in Germany had already received attention and care: the picturesque Drachenfels (dragon's rock), the ruins of a twelfth-century fortress on the banks of the Rhine near

Bonn, was saved from destruction by a group of concerned citizens in 1836 and declared one of the first protected natural monuments of Prussia.[4] For its defenders, Drachenfels, alongside other natural monuments in this region, was a symbol of pride as well as an expression of uniqueness, rootedness, and durability in the face of an accelerating, homogenizing modernity.[5]

By 1900, as the full scale of ecological destruction wreaked by industrialization was becoming clear, Denkmalschutz (again, the protection of natural monuments) became more institutionalized. The Prussian Ministry of Culture hired botanist Hugo Conwentz (1855–1922) to realize such a program in Germany. By 1906, Conwentz was able to move forward with his vision as director of the newly established Prussian State Office for Natural Monument Care (Staatliche Stelle für Naturdenkmalpflege). His interpretation of this key term was broad and allowed for his office to even protect living organisms or landscape elements.[6] Conwentz was no radical and certainly no romantic; he saw the state as a crucial actor in nature preservation and sought compromise and reform rather than deep, structural change. That same pragmatism also led Conwentz to preserve small tracts: "It is much more correct, and practically easier to carry out, to maintain smaller areas of different characteristics in their original condition, scattered throughout the entire area, and if possible in every part of the country."[7] In this way, Conwentz introduced a form of nature conservation at the highest levels of state administration, offering a tangible and realizable approach, and his concept of natural monument preservation continues to inform German conservation policy to this day. In fact, by the time Germany reunited in 1989/1990, the FRG had thirty thousand and the GDR had ten thousand natural monuments under state protection.[8]

The desire to protect natural monuments is closely connected to another founding movement of German conservation: Heimatschutz, or again, the preservation and protection of the German homeland. Starting in the 1830s, Heimat evolved into a keyword of the German language. In the midcentury decades, Germany transformed from a predominantly agricultural and crafts-based society, organized in a patchwork of small fiefdoms and feudal estates, into a technologically, socially, and politically much more modern, urban, and industrial society marked by intense class conflict and mass emigration. These same years also saw the formation of a "bourgeois, national, partly liberal and partly democratic movement that sought a nation-state," and in its critique of the status quo linked the essentially antimodern idea of Heimat to the ideals of freedom and fatherland.[9] Whereas the French Revolution had wedded French national identity to the state and its constitution, in a much more splintered Germany any sense of nationhood would need to fall back on prepolitical commonalities in culture, language, origin, and traditions—including those expressed in land use. In this context, Heimat was able to symbolize connection, stability, and community, and thus formed a model for nation building. Heimat expressed a search for identity, initially a local or regional one, and later a national one. The invocation of Heimat as "a selectively idealized memory of the past" was therefore meant to heal the rifts of alienation or estrangement from the bonds of human and ecological community.[10]

The threat of loss galvanized a group of again mainly urban and middle-class citizens to organize and protect Heimat from further destruction. Their work resulted in the 1904 founding of the Association for Homeland Preservation (Bund für Heimatschutz), spearheaded by composer Ernst Rudorff (1840–1916), who for years had written passionately about the losses he witnessed and the past he grieved. His was as much a movement against the increasing industrial exploitation of nature as it was for the preservation of older, premodern landscapes—forests, rivers, bogs, and heaths. Channeled through the notion of Heimat, though, conservation also meant protecting the *entire* landscape, including peasant cottages, crafts and folkways, and poetry and stories in regional dialects. The contrast to the US conservation movement could hardly be clearer: here it is not a wilderness that must be safeguarded from an ever-advancing frontier, but instead a landscape that "nature" and humans had cocreated over millennia to form an arcadian, aesthetically pleasing whole—one requiring protection from a rationalizing, industrializing, urbanizing, materialistic consumer society.[11] In both cases, however, nature was seen to be a shaper of human character, whether a masculinizing force or one that rooted its people in the soil of their homeland.

Both the monument preservation and Heimat movement carried the conservationist ethic into the twentieth century. Within decades, a whole cluster of nature conservation organizations had sprung up, at once manifesting a new vision and reflecting an already existing, broad concern. Heimat acquired validity through natural beauty since both nature and Heimat "invest an inanimate Other with shining subjective qualities that reflect themselves back as identity." The concepts reinforce each other since "*Heimat* has absorbed the beauty of nature and given it a geographical grounding."[12] Yet by the early years of the twentieth century, the notion of Heimat had been colonized by nationalistic political interests, and in the 1930s most infamously reached its nadir in its strong resonance with the blood-and-soil ideology of National Socialism.[13] Along with the movement that advocated for it, the concept practically disappeared from the German political stage. To this day, however, it remains an important (under)current in German place attachments and understandings of nature, influencing both Green Belt policy and community responses to them.

It also helped shape the parent organization of today's BUND Green Belt project office, the BN. The BN was formed in 1913, the heyday of the Denkmalschutz movement under Conwentz and Heimatschutz movement under Rudorff, and is linked politically and ideologically to both. The organization was primarily an outgrowth of the urban and educated middle classes. Like others at the time, the BN was carefully contrarian: it critiqued the ecologically destructive excesses of modernity, and focused its energies on safeguarding relatively intact natural areas and preserving the landscape of Heimat. Strong alignment with the Bavarian government allowed it to lobby for policy change, but its efforts were reformist, emphasizing discussion and compromise—and in the eyes of critics, a distinct loyalty to the state.[14]

In sum, the early German conservation movement had three major directions. First, it was a movement to protect natural monuments advocating a historicist, nature-based memorial culture. Second, it advanced a Heimat preservation interest that aimed to protect a threatened preindustrial, agrarian, cultural landscape. Third, it offered a vision of conservation centered not on "memorials to natural history" but instead the living, breathing, and increasingly rare plants and animals that needed spaces free from human intrusion. All three directions were deeply shaped by the industrial transformation, concerned with safeguarding what was, or at least what was perceived to have been, and guided by romantic notions of sublime nature and Heimat. All three were rooted in a sense of loss. In the decades after World War II, though, all energies went toward reconstruction, and Germans were eager to leave Nazism behind. Unlike the earlier movements, postwar nature conservation retreated into empiricism rather than attempting to make ideological arguments. Sidelined by economic imperatives, conservation struggled for relevance, remaining relatively reform minded and apolitical for decades. This changed drastically in the 1970s.

THE POSTWAR BIFURCATION: CONSERVATION AND SCIENTIFIC ENVIRONMENTALISM

The Green Belt today is a composite of old and new, a product of a backward-looking nostalgia and, more recently, range of future-oriented, scientific concerns that crystallized in the postwar decades. By the late 1960s, student movements for peace and against nuclear proliferation and a newly scientized environmentalism all came together. Willy Brandt, a member of the center-left Socialist Democratic Party, became chancellor in 1969, and under his leadership, more space opened up for more broadly democratic debate and a resurgent Left that had been sidelined during the years of economic recovery. Protest and criticism of the state became more acceptable.[15] Meanwhile, West Germany was receptive to international impulses, and consequential books like Rachel Carson's *Silent Spring* (1962) and the Club of Rome's *Limits to Growth* (1972), alongside the first United Nations Conference on the Human Environment in Stockholm (1972), fed the German public's curiosity and concern about the dark underbelly of a seemingly comfortable, "postmaterial" world. The feeling of ecological precarity was driven home not just by a possible nuclear war—in which the divided Germany would occupy the front line—but by the oil shocks of the early 1970s as well. Under the influence of international ecological science, and propelled forward by a restless and querulent spirit, "a patriarchal, elitist, conservative, state-oriented, partly neo-romantic, partly technocratic project was reimagined within a few years as an anti-establishment, anti-technological, critical and radical effort."[16] A new anthropocentrism emerged: rather than protecting nature for its aesthetic, spiritual, or memorial qualities—as was the case in the early Denkmalschutz, Heimatschutz, and Naturschutz movements—more and more people pointed to the human dependence on nature. No longer was the rallying cry about nature alone; it was about preserving the foundations of human existence.[17]

The newer, science-based environmentalism of the 1960s and 1970s was less attached to the romantic inheritance than its conservationist predecessor. Other issues, previously ignored, moved into focus, including air and water pollution, population growth, and radiation poisoning. For German environmentalists, the nuclear question in particular was a catalyst for a less compromising and amenable movement. All in all, environmentalism entered a new phase after decades of stagnation, invigorated by a return to politics.[18]

At a more local level, the BN observed this cultural and political shift. In 1969, the organization hired Hubert Weinzierl, an activist with a background in forestry, to spearhead the organization and help it adapt to the new age. Within a few years of Weinzierl's arrival, the BN decided to create a new organization, one based on ecological science, lithe and aggressive, able to attract the younger, more radical generation to the environmental question, and all the while maintaining a critical stance toward technology and modernity. Members of the BN founded the BUND in 1975 and thus institutionalized the new movement:[19]

> To a certain extent, the BUND formed the sum of the modernization processes in nature conservation. It was both an umbrella organization and a member association, an elite creation "from above," but also included local and regional organizations that had grown "from below." It connected the traditional audience with the younger generation, combining elements of classic programming and familiar lobbying with the appearance and self-image of citizens' initiatives. From the beginning it aimed to be an association that dealt with all environmental policy issues. It intended to emotionalize as well as scientize the debate. The example of the BUND illustrates the flexibility and stylistic breadth of nature conservation/environmental protection.[20]

The founders had understood the moment well. In the 1970s and 1980s, while membership in traditional Heimat and conservation organizations languished, the newer environmental groups attracted intense interest. In 1976, with its membership having grown into the tens of thousands, the BUND received a national office in Bonn, the West German capital, and acquired a board of directors, scientific advisory board, and thematic working groups.[21] Offices emerged little by little in other federal states, and today they exist in all sixteen *Länder* (federal states) and over twenty-two hundred local and regional affiliates. Now headquartered in Berlin, the capital of reunified Germany, the BUND has nearly half a million members, making it one of the largest and most powerful environmental organizations in Germany.

Conservation versus Environmentalism

In the 1970s, *ecology* became political. An increasingly confident, science-based consciousness, already in formation in the 1950s and 1960s, emerged onto the international and national stage, and began shifting the activism and discourse of German conservationists, both opening and closing possibilities. Closely related to ecology, the Germans imported from the United States the concept of *environment*, transliterated as *Umwelt*, or "the surrounding world." In contrast to its predecessor, it emphasized abiotic components like water, air and soil, toxins, and emissions. Environmental protection (*Umweltschutz*) increasingly edged out any remaining notion of nature conservation along with its central concepts like natural monuments, Heimat, and landscape. The key difference between the terms was not just differential scope but rather that Umweltschutz placed humans at the center of consideration. It was about protecting the environment for human well-being and minimizing health risks by reducing toxicants and pollutants. Umweltschutz was informed by a criticism of some technologies' role in environmental destruction and simultaneous faith in the utility of other technologies for environmental rehabilitation. All of it rested on a vision of human beings as prudent managers of natural resources.[22] Meanwhile, Naturschutz and its imperative of safeguarding nonhuman species from human activity was relegated to the back-burner, vaguely included in the catchall of Umweltschutz yet never clearly articulated. Umweltschutz became a West German policy priority in the 1970s and 1980s, and protecting the environment was increasingly anchored in the state through federal laws and regulations as well as a growing cadre of agencies dedicated to controlling pollution and waste, all supported with tax money. The scientific concepts of *ecology* and *ecosystem* held Umweltschutz and Naturschutz together, however awkwardly, and kept conservation interests alive, but mostly on the terms of a more and more technocratic, scientized, anthropocentric, and reformist environmental movement. In 1976, the West German government overhauled the Nazi era *Reichsnaturschutzgesetz* (Reich Nature Protection Law), included in the new version a recognition of the diversity, uniqueness, and beauty of nature and landscape, and introduced national parks as new forms of protection. To the extent that Naturschutz was pursued in West Germany, its connection to the encompassing notion of Umwelt (environment) made for more expansive approaches, away from individual natural monuments and toward ecological processes at the landscape scale.[23] Nonetheless, even as the science of ecology began shifting in response to nonequilibrium insights, political organizations like the BUND held onto the older balance-of-nature discourses to mobilize support.[24]

Conservation took a rather different turn in socialist East Germany. For the government of the GDR, the environmental crisis, to the point it was acknowledged, was not a result of socialist mismanagement or overexploitation but rather a holdover symptom of capitalism. By definition, so the argument went, socialism was entirely compatible with high environmental quality—in fact, socialism was going to clean up the mess that prewar capitalism had left behind. But East Germany had drawn the short straw when it came to natural resources: much of its territory was located on land that lacked minerals of strategic importance, and it was cut off from supplies of wood, aluminum, or cotton in the West.[25] Instead, East Germany relied on the Soviet Union for oil, and as that became too expensive to import, it turned to what it had in abundance: lignite coal. Coal powered and heated homes and businesses, and formed the basis for a domestic plastics industry that allowed the GDR to partly emulate the high-consumer lifestyle emerging in the West. The GDR had neither the funding nor technology, however, to update the dirty manufacturing technology it had inherited from its prewar past. At one point, East Germany mined more coal than any other country in the world, surpassing even the Soviet Union. Dark clouds of sooty air hung above East German cities, and unprocessed, toxic by-products poured into rivers and streams, leading to environmental catastrophe.[26] To the extent that pollution was recognized as problematic by the 1970s and 1980s—a progressive national environmental law, the Landeskulturgesetz, was passed as early as 1970—the GDR's Environmental Protection Ministry (itself created a year later) was not even able to enforce better environmental behavior: the costs of upgrading factories were so high that no state fine could realistically incentivize businesses to clean up.[27]

By 1971, there were first signs of environmental organizing in East Germany, and as books and media information (including the 1972 Club of Rome report) filtered in from the West, activism accelerated. Given state repression of any organizing, much of that work occurred under the protective arm of the Protestant church.[28] A 1978 landmark meeting between the church and state formalized a new relationship, and "gave the church significant freedom to pursue social goals, while the regime's increasing dependence on its ties to the West further entrenched the church's liberty."[29] The environmental movement expanded slowly in the 1980s, partly aided by the church, but faced significant repression as the Stasi infiltrated and sabotaged the movement.[30] The state was caught in a bind, though: do nothing and environmental activists would publicize the state's failings, or decide to repress the movement too harshly and the state would draw even more attention, this time from the Western media, to the movement it was trying to quash. Its answer was to engage in as low-profile repression as possible, including intimidation, stalling, subtle prevention, sabotaging communicative efforts, and enacting pressure on the church to withdraw its support for the environmentalists. By the latter part of the decade, more and more "solidarity channels" had been crafted between East and West Germany. By the time of the SED's collapse and formal end of the GDR, however, the Stasi had left much of the environmental movement hobbled and unable to seize its moment of freedom when it finally arrived.[31]

Meanwhile, little was left of the conservation movement. Just like in West Germany, it stagnated in the postwar decades, and despite smaller successes struggled for legitimacy against the imperative to rebuild and reemerge stronger from the midcentury ruins.[32] Yet compared to its politicized cousin, conservation was able to continue relatively unmolested by the SED regime. Conservation was not threatening in the way environmentalism was: while the latter had the potential to launch incendiary critiques against the state for ecological mismanagement and the poisoning of entire communities, conservation was defined in more narrow terms and remained small.

It bears mentioning that in comparison to West Germany, the concept of Heimat protection survived in the GDR as a viable framing for environmental struggles. While in both parts of Germany the idea had lost much legitimacy due to its entanglement with fascism, it was revived in the GDR and reinterpreted through a socialist lens "in which the natural resources and places of production, the forests and fields, serve those who work." Protecting nature was integrated into a larger need to build and defend a "peace-loving Heimat of patriotic socialists."[33] State and media presented history as a righteously overcome feudal and then capitalist past, and Heimat would be created as something new, progressive, and positive; only socialism could offer real Heimat, free from the burdens of the past and in harmony with nature.[34] More pragmatically, the SED leadership was under no illusion that a love for Heimat acted as a powerful incentive for people to stay in the East.

Conservation and Environmentalism in a Reunified Germany

Reunification shifted the terrain once more. While the first few years of the *Wende* (German for "turning" or "transition") found East German environmentalists riding high, the momentum was ground to a halt by the tumult of reunification. And yet in the final days of the GDR, a dedicated and driven group of East German environmentalists managed to do something nearly unthinkable during the previous four decades: under the leadership of Michael Succow, the GDR's recently hired deputy minister for the environment, nature protection, and water management, the government set aside an astonishing 4.5 percent of the territory of the GDR as nature reserves.[35] Many of these spaces were former military training grounds and other areas near the inter-German border. All in all, with a law that went into force on October 1, 1990, the outgoing government created five national parks, six biosphere reserves, and three nature parks.[36] Quite a few of these protected areas help constitute today's Green Belt. In a harbinger of conflicts to come, though, the explosive growth of protected areas in the GDR went against the sensibilities of many locals. While West Germans could now bask in the wide open spaces and scenic landscapes of Brandenburg, for instance, many locals resented their home becoming a "Serengeti for Wessis," preferring jobs and livelihood instead.[37] Yet in these rural and remote areas, industry usually did not settle so that even today, nature tourism is one of the region's main economic pillars.

In the decades after reunification, West and East German environmental groups merged, although perhaps it would be more accurate to say that East German groups generally were assimilated by their well-funded western counterparts as the latter tried to establish themselves in the east. Other groups, especially those allied with the church, dissolved entirely. To this day, many environmental groups in the former East Germany have a strong former West German presence rather than deep East German roots—a pattern that includes the BUND as well and continues to shape the potentialities of conservation work there.[38]

GERMAN CONSERVATION TODAY

The complicated history of conservation in Germany puts projects like the Green Belt before two significant challenges: the often-unacknowledged tensions between Naturschutz and Umweltschutz, conservation and environmentalism, that confound and stymie progress; and the scientization of the movement that hampers its capacity to connect emotionally to people in the places they inhabit.

Today, German nature conservation and environmentalism continue to exist in uneasy relationship to one another. There is a frequent lack of clarity about what is meant with either of these terms, and in some cases, the two are in overt and tragic conflict with each other. To illustrate the irony, consider this statement by a prominent German conservationist: "Environmental protection has become a formula for the effective destruction of nature. We save the climate and accept that the last remnants of wild river landscapes will disappear." Conservationists even half jokingly exclaim that "nature needs to be saved from the environmentalists!"[39] In present-day Germany, for instance, protected areas along the Green Belt and elsewhere are threatened by expanding power transmission corridors central to the country's ambitious clean energy transition. Monoculture cornfields are displacing more and more mixed-use pastures to produce biofuels and help meet Germany's emission targets. For activists in a political movement, this contradiction can sometimes be ignored, but when it comes to the creation of institutions, agencies, and policies, any conflicts glossed over earlier will reemerge. Conservation centers on living organisms, natural monuments, and landscapes; environmentalism foregrounds natural resources like air, water, and soil. Ecological framing can offer some bridging between the two, but it cannot address what is underneath: different philosophies and value systems. There is incommensurability between the urges to protect nature *from* humans and protect it *for* humans: one gives rise to a land-sparing strategy, and the other to prudent land sharing. Both movements' reference to scientific concepts like *ecology* and *biodiversity* hides the tension between them, but in conservation praxis—its implementation and incentivization—this basic conflict rematerializes. It becomes particularly fraught when the spaces to be protected are themselves questionable in some ways: they are not perceived to be beautiful or otherwise remarkable, or carry the weight of historical traumas. Even back in the 1970s, Weinzierl, head of the BN, warned that in the enthusiasm to push the movement into more scientific and anthropocentric spheres, one risked losing sight of how important "places of natural beauty" were. He called on people to have both "the courage to remain romantic and . . . to think in modern and realistic terms."[40] But it turns out that this combination has been hard to maintain in a world that tends increasingly toward the scientization and quantification of environmental concern.

That same dominance of scientific discourse may be a strength in the offices of powerful and distant decision makers, but it does not bode well for conservation on the ground. The older conservation movement had elevated aesthetic and emotional aspects over others, and that framing lost power in the economistic and technocratic postwar decades, yet that did not mean that the original concerns were irrelevant. Protecting nature is not just a scientific endeavor; it is a cultural and emotional one too.

The Contested Place of Heimat

It is hard to overstate the complexity of Heimat in the German context. As I explain above, by the end of the Second World War, Heimat had been thoroughly discredited as an environmentally viable concept as it carried the burden of National Socialism, a near-atavistic urge to preserve a parochial, premodern past. Yet what does conservation lose without Heimat? Some thinkers, inside and outside the natural sciences, have argued that the rejection of Heimat threw out the proverbial baby with the bathwater. In its effort to distance itself from the Nazi past, the environmental movement instead adopted colder, more sober scientific and economistic arguments. This disengagement with history and culture may have bought the movement greater legitimacy with high-level policy makers interested in objective fact and decision-making. But it has also alienated environmental and conservation concerns from the average individual. A survey conducted in Germany in the early 2000s already pointed to this problem: "There is a clear gap between what the population and what the conservationists understand by nature conservation. While the population accepts *Heimat* and sustainable use as justifications, the majority of conservationists rely on science and emphasize the ethical value of their cause. Here the communication problem of nature conservation becomes palpable."[41] A deeply scientized, acultural movement simply cannot meet people—in a literal sense—where they are. By erasing Heimat, conservation has excoriated itself. Without historical and cultural concepts, conservation becomes simply applied ecology. What is needed, so the reasoning goes, is conservation embedded in a larger meaning-making effort connected to values, identity, and emotion. And in Germany (as elsewhere), conservation has also always been about something bigger than the place conserved: it is about local and national identity, the anxieties of modernity, and the reactions to a shifting political and economic order. Conservation is thus always an emotionally textured politics as well.

The answer to this, according to several people in the field, is to reintegrate Heimat, both discursively and in practice, into the work of environmentalism and conservation. Heimat is "the place where you were born, is for every person the centre of the world," and yet "the concept is not simply territorial, but rather invokes a 'memory of origin' and inevitably involves the notion of an 'impossible return' to (imaginary or real) roots or origins."[42] Everywhere except conservation, Heimat received increased attention by the 1980s because it was through this lens that Germans could begin reckoning with their recent past and learn to understand themselves. Heimat, "like nature, religion, language, and the mother, is for German-speaking middle-class citizens something larger than oneself, something worth caring for."[43] In other words, doing the hard and delicate work of reinserting Heimat into conservation could literally make space for the deep emotional bonds people have with the places they live. Heimat's evocation of the past, embodied (if idealized) memory, and nostalgic longing offers the possibility of honoring love for the community and land.

But Heimat also bears serious risks and, in twenty-first-century Germany, it has acquired a layer of fear, anger, and urgency amid the tensions of reunification, greater geographic and economic polarization, high levels of immigration, and a retrenchment of (ethno)nationalism in Germany and Europe more broadly. The diversification of German society—particularly in the wake of Chancellor Angela Merkel's decision in 2015 to admit over one million mostly Middle Eastern refugees—has provoked renewed xenophobia and racism, especially (though certainly not only) in the former East Germany. To what extent can conservation speak to the dislocations so many Germans seem to be experiencing and not exacerbate them? The defense of Heimat here has the potential to become a new wedge that can be driven between not just former West and East Germans but between "old" and "new" Germans as well.[44] Conservation in this manner can quickly become a metaphor for exclusion, illustrating who or what "truly belongs" or not. Heimat may help some people make sense of their lives, but it can also act as a justification to threaten the lives of others. Nevertheless, the Green Belt as currently conceived continues to explicitly and implicitly engage Heimat as a narrative construct as well as an embodied reality through its marketing materials and ecological management strategies. These are the subjects of later chapters.

The German conservation movement today has a complicated ancestry, and the Green Belt cannot easily be separated from it. It emerged in the late eighteenth and early nineteenth centuries from the alienation and upheaval caused by industrialization. First articulated as an object of romantic longing, nature was also the grounding for feelings of loss and dislocation, which then informed the efforts to preserve natural monuments. Ideally, such places expressed the German national character, where strength, longevity, and deep roots in nature came together. Closely related yet more expansive was the emerging Heimat movement of the eighteenth century. Heimatschutz attempted to safeguard and set aside traditional cultural landscapes, which included the plants and animals that had adapted to them along with the human communities—with all of their crafts, rituals, and celebrations—that called these places home. Finally, Naturschutz congealed in the early twentieth century, remaining largely apolitical and quite marginal through the war years, economic reconstruction, and even into the German partition. In both Germanys, the 1970s saw the beginning of a new, scientific environmentalism premised on a broader, anthropocentric understanding of the limits of natural resources and need for sustainable human development. Armed with science and wielding powerful ecological concepts, environmentalism (Umweltschutz) was catapulted into West German politics in the 1970s and continued to run strong through reunification. But its presence came at the cost of absence: environmentalism's older relative, conservation (Naturschutz), was sidelined. Today, conservation derives considerable legitimacy and crucial guidance from the ecological sciences. Ecology, ecosystems, and biodiversity, core concepts of environmentalism, are guiding precepts for the Green Belt. Yet people within the conservation movement know that something is missing. By ecologizing conservation, we have lost emotion— the acknowledgment of grief and sorrow along with the honoring of love and hope.

The Green Belt project is an outgrowth of a tangled set of roots, and in the end, this can be a strength. It can dissolve what seems like a contradiction: based in ecological science, this project attempts to make emotional connections to people's deep ties to place, the past, and home. As I will discuss, conservation's emotional and aesthetic demands are partly answered by the Green Belt's emphasis on the human memories of the borderlands alongside the more-than-human pasts that shape their emergent ecologies. At the same time, however, the material and storied, the managed and wild borderlands of the Green Belt also carry within them various important features that shape the potentialities for mnemonic ecologies along the former Iron Curtain and beyond.

4 MNEMONIC ECOLOGIES IN THE MATERIAL AND STORIED BORDERLANDS

The border as a material, discursive, and cognitive construct is a site where memory crystallizes. Ecological work conducted in its considerable imprint has the challenging task of reconciling past and present, safeguarding and memorializing, healing, and attending to human and nonhuman needs at the same time. The early years of the Green Belt focused on acquiring and protecting land above all else; memorialization was hardly anyone's concern. By the early 2000s, criticisms over greenwashing the border and erasing the past had become louder. The BUND has responded to conflicts and critiques by reckoning with memory much more overtly than in earlier years. This chapter discusses the mnemonic ecological project of explicit commemoration, where nature is marshaled as a strategy for remembrance, and both human and other-than-human agencies are fused together to craft hybrid monuments for the present and future. All the examples in this chapter are more official, formal, or at least publicly recognized forms of memorialization, and are aimed at a broader public even as their symbolism, messaging, and curation may be ambiguous or open-ended.

ECOLOGICAL ART ALONG THE BORDER

Landscape art has been one of the salient mnemonic tools for ecological work in the borderlands. Two examples illustrate this strategy. The *Tree Cross of Ifta* (*Baumkreuz von Ifta*) is a piece of dynamic landscape art that straddles the former border between the two Germanys. It began in mid-November

1990, just over a year after the fall of the Berlin Wall, with the planting of 140 trees along the former border in the center of the country. This was the start of a west-east line of linden trees that was envisioned to reach along federal route 7 from the western German city of Kassel in Hesse to Eisenach in Thuringia in eastern Germany. It is cut perpendicularly by three parallel lines of European ash trees that run alongside the former border, with one line on the fence's west side, and the two other along its eastern side (figure 4.1). Since then, each November volunteers gather to care for the trees and plant new ones; well over 1,000 have thus been planted over the past decades.[1] The 300-meter-long fence that the ash trees frame is likely the single-longest segment of border fence still standing in Germany. The *Tree Cross of Ifta* today is administered by the BUND office in Thuringia.

The project was the brainchild of a group of western German artists and eastern German environmental and social justice activists. Using trees as

Figure 4.1

Tree Cross of Ifta. Visible on the left is the rusting border fence and alongside it are two rows of trees with a path leading through them. *Author*: Heinz K. S., May 7, 2020. *Source*: Wikimedia Commons, https://commons.wikimedia.org/wiki/File:Baumkreuz_bei_Ifta_am _%E2%80%9EGr%C3%BCnen_Band%E2%80%9C_(2).jpg, Creative Commons License CC-BY-SA 4.0. Reprinted by permission.

their focal element, the group saw itself as heir to contemporary performance artist Joseph Beuys and his "expanded concept of art" (*erweiterter Kunstbegriff*): his sense that art's purpose should be to transform society. Beuy's 1982 installation *7000 Oaks* in Kassel, Ifta's artistic predecessor, consisted of planting thousands of oaks across the city, each accompanied by a basalt stele. For Beuys, this was an attempt at an "ecological intervention": a way to posit nature's flourishing and emergence against administrative state inertia, all to help create a more livable and sustainable society.[2]

At Ifta, similar oppositions are evident. The hardness of the rusting steel fence—a remnant and increasingly symbol of the violent partition—is set against the softness of the trees, part of the Green Belt's ecological refuge. It is decay against emergence, inertia against movement, death against life, end against beginning. Visitors can park near the *Tree Cross of Ifta* and walk for miles on the old concrete slabs of the patrol road, or stay within the ambits of the art project itself and experience the line of trees alongside the fence. They can feel into the quiet and listen to their own breathing all the while aware that they stand on land that was dangerous, off-limits, a place where violence was condoned and enacted. The Omnibus for Direct Democracy, one of the activist organizations involved in maintaining the *Tree Cross of Ifta*, calls this "a place where the soul can follow."[3] The annually recurring, collective efforts of care for the trees—set alongside the emphasis on individual place experience of emotion and memory—connect the political components of democracy. The inscription at the project site, signed by the mayor of Ifta and district administrator of Eisenach, explains that the *Tree Cross of Ifta* is "the sign of overcoming death, of a new idea of economy and of an expanded concept of art."

Because the remainder of the border fence is embedded in an ecological context, it is not simply oriented toward the past but rather points toward coming times. This means that ecological art as memorial can "proffer a future-driven strategy to reimagine oneself, one's community and its practices . . . where even death is not the end of bodily existence and physical presence can endure in salutary ways."[4] If one imagines the project extending decades into the future as its supporters would have it, the line of trees will outlive the rusting fence. The trees' linear arrangement may give rise to questions that future generations might ask: Why is this here? Ultimately the fence will only be present in its absence, its traces suggested by patterns of vegetation. The oxidized metal will, over long enough periods, return to the earth, its molecular components absorbed by the soil, plants, and microorganisms. In this way, the existence of the row of trees initially relied on the border and its fence as referent, but moving onward, it will create its own future with and without the help of its human caretakers. It thus becomes a metaphor for Germany's past, present, and unified future, a society tethered to history, a reunification dependent on a prior partition, but a country now growing into a different kind of future that is cocreated by individual and collective action.

But nonhuman life has a mind of its own, not always anticipated, that disrupts and changes memorial meanings: since the 1990s, ecologists have noted an accelerated ash dieback caused by a newly documented fungal pathogen, possibly aided by warmer temperatures in central Europe.[5] The volunteers for the *Tree Cross of Ifta* have been replacing dead or moribund ash trees with Norway maples, also native to the region.[6] Time will tell how well the new plantings survive and thrive, and how they continue to interact with the remains of the border and their human helpers.

The *West-East Gate* (*West-Östliches Tor*) is another example of landscape art, this time sponsored by the BUND itself. Conceived in 1996 and installed by its creators in 2002 in the geographic center of Germany, near Teistungen in Eichsfeld, the project consists of two twelve-meter-tall oak trunks, placed upright at the top of a local hill, the Kutschenberg, with views all around. The tree trunks, cut by a family-owned, formerly East German sawmill in existence since the nineteenth century, stand several dozen feet apart and are connected to each other via a heavy band of steel, symbolizing the fusion of the two Germanys. This tree "gate" is surrounded by sixty-six red oaks, which are expected to grow taller and larger over time as the dead trunks in their midst decay.[7]

Unlike the *Tree Cross at Ifta*, which was developed independently of the Green Belt and was only later formally integrated into it, the *West-East Gate* was a BUND initiative from the start. It formed part of a concerted campaign in the 1990s to publicize and increase acceptance of the Green

Figure 4.2
The *West-East Gate* with the two decaying oak trunks, the smaller trees surrounding them, and an explanatory sign in front of the monument. *Source*: Beckers Blockhaus, used with permission.

Belt under the slogan "From Death Strip to Lifeline." The *West-East Gate* emphasizes not just the past but also the beauty of the surrounding landscape in hopes of increasing the public's interest in preserving it. The 2002 inauguration of the gate was a major public relations coup: the guest of honor was none other than Gorbachev, the former leader of the Soviet Union who presided over its dissolution and facilitated the fall of the Berlin Wall. Signage explains the *West-East Gate* to visitors:

> Two oak trunks, as an open gate, connect the once two German halves, which for 40 years bordered one another along this line. A gleaming threshold made of stainless steel, welded together from a western and an eastern part, symbolizes the common present since the opening of the border in 1989. A grove of young oaks represents that hope that West and East in Europe grow together and that the natural treasures of the "Green Belt," created in the former borderlands, are treated carefully.

The gate is open and will remain so through its existence. It has been symbolically pushed open with the fall of the wall, and it lacks any mechanism or desire for closure, expressing the hope for freedom. But the shape of the sculpture is also significant. A gate has a threshold. The west-east axis is marked by the steel band, uniting what was once separate. Visitors can step across this band, but in part because the gate is not actually located exactly on the former border,[8] the meaning of this movement remains as open as the gate itself: What kind of a transition might it be? Stepping from present into future? From one mindset into another? It is not clear whether this was the artists' intention, but it does have the effect of opening space for individual experience, interpretation, and feeling.

Colors are also integrated into the project concept: around the anniversary of the fall of the Berlin Wall every autumn, a field of late-blooming wildflowers—autumn squills (*Scilla autumnalis*) planted along the border's traces—celebrates the season's significance.[9] Transformational ecological processes are marshaled in remembrance of a transformational human event. With the passage of time, however, the initial artistic vision has gotten muddied by ecology's own dynamics. The grove of red oaks was meant to mark the space and differentiate it from the surrounding green trees and shrubs. Yet some observers noted that the realization of this effect was not immediate: due to either soggy weather or poor landscape planning, the northern red oaks (a species native to eastern North America) languished and died from too much water. By 2005, they were removed and replaced with local trees.[10] Compared to the *Tree Cross at Ifta*, where the border fence is a prominent and stark reminder of the past, and the trees will continue to echo the border's course for decades to come, the *West-East Gate* lacks a clearly visible, palpable historical component. The past is suggested by the decaying oak trunks and, more directly, by the steel plate that binds them together, but for better or worse, that band—a symbol of union—disappears all too readily under a mat of grasses and shrubs, giving the structure an unintentional, opposite meaning to what was originally planned, though perhaps more accurately reflective of the complexity and fraught nature of reunification.

Both works of landscape art directly engage ecological elements to mark place and past. For eons, trees have had a unique importance in human culture, including memorialization processes.[11] German culture especially is historically and mythologically connected to the forest; one need only think of Brothers Grimm fairy tales.[12] The *Tree Cross at Ifta* and the *West-East Gate* use trees as architectural and structuring components, artistic elements, and symbols and messaging devices. As symbols, trees are "physical manifestations of ideas" that "aid the process of gaining access to and of manipulating otherwise abstract concepts." A tree "also stands, both literally and metaphorically, as a living entity spanning many human generations. As such it avails itself as a historical marker and social focus of events. As links with the past, be it actual or mythical, particular trees make ideas more realistic and dynamic in the present."[13] Ultimately, among their many ecological functions, trees influence human identity formation at the individual and collective, or even national, level.

Both projects rely on tree growth as core to their message: their (hopefully) continued development represents living and flourishing, a wish for Germany's present and future. Trees can be personified too, so some visitors may even see themselves or their communities in the trees that now frame the border fence or grow in a circle around the two oak trunks, signs of a formerly divided country.[14] In their growth—the repeating seasonality of branching and leafing out, and growing one ring after another—the planted trees record time; time is for many a measure of their healing. Trees also act as signals to coming generations that something important happened here, that their peculiar, "unnatural" arrangement in this place marks something worthy of remembrance, even if the object of that memory becomes more and more remote to future visitors. This may be intended, but trees, of course, through their "living, growing, changing presence can outgrow the original intention of their planting and contribute to a wider portfolio of memories and unfolding emotional geographies."[15] Meaning-making is always contextual, and that is true for art, especially landscape art, which uses such unpredictable ecological cocreators in its work. Unruly nature, to the extent it interferes with the artists' message, must often be disciplined and realigned: dying trees are cut, healthy ones are replanted, grass is mowed, and shrubs are pruned back to size. In the case of the *Tree Cross at Ifta*, this has been integrated into the art itself, becoming an annual community event.

The *West-East Gate* uses trees specifically as representational symbols. The two large oak trunks represent a people formerly divided and even division itself. Here as well the passage of time matters, not just in terms of giving the ring of oaks, symbolizing unity and harmony, a chance to grow large and overshadow the symbol of partition, but to allow the latter to slowly deteriorate. It is the oak trunks' long-term death and decay that matter, since "objects generate meaning not just in their preservation and persistence but also in their destruction and disposal."[16] Stripping these two large oaks of their "treeness," reducing them to trunks, forces "the material, wood, [to draw] back into itself. When the tree reached out with life, we missed its innerness. Ironically, the dead tree has more life when it has ceased to be biological and turned to inanimacy. It turns inward as complex object."[17] The tree becomes more humanlike, drawing our sympathy as we witness the passage of time in it too. The oak trunks' slow attrition by the elements brings dignity to aging and death while the trees planted around them supply the relief of a counterpoint: renewal and immortality, offering new lifelines for others.

The presence of absence is a significant component of these examples of landscape art. At the *West-East Gate*, it is the slow disappearance of the two oak trunks that compels our emotional response, as their decline leaves behind a steel plate threshold and ring of red oaks. At the *Tree Cross at Ifta*, it is the dissolution of the border fence, outlasted by the rows of linden, ash, and maple trees, that makes meaning. As is the case elsewhere along the Green Belt, what is managed is not so much the border infrastructure but instead what is and will be there in its absence.

One of the reasons that the Green Belt is so evocative as a memorial landscape is that visitors can see the ecological traces that the destroyed border has left behind: different tree species have filled in the swath of clear-cut forest and are visibly distinct from the older growth on each side; shrubs remain stunted in areas heavily sprayed with herbicides for decades. These allow us to still "see" the border, even in its absence. The *Tree Cross at Ifta* builds a version of this into its art. Once the fence is rusted away, the trees, arranged in parallel lines, become the proxy for what was. In these cases, "the absent elements are sensuously, emotionally and ideationally present to people, and are articulated or materialized in various ways through narratives, commemorations, enactments of past experiences or visualizations of future scenarios."[18]

It is the present as well as the absent that has power, and it is the witnessing of "absencing" as a process, a verb, that can allow for powerfully evocative and commemorative experiences, allowing for self- and collective reflection. What does the absencing of one thing mean? What is the significance of a void? How is absence productive of emotions, imaginings, actions, and not least, new ecological relationships? Absence is thus not simply the binary opposite of presence. It is "a corporeal, emotional and sensuous phenomenon articulated in distinctly concrete, political and cultural registers. The agency of the absent . . . is never finite, but entangled in the dynamics of potential reverberation, reappearance, transformation and return."[19] Perhaps more than anything, absence can make us humans more present to ourselves and each other.

Ruin Sites

The construction of the GDR's border system was predicated on removal—not just of forests and fields, but of people and their homes. Dozens of towns and villages were destroyed over the course of decades as the militarized zone grew larger and more intimidating. Today, some of those sites have disappeared into near oblivion, while others are marked with a commemorative stone. Still others have as their only trace a small cemetery sitting in the middle of agricultural fields, a poignant reminder of the lives lived and honored here. One such ruin site—the north German village of Jahrsau—is particularly moving and presently featured in many Green Belt travel brochures. It is a case of presencing absence through ecological relationships.

Official records of Jahrsau's existence go back to 1375, but in 1952, the GDR ordered the first families to leave. The remaining families were pushed out in 1961, and by 1970, the buildings were destroyed.[20] Since 1989, the remains of the village have been reclaimed by forest, leaving ghostly traces of previous human occupation. In 1993, a few years after reunification, the German government included the site in its index of monuments of Saxony-Anhalt.

The memorial site today is powerful in its understatement. As one approaches by car on the local road, the usual directional signs point toward Jahrsau. But one never gets there: the old cobblestone road ends in shrubs and woods. Jahrsau itself is gone. No major parking lot or entrance building draws attention to the site. Next to an explanatory panel put up by the BUND, a small welcome sign, handmade by a local, greets visitors with an explanation of the village's six-hundred-year existence and twentieth-century demise. A deciduous forest has grown over part of the past, quite literally. Between specks of light and shadow, among tangled roots, nettles, moss, and leaf litter, visitors can still find traces of rock walls, rusting tractor parts, the rotting wood of an old wagon yoke, the faint outlines of a home, parts of a chair, the lid of a cooking pot, and even a shredded rubber boot. There is no starker way to narrate the conditions of removal. Narrow trails through woods and brush take visitors from one site to another with small signs, not bigger than letter paper, indicating by name whose home stood on which street. Among the ruins are also the markers of the Cold War itself: sections of shredded border fence, half buried in humus, or pieces of rebar, rammed into the trunk of a tree to form a makeshift ladder for GDR border agents to watch for escapees from a leafy hiding spot. Even this assault is being tamed by the tree, however, as its bark slowly folds itself around the corroding metal.

There is something profoundly ambivalent about the site: it is sorrowful, heartbreaking, and haunting—a cemetery of sorts. And yet especially during spring and early summer, as birdsong echoes through the woods and small wildflowers show among the dapples of sunlight, it is equally apparent that this site holds something more. This is a place where the Green Belt is at its most poignant: amid the contradictions of dissolution and emergence, transition and metamorphosis, past and future, right along the gossamer-thin edge of dying and living.

The remains of Jahrsau, as those of many other places, invite us into an intimate relationship with past human lives. The experience of ruins is somatic and sensual, not merely intellectual. In these tangled woods, there is no clarity about where to go, what functions certain structures had, or what meaning they held, and little sense of orientation. Visitors must craft their own logic from these shattered things. They walk into old basements, touch rusting equipment, and run their hands against mossy walls whose stones were placed there, one by one, by others long gone.

Part of Jahrsau's magic is that it is so minimally curated. There does not seem to be a drive toward stabilizing the thing or its meaning. This runs counter to the interest many museums have in ensuring the physical permanence of their artifacts so that their meaning and significance can be sustained and preserved for those who come after. Without such effort, Jahrsau will continue to disappear, its walls will crumble, the cobblestones will be broken up by root systems, and wooden beams once hewn with much effort will succumb to rot. Ruination changes meanings since it "liberates matter from its subservience to form. . . . Matter flexes its being in the absence of the formal whole."[21] Ecology blurs the boundaries between the human and nonhuman, creating joint yet unsteered and unnamed futures.

Decades hence, beyond perhaps a few signs indicating otherwise, there will be even less to remind passersby that Jahrsau existed, that it was a home to people for six centuries. Over time, this progressive absence becomes a new form of memorial device. It is so precisely *because of* ecological change: nonhuman nature is what makes this a place of reflection and commemoration. The overgrown remnants of this village are now homes for others—chaffinches and lichen, foxes, oaks, owls, and bats—forming part of a landscape that allows them to survive and endure.

Telling Stories in the *Green Belt Adventure*

Art and ruins are potent forms of commemoration, and both explicitly rely on ecological processes to carry their messages. Memory is a social activity, though, and most memories exist in relation to what is shared with others: events, rituals, and symbols as well as language and stories. More recently, the BUND has successfully engaged human storytellers to advocate for the Green Belt and make the connections between ecology and memory explicit. One of the more famous ones is Mario Goldstein, known to many Germans from his nature and adventure documentaries that show him navigating the Yukon River on a self-made raft or driving across Eurasia to meet the Dalai Lama. Goldstein has made his career by defining and circumscribing ideas of "wilderness" and "adventure," and drawing on what Germans call *Fernweh*, or the yearning for faraway places.

It is therefore significant that Goldstein turned his attention to the inter-German border because his brand travels with him. As such, the Green Belt becomes the subject of the same kinds of imaginations: a blank space on the map to be discovered and known, a place of wonder and mystery, and ultimately a wilderness to be encountered, experienced, and felt. His 2016–2018 project to travel along the entirety of the Green Belt and report back on both his human and nonhuman encounters resulted in the publication of a coffee-table book titled *Green Belt Adventure: 100 Days by Foot along the Former German-German Border* (*Abenteuer Grünes Band: 100 Tage zu Fuss entlang der ehemaligen deutsch-deutschen Grenze*), produced in part with support from the BUND. Goldstein is a former East German—himself twice imprisoned and interrogated by the Stasi for his escape attempts—and yet he is also a stranger to many of the places and people he visits. His relation to the border itself is understandably troubled, as he states in his work, and he saw his return to Germany as a way to finally confront his own history.[22]

The book's central axis is Goldstein's travel narrative: his descriptions of landscapes and communities, and his felt experience hiking along the old GDR patrol road, always within immediate proximity to the border. From this main line, three kinds of informational insets branch off; they are labeled "portrait," "flora and fauna," and "history." The twenty different portraits introduce the reader to people Goldstein meets on his travels. They range from BUND staff (Frobel being one of them) to traditional craftspeople and contemporary artists, to former East German border police officers, to shepherds and fishers. They offer different perspectives on the Green Belt, whether about its creation and maintenance, ecological management, or past as a militarized zone, or the ways in which people today make a living nearby.

Two of the portraits focus on the dead: East German men who were killed during their attempted escapes. By including these two figures—thirty-four-year old Heinz-Josef Große and thirty-two-year old Michael Gartenschläger—the book wades into the complicated arena of lost lives and their remembrance. Große was an East German construction worker hired in spring 1982 to repair a section of the border fence. He used his backhoe loader to climb over the fence and ran up the slope on the other side, still on GDR territory but in the no-man's-land and closing in on the demarcation line to West Germany. After an initial warning shot, a GDR border guard fired his Kalashnikov nine times at Große's back. One of the bullets hit Große in the pelvis, shredding a main artery. He bled to death lying prostrate in the grass and just within sight of the West. Gartenschläger's story is more complex, but his victimhood is not. Also an East German, he had started publicly questioning the border regime as a teenager and served ten years of a life sentence before West Germany bought his freedom in 1972. From the West, he continued his work against the GDR, helping East German refugees escape. In 1975, Gartenschläger decided to approach the border from the west to defuse and disassemble its spring guns and show West German officials (the GDR was denying that it had installed such technology). He quickly became a Stasi target. When he approached the border yet again in spring 1976, GDR border forces fired between 120 and 140 rounds at him and his two friends. Gartenschläger died that night, hit by 9 bullets. The Stasi burned his body and buried his ashes anonymously in an East German cemetery; his sister did not learn of his fate until after reunification.[23] Both stories underscore the message of the border's brutality, and in both cases, the book is careful not to paint with too broad a brush: the biographies denounce the border regime rather than the GDR as a whole.

In each of the twelve chapters of the *Green Belt Adventure*, between segments on "flora and fauna" and "history," several passages of text are visually set apart from the rest of the travel narrative. In what seem to be journal entries made from the trail, Goldstein grapples with his memories and emotions. Two examples from the first half of the book illustrate the interweaving of deeply personal reflections on the past with the experience of nature along the Green Belt:

> While listening to the forest and myself, I suddenly feel with overwhelming clarity that this journey will become an encounter with my own past. This is what connects me to the Green Belt: my own escape story. There is still a lot to work on, with time and calm. And both are now sufficiently available to me. I haven't seen anyone for hours today. Only hikers can make progress on the *Kolonnenweg*, any other form of movement is uncomfortable on the per-

forated concrete slabs. This path literally forces you to move slowly. But it is precisely this slowness that also brings time that one does not have in normal, everyday life. What a gift! What a beautiful moment![24]

Being alone for hours, sometimes even days, puts me in an almost meditative state. I see the thoughts come and go, I give them space, and in the moments of reconciliation I feel that all past pain simply takes time until it is finally overcome. After all, I haven't been at this border for over 28 years. That is repression in its purest form. Sometimes I feel like I've been racing against myself. But in the end, no one can escape from their own story. [A recent conversation with a survivor of the border regime] made me aware again that I share my pain with many other people, all of them linked to the Green Belt in their own way and who have their very own history. With every meter of this damned patrol road that I put behind me, my pain disappears. The incessant tock-tock-tock of the tip of the walking stick on the concrete slabs slowly but steadily drills a hole into my thick armor; it is the metronome that keeps the rhythm while my past is being stripped away.[25]

The somatic experience of walking, moving one's body through space, feeling one's feet touch the ground, one before the other in an ever-repeating succession, becomes a form of meditation. Through it, and his experience of walking with complete impunity on the patrol road (a key infrastructural piece of the border regime that contributed to his own arrest and imprisonment decades earlier), Goldstein interweaves ecological beauty and inner peace.

Adding to this experience is his sense of deep connection and solidarity with others, not just because they might have shared experiences, but because their experiences have been *different*; their attitudes, perspectives, and choices of how to deal with the past have not always been the same as his. Meanwhile, it is also the sharing of memories, being able to talk through one's hurt and have it be deeply heard and felt by others, that offers a real possibility of release. As the poet Rumi reminds us, the healing from the pain is in the pain. The reencounter with trauma and anger, often lodged deep in one's cells, happens for Goldstein through his mind and body. His walk along the patrol road spurs catharsis and resolution, allowing him to cast off the weight of a painful past. But the trauma is not just his own; it is collective. And the healing is not just a solitary journey but also a shared one.

In this, the narrator's story invites readers in as witnesses to a personal metamorphosis, catalyzed by nature, mind, and body. His openness and vulnerability thus become a model for others, and he manifests the kinds of hopeful transformations that the Green Belt might prompt. He becomes, perhaps unwittingly, a symbol of a new Germany too. His personal reflections express the reconciliation that still eludes the German nation as it continues to grapple with the fallout of reunification and persistent inequalities between the former East and West Germanies. The fact that his confessionals are set into a larger narrative mosaic that also includes observations on fauna and flora makes the links between memory, nature, and nation all the closer.

Goldstein continued his advocacy of the Green Belt after his travels concluded by returning to the borderlands and launching a speaking tour in Thuringia, supported by the BUND. He accompanied his storytelling with photographs and snippets of film as he switched back and forth between landscape aesthetics and history, between stories of animals and stories of human experiences along the border. The evenings had a welcome side effect: they increased not just public awareness of the Green Belt but also became meeting and exchange places where the storytelling went far beyond Goldstein. As a lead BUND staffer in Thuringia who helped organize Goldstein's tour explained to me,

> Those evenings were never located farther than 20 km from the Green Belt, sometimes really close. We noticed that the local people were very grateful that their stories were told and that the beauty of their landscapes were shown. . . . As I said, there are definitely those who work against the Green Belt, and also against the National Nature Monument, but basically as far as this topic of memories via the Green Belt is concerned, we have received very, very positive feedback. So [with] the multimedia show, it was exactly this combination, when we made it clear with pictures and stories . . . , this idea that one comes to tell stories *through* nature, so to speak, and also to get generations to talk to each other about it. People came with grandchildren and grandparents and so on. . . . That was received extremely gratefully.[26]

Goldstein's speaking tour made room for conversations that needed to happen—on the ground, in real time, and person to person. Perhaps there is a way, then, to further widen the aperture by multiplying the stories, such as by inviting to the table—or the publication of another book—people who are often overlooked: those of industry and agribusiness, hunters, or owners of working forests. They form part of the network of interests as well, and to some extent they, too, have helped create or expand the reach of the Green Belt in their collaborations with the BUND and local environmental agencies.

In an effort to elevate alternative histories, there may also be an opportunity to look at other border deaths. The stories of border fatalities that form part of the Green Belt materials tend to enact a politics of morality by elevating the kinds of deaths deemed reprehensible and hence worthy of remembrance.[27] The deaths of Große or Gartenschläger, for example, are directly, incontrovertibly, and causally connected to the border regime: neither would have died in the way he did if the border had not existed. This adds to their tragedy. Moreover, both men were seen to be honest and good, each of them innocent and blameless, and therefore their deaths become killings—state-sanctioned murders—that illustrate the disproportionality and absurdity of the border's violence. It is important to raise these points, but as narrative instruments, such stories sidestep the gray areas that continue to complicate our understanding of the GDR, West Germany, and the border in their midst. It may be precisely the gray areas that need elucidation to help develop a more nuanced and indeed layered accounting of the Green Belt.[28]

The multimedia tour formed part of the BUND's campaign to have the Green Belt declared a national nature monument (*nationales Naturmonument*), a new protected area category in Germany, thereby giving it countrywide recognition and additional layers of legal protection. It has been a struggle to get this far, and the BUND has relied on various strategies, from the speaking tour described above to particular forms of selective curation, narration, and representation. The following section takes a closer look at the latter, emphasizing the significance of how stories of people and places are told. The resistance to the Green Belt—seen here primarily as a conservation rather than memorial project—shifts our attention to the unavoidability of affect. Drawing their strength from memories, fear, and long-held trauma, emotions matter to conservation. Not just this, but the materiality of conservation—land and our varied relationships to it—literally "matters" as well.[29] The stakes increase further if conservation is brought into the ambit of the state as well as its national and international ambitions.

THE NATIONAL NATURE MONUMENT

While expanding protected areas, the BUND has sought to create greater awareness of and appreciation for the border region's ecological riches. It has also become increasingly obvious, however, that the Green Belt is not an easy conservation target: it is a complex mosaic of habitats cutting through many cultural regions and administrative districts, and has been shaped by violence. Curating the Green Belt and telling its stories is difficult due to four decades of GDR rule and the attendant trauma, both under Communism and then from the sudden reunification and transition to capitalism. The BUND's struggle to have the Green Belt recognized as a national nature monument offers a closer look at those challenges. It brings to the surface both how the borderlands' socioecologies are narrated and branded and how the Green Belt's implementation can spur considerable conflict in particular places.

Unlike other kinds of mnemonic ecological work along the Green Belt, this section concentrates specifically on how the BUND speaks.[30] If we consider environmental managers to be authors of text, then we realize that stories inform their work. In the case of landscapes with layered pasts, "narratives can be used in restoration to explore and negotiate the meanings of complex landscapes. . . . Narratives can reveal and enable more careful consideration of diverse values. As such, they can play an important role in the process of identifying plans for restoration, management, and interpretation that acknowledge the richness of a layered landscape and the complexities of its past."[31]

Conservationists of the BUND have worked hard for decades to slowly and incrementally realize their vision of an uninterrupted ecological corridor along the former inter-German borderlands. To help gain even greater recognition and improved legal protection for this space, the BUND launched an ambitious push to get the Green Belt designated a national nature monument. Germany's newest conservation category is an adaptation of the IUCN's protected area category III, the "natural monument or feature."[32] Here the Green Belt falls under "cultural sites with associated ecology: where protection of a cultural site also protects significant and important biodiversity, such as archaeological/historical sites that are inextricably linked to a natural area."[33] Meanwhile, Germany's 2010 Federal Nature Conservation Law defines national nature monuments as areas "that are of outstanding importance due to 1. scientific, natural-historical, cultural-historical or cultural reasons, and 2. their rarity, uniqueness or beauty." The Federal Ministry of the Environment, Nature Conservation, and Nuclear Safety (Bundesministerium für Umwelt, Naturschutz, nukleare Sicherheit und Verbraucherschutz) offers additional elaboration:

> National nature monuments are unique natural phenomena of nationwide importance. They can be important examples of natural and cultural history and provide habitat for rare plants and animals. National natural monuments . . . can contribute to greater understanding of nature for many people.
>
> National nature monuments protect landscape sections or natural phenomena that are of outstanding scientific, naturalistic, cultural or of regional landscape interest because of their rarity, uniqueness, or beauty. Often created through the interaction of natural and human influences, they are frequently refuges for very special communities.
>
> A national nature monument is subject to strict protection, which excludes any change in the protected natural feature. . . . National nature monuments encourage us to deal carefully with what has been handed down to us from the cultural and natural heritage of past times.[34]

This new protected areas category is understandably appealing to the BUND. It offers an appropriate frame for what the Green Belt is—both an ecologically and culturally significant space—and provides additional layers of safeguards by further restricting industrial and infrastructure development as well as limiting more local land use changes. Achieving this designation in Thuringia elevates the conservation project to matters of state and national importance, makes it an even more attractive target for long-term financial support, and creates a beacon for other federal states to follow.[35]

In Thuringia, the two main conservation actors are the BUND and Thuringian Foundation for Conservation (Stiftung Naturschutz Thüringen), with the latter funded by the federal state of Thuringia. There are two major arenas of struggle: the winning of hearts and minds among local communities and supporters, and the legal changes needed to realize the new protected area designation. In what follows, I highlight both the discursive strategies the BUND used along with the actual and possible practical consequences of elevating some kinds of Green Belt narratives while erasing others. Meanwhile, the legal process in general and language of the law specifically in Thuringia offer interesting insights into how the Green Belt's nature interplays with questions of nationhood, on the one hand, and local concerns and fears, on the other.

Aside from the activities of Goldstein already discussed, the other main publicity vehicle for the BUND's campaign for national nature monument is its web interface.[36] Under the heading "Monumental: The Green Belt on the Way to a National Nature Monument—Thuringia Sets the Tone" (Monumental: Das Grüne Band auf dem Weg zum nationalen Naturmonument: Thüringen hat den Anfang gemacht), the BUND website celebrates and promotes the naming of the Green Belt as a new conservation category in Germany. The website's design and aesthetics are striking. The picture dominating the top of the site shows a small, white flower (*Anemone nemorosa*, a springtime bloom) growing in the shadow of a towering border fence (figure 4.3). The image's strong narrative qualities point to one of conservation's major themes: peaceful ecological resurgence in the wake of military violence.

From this opening photograph, visitors scroll down to reveal multiple sections with bold single-word headings: "Phänomenal," an interactive map of the Thuringian Green Belt; "International," an explanation of the European Green Belt for which the Thuringian portion forms but a small part; "Denkmal!" (memorial), a brief discussion of the US-based conservation idea of a natural monument; "Merkmal" (characteristic or feature), an explanation of why the new conservation category is appropriate based on the conservation value of this corridor; and "Brutal," a post–World War II time line of the GDR wall and its demise. In this last portion, the time

Figure 4.3
The main web page of "Monumental" illustrating the use of narrative opposites: the imposing metal border fence against the delicate and emergent flora. *Source*: BUND Fachbereich Grünes Band, used with permission.

line moves from the keyword *brutal* (the building of the wall) to *final* (the fall of the wall), to *zentral* (how the central death strip becomes the site of ecological resurgence), and then *monumental* (how the Green Belt memorializes both the end of the GDR and celebrates the transition from "death strip to lifeline").

In the accompanying video, developed in 2017 by the BUND and available on YouTube under the title *Green Belt: On the Path to a National Nature Monument* (*Monumental: Das Grüne Band ist auf dem Weg Nationales Naturmonument zu werden*), a voice-over narrator says,

> It was created by tanks. It is 1,393 kilometers long but only 50 to 200 meters wide. It separated families, loved ones, villages, and it has seen many dramas and witnessed many turns of fortune. It became a refuge for plants and animals. Since 1989 it is once again part of the country and must be preserved as a habitat and as a place of remembrance. It is—your history. It is—your nature. It is—a part of you. It is—the Green Belt. The Green Belt is on its way to becoming a national nature monument.[37]

We see the intertwining here of the themes of separation and joining, loss and recovery, and the dual role of the Green Belt as an ecosystem and memorial. The video's attempt to make viewers identify with—and even take ownership of—the Green Belt is particularly notable, underscored by significant pauses (indicated by the hyphens above) and dramatic cinematography showing flyovers of the Green Belt and border infrastructure, close-up shots of endangered species, and portraits of people including traditional land users like shepherds (the parallels to Goldstein's *Green Belt Adventure* are evident here). These themes are expanded in numerous Green Belt informational brochures distributed by the BUND. The flagship website, video, and this additional material showcase the major narratives.

The first is what I call the story of ecological resurgence. Its underlying plotline plays on the idea of renewal and resurrection, a movement out of shadow and into light. One of the BUND's publications that most directly discusses the project's history and significance in Thuringia is a 2012 booklet called *Trace in the Landscape* (*Spur in der Landschaft*). Here are some examples of how it describes this transformation: "A Green Belt across Germany, a living memorial of German history and a natural pearl necklace in the middle of densely populated Europe—and all [of] this where other people not long ago wanted to separate each other with lethal perfection: in the inner-German border strip. . . . The Iron Curtain, for humans a source of fear, created a last refuge for nature."[38] Similarly, another publication by the BUND, this time from 2015 and focused on "ecological management along the Green Belt," states,

> The Green Belt—the habitats along the former inner-German border—is the largest and so far only existing cross-border biotope network in Germany. It was created by the decades-long border situation in which the areas were hardly or not at all used (fallow land) or were kept open by the GDR border troops every few years, in order to have a clear view. Wilderness areas have been created in numerous areas of the Green Belt that had been left to their own devices, especially in forests and wetlands.[39]

The border situation and border patrol forces with which this passage begins transitions to the natural areas "left to their own devices" that produced forests and even wilderness areas. The brochures and flagship website underline this with one of three kinds of images: flyover shots of the Green Belt showing up literally as a green belt through yellow fields of wheat, pictures of decaying border infrastructure, and images of people in this landscape—either tourists or participants (ecological managers and volunteers). The implicit dualisms between war and peace, death and life, (human-imposed) monotony and (natural) diversity create narrative tension.

The second main story line of the Green Belt, and the narrative opposite of the story of resurgence, is the border's past as one of the most fortified military spaces on earth, the ground zero of the Cold War, and a symbol of what is said to be the inhumane and oppressive GDR regime. The BUND's *Trace in the Landscape* describes the border regime in the following way:

> Today one can hardly imagine how the former inner German border cut through the landscape. It was a barely surmountable dividing line between two social systems and the people living in them. Many human fortunes and much suffering were connected with this border: families were torn apart, people forcibly relocated from their homeland. Any approach of the border led to extensive checks in the surrounding areas. In their attempt to escape this social system or simply to live with friends and relatives on the other side of the "curtain," more than 700 people died in the period from 13.08.1961 to 09.11.1989 alone. The cold perfectionism—for which 2.2 billion DDR Mark were spent for the "protection of the state border," more than 50,000 men were hired as border guards, 60,000 auto-firing systems were installed, and 1,322,700 mines were laid—continues to shock us.[40]

"Monumental" takes up this narrative theme about two-thirds down on the web page (the page begins with the ecological resurgence theme), and in its stark black-and-white rendering the section is visually set off from the rest of the page (figure 4.4), which keeps to shades of green and tan. In four segments, a time line chronicles the creation of the border regime in the 1940s, its strengthening in the 1950s and 1960s until its sudden dissolution in the 1980s, the border region's transformation into the Green Belt throughout the 1990s, and finally the expansion of the Green Belt in the 2000s and 2010s. Reading through the short summaries, the following keywords are used to highlight the Green Belt's history: *occupation zones, demarcation line, small border traffic, Iron Curtain, Cold War, interzone passport, watchtowers, barbed wire, roadblocks, exclusion zone, passport controls, travel permits, forced displacement, death strip, firing order, mass exodus,* and *peaceful revolution.*

Figure 4.4

"Monumental" offers commentary on key historical moments in the border's creation under the heading "Brutal: The Inter-German Border." *Source*: BUND Fachbereich Grünes Band, used with permission.

Much of the narrative thus turns on physical infrastructure, on the one hand, and references to restricted mobility, on the other, both of which find their narrative opposites in the concepts of the *ecological refuge* and *ecological corridor*.

It is worth noting here that for some critics, this kind of narrative constitutes a narrow, one-dimensional, and ultimately West German perspective. It suggests that people in the GDR only ever suffered, and people in East and West Germany only ever hoped for reunification. Many—and perhaps even most—people on both sides of the border, however, eventually accepted it as a fact of life or even helped maintain the wall. The West German view of the border was not simply one of compassion for the East German people and anger at militarization but also significantly shaped by voyeuristic curiosity, self-affirmation, sensationalism, and stereotypes as well as indifference and disinterest.[41] Yet the clarity of the BUND's narrative of GDR offers a more powerful frame for the Green Belt, though the BUND has been careful to mostly limit its geographic scope to the borderlands rather than attempt to speak for the GDR experience more broadly.

A third narrative exists alongside these first two: that of the rural idyll, understood as "an idealized, romanticized construct. . . . The rural is cast as an idyllic place to live, portrayed as having beautiful landscapes, more neighborly communities, and a better quality of life."[42] Most of the Green Belt moves through rural areas. Conservationists are attempting to connect the Green Belt to the rural Heimat, expressed in traditional crafts and land use, rural folklife, and regional identity. This can be understood in part through the BUND's interest in creating value-added conservation that contributes to the economic growth of the areas near the Green Belt, and this happens largely through tourism. The rural idyll is underscored by photographs that focus on "dying" rural crafts and foodways along with otherwise-outdated land use traditions like sheep herding. It also relies on reference to a traditional cultural landscape, where fields are small and patchworked, hedgerows provide refuges for animals, agriculture still knows its limits and adapts to the local landscape, and German identity is "authentic" and untroubled.

The flagship website for the national nature monument features an interactive scroll-down map, with small pictures popping up at different places along the Thuringian Green Belt featuring both "natural" and built landscapes, scenic views, and local people visibly involved in some form of caretaking like ecological management, environmental education, or wildlife rehabilitation. Notably absent from representations of the rural, though, are depictions of contemporary—modern—human pursuits (whether it be industrial production or farming, both of which can have major ecological components).

When considering memorial landscapes, those layered spaces with traumatic histories, it is imperative to think about whose stories are told in conservation and whose are not. And what might the implications of certain selective silences be? The ways in which the Green Belt project unfolded in one small part of Germany is emblematic of how the past continues to haunt the present and what is at stake when conservation ignores human memories.

LAYERED LANDSCAPES AND STORIES UNTOLD

The Eichsfeld region lies in the geographic heart of Germany, a quiet, rural space between the industrial cities of Kassel, Erfurt, and Hannover. It possesses some of Germany's best soils, and intensive, industrialized agriculture is one of the important economic drivers. In the west, agricultural lands used to be relatively small parceled but are becoming increasingly consolidated in part due to rural–urban out-migration. In the east, huge tracts are holdovers from 1950s' collectivization.[43] Monocultures are the norm in both cases. While seasonal migration has been a livelihood strategy in the region since at least the Industrial Revolution, permanent out-migration has accelerated since the 1990s in an imitation of national trends.[44] For instance, between 1993 and today, the number of people employed in agriculture and forestry here has declined by 42 percent. The remaining lands are farmed by fewer and larger farms, overwhelmingly using high-input methods.[45] A local nature conservation and education organization, the Sielmann Foundation, located just outside the town of Duderstadt, has been the BUND partner and key project coordinator here for the Green Belt.[46]

The official beginning of the foundation's work to conserve the Green Belt in Eichsfeld was in 2009 when the federal government granted it 1.1 million euros to develop an ecologically based project implementation plan. Initially the foundation thought big: it wanted to put over 33,000 acres under protection, including the actual borderlands themselves, but in addition, some other areas of conservation value farther afield that could be linked to the Green Belt.[47] The foundation hired a planning firm from Munich to develop the implementation plan based on the foundation's (and BUND's) ecological guidelines. The plan was finalized in 2012. Unfortunately, that document at first surprised farmers in the region and then galvanized them into resistance. A significant part of the land slated for conservation was either then in agricultural use or near it. Even conservation activities in neighboring fields can jeopardize current farming practices. The fact that perceived "outsiders"—both the biologists on the board of the Sielmann Foundation and the Bavarian planning firm—were about to make decisions that would impact local livelihoods raised hackles.

The conflict got so heated that in 2013, a 250-tractor caravan rolled into Duderstadt in protest. Signs read "forty years of the border is enough," "expropriation in secret—against our will," and "no new border after reunification," using the memory of the GDR as a rhetorical cudgel.[48] The Sielmann Foundation backed away from the project and called on local consultants to help take the pulse of local opinion. According to my interviews with local stakeholders, families along the Green Belt today still feel deeply attached to their lands and property—a point confirmed as well by scholars, who describe attachment to landownership historically as an "important economic resource and as an anchor of self-esteem."[49] Farmers suffered land seizures, displacement, destruction of livelihood, and persecution, and thus the border helped form a mnemonic community that is triggered by the conservationist need for land. To understand current farmers' objections better, I spoke with members of two farmers' unions, one on each side of the Green Belt, in Lower Saxony (the former West Germany) and Thuringia (the former East Germany). A range of grievances were articulated, some of which seem like reverberations of older wrongs: conservation was being forced on farmers from above without local participation or consultation; it was being imposed by outsiders—urban professionals without roots in the region; conservation would justify a form of expropriation, limiting the farmer's "entrepreneurial freedom"; and ultimately, farmers are entitled to have agency in this because farming activities for the last centuries have cocreated the cultural landscape that now is seen to have conservation value.[50] As one person put it, "That [implementation plan] came from above, from the professional greens. They want to impose an ideology on us: 'What you guys do is bad and what we do is good, we come from Berlin and know better.' But the landscape here didn't emerge on its own, this is a cultural landscape that was made by farmers!"[51] In Thuringia, in the former GDR, farmers are feeling even more cautious about the possible loss of control over their lands given the memories of past expropriations and overall decline of the agricultural sector in Germany.[52] With the uneven track record farmers have had with conservation in the area, there exists, according to a representative from a farmers' union, a "vigilant defensive" position—something that has only increased with the additional layer of EU-level laws like Natura 2000.[53]

The attempt by Thuringia to declare the Green Belt a national nature monument is, to them, an overreach as well as an attempt for others to "once again tell us how things need to be."[54] Again and again in my conversations with farmers in Eichsfeld and elsewhere in Thuringia, I heard how misunderstood they felt, from their daily work to their role in the German economy.

Farmers see the cause of this largely in Germany's urbanization that removes people from rural areas and the natural resource base. They bemoan the fact that renderings of German agriculture continue to favor romantic images, and many urban consumers might say they want ethical production but remain ignorant of rural life and are unwilling to pay farmers fair prices for their products. As Germany continues to urbanize, questions emerge for those left in rural areas about what role—if any—they will have in shaping the future of the country and its national identity.

Many of the points made by the region's farmers were also raised, albeit in slightly different terms, by one of Eichsfeld's most vocal Green Belt opponents, district administrator Werner Henning. As a former East German, he offered a broader perspective, pointing to deep historical ties to land and community in the region, and a strong sense of lingering injustice relating to GDR land seizures. To him, reunification did not end the oppressive presence of the state but rather shifted it from a state based on and shaped by ideology to one that was ostensibly "free" yet structured by a rigid system of rights. In his view, this "political state" uses the legal system to advance its policies, and just like its socialist predecessor, has a way of erasing local identities, cultures, and needs: "The 'Green Belt' . . . for me, this term derives from art, from Sielmann, the artist-filmmaker who created the term. But from there, the Green Belt has been redefined as a political term, and that becomes a threat here. . . . Here the state rises again above the people, the state defines nature, and the functionary of the state is the nature conservationist." Seen through decades-long experiences with a repressive and controlling political apparatus, conservation for many East Germans becomes linked with the state, and through this association, evokes anger, fear, and resistance. While the BUND is technically a private NGO, its close collaboration with the state agencies in Thuringia and federal government in the effort to create a national nature monument does lend credence to the administrator's complaints. For him, the drive to declare such monument status amounts to "militant affectations of the state":

> The politics of the Green Belt is not credible because it does not arise out of deep love for the homeland [Heimat], love for the landscape. Instead, it is

"law and order." . . . I am in favor of nature conservation and that it has to be organized, but I am against being used, against expropriation, and against alienation. . . . The Eichsfeld, that is love for Heimat, where Heimat equals relationships, exchanges with ideas, with nature, with landscape. . . . The communities should be able to do this themselves.[55]

It is evident that in the conflict over conservation, different experiences with the state and different hopes for state-society relationships postunification shape levels of acceptance, and ultimately the outcome of any conservation or restoration project. Land—its seizure, repurposing, clearing, and defense—was central to the border's construction, and land is central to conservation. The Green Belt's whole premise is the creation of a single, uninterrupted ecological corridor, and that cannot happen without land. So land is literally the terrain on which the East-West divisions of the past continue to play out.

Conservation science itself also contributes to the sense of alienation that local communities feel. A staff member at one of the municipal environmental agencies who has accompanied the Eichsfeld portion of the Green Belt since its inception in 1989 and remains generally supportive of the project explained the farmers' resistance to me based on his experience:

The Green Belt is an artificial construct; unlike other protected areas it is not a visible, naturally bounded space. It's all over the place. They suddenly want to protect things that never before had any conservation value. This feels arbitrary. The *border* was arbitrary, and the Green Belt is therefore an artificial construct. The Green Belt makes sense for the biologists because it's an ecological network, but not for the rest of the population. One could indeed create such a network anywhere; the Green Belt is there only because of the former border.[56]

In some ways, then, the conservationists' narrative of the Green Belt seems an exclusionary one based on a vision grounded in the ecological sciences and not necessarily legible (or narratable) in this way by others who do not share the same epistemological frame. In other words, various stakeholders construct landscape quite differently from one another—and partial perspectives make for unstable meanings. Farmers' relationships to land, different from that of ecologists, produces a tension that, while seemingly recognized by both parties, so far has not been articulated and included in the official Green Belt story.

In addition, the conservationist story of a layered landscape, comprising both living memorial and resurgent ecologies, obfuscates others. The reasons for this appear obvious, at least to some extent: if the point is to brand this space to attract tourists, supporters, and donors, increase enthusiasm among local, regional, and national agencies, and persuade remaining private landholders to collaborate with environmentalists, the story's engaging plot has clear advantages. But in parts of Eichsfeld and places like it all along the Green Belt where there is resistance to this project, other story lines might need to be brought to the surface, other histories need to matter, and conservation praxis needs to shift even more toward building local relationships by elevating local landscape meanings, and importantly, understanding and honoring local people's memories of the past and their lingering traumas.

The levels of resistance and antagonism toward the Green Belt came as a shock to the BUND, and led to reflection both internally and in relationship with the project's critics. Over months, conservationists recalibrated their approach. They drew on the expertise of the Thüringer Landgesellschaft (which translates loosely to the Thuringian Society for Rural Lands, or ThLG), whose staff have much closer ties with—and greater understanding of—the farming community and state of the agricultural sector in the region more generally.[57] The ThLG began to gather information by surveying locals, and eventually crafted a new, more participatory and transparent strategy for land-based conservation. A staff member at the ThLG who oversaw this process recounted it to me. The organization was brought in at the request of the Thuringian farmers' association to help moderate—in partnership with local farmers—discussions for one of the southern Thuringia–northern Bavaria Green Belt sections. In a series of one-on-one conversations, the ThLG staff first explained the ecological care and management plan (Pflege- und Entwicklungsplan) that the BUND affiliates had prepared. This technical and scientific document is generally illegible to nonscientists even while it can have significant repercussion for people's livelihoods. It helped, the staff member said, that they and their partner "weren't seen to come from

Bavaria or northern Saxony [West Germany], we were seen as the *Thuringian Society for Rural Lands*. That was an advantage." My interviewee felt that even though they were born in West Germany, their longtime work in the East allowed them to be seen as "holistically German" (*gesamtdeutsch*).[58] Discussions were held at the farms themselves, and meetings were open to all. The maps of the management plan were all reprinted in much larger format, and the obscure numbering system was replaced with clearer, multicolored labels that indicated which ecological changes were being proposed on or near whose land. Meeting participants could then indicate their response with differently colored stickers: red for rejection of the measure, yellow for undecided but open to discussion, and green for approval. The finished maps were reproduced, and copies were handed to the participants. The claim that this process seemed to create trust, transparency, and legibility was confirmed by the farmers whom I asked about this process.

In my conversation with the ThLG member, I commented on how complicated conservation could be sometimes, considering that it exists across so many different scales, interest groups, and the west-east divide. Their response was disarming: "Maybe, but conservation doesn't have to be difficult because of that. All we did was get into the car, we drove there, and we talked to people. And it worked. No big mediators or facilitators were needed, just lots of one-on-one conversations. It was less threatening, more human." As is clear with other places along the former border, the interpersonal relationships that grow through speaking and listening are crucial to conservation: "What really surprised us was how much need for conversation people had. It was almost like therapy. We really just listened to what people recounted about how things were back then. They did that to explain to us why their attitude toward the Green Belt was what it was."[59] The conservation project in this region has moved along much more rapidly and with much less conflict than in Eichsfeld—reason enough for the BUND to reconsider its approach there as well.

Despite the successes that the ThLG helped generate in the Thuringian-Bavarian borderlands, land and history still became a topic in the Thuringian parliamentary debates over the strengths and merits of the draft National Nature Monument Law in 2017–2018. Position statements submitted during the comment period show mayors and officials from twelve munici-palities affected by the designation unanimously opposed to the law as orig-inally drafted.[60] Two major concerns rose to the top of the many articulated: the new law would de-historicize the landscape through an overemphasis on ecology, and as discussed already in the case of Eichsfeld, it would jus-tify a new wave of expropriations, but this time for conservation purposes. Beyond that, municipal officials were unwilling to accept additional financial burdens for the Green Belt's maintenance, and they pointed to the lack of transparency in decision-making, demanding better flow of information and greater participation in matters of conservation governance.

The first point of concern was that the planned "nature monument" would prioritize "nature" at the expense of "monument"; in other words, this would simply be a protected area in disguise and there would not be enough attention paid to the historical components that gave this new con-servation category its name (a fear that the BUND's media campaign—both on the web and through Goldstein's speaking tours—tried to allay). Another position statement by the Regional Commissioner for the Study of SED Dictatorship (Landesbeauftrager zur Aufarbeitung der SED-Diktatur) even pointedly commented on the BUND's willingness to spend over 200,000 euros on a publicity campaign to build awareness and acceptance of the Green Belt when it had not (yet) approached the commissioner to develop anything similar to this with respect to GDR history.[61] Several years prior, in 2016, as the Thuringian environmental agencies started alluding to this designation effort, that same official had published a critical response in a local outlet. Titled "An Ecologizing of History Must Be Resisted," the article stated,

> The metaphor "pearl necklace of nature" ecologizes the Iron Curtain. The monstrosity at the external border of the Soviet Empire with the GDR border regime, the mines, spring guns, fences, and the strip that was cleared of vege-tation, was and is "unique." The old and new biotopes are only conditionally so. What should have priority are the regional significance and distinctive qualities of the former death strip. That should be reflected in the law for the national nature monument.[62]

Cultural history, not ecology, should be the orienting principle for any inter-ventions along the former border.[63]

The second major point of friction that appeared in the position statements by local mayors and municipalities was the fear of land seizure—this time for conservation: "In our community, many property owners who had their land expropriated before 1989 bought it back after reunification. . . . The proposed bill means the same treatment for private owners as it did before the fall of the wall, namely the expropriation of their private property."[64] The de-historicization or erasure of memory, alongside the threat to privately owned land and feeling that one's voice is being silenced, are all reminiscent of older traumas. They reemerge here in a conflict over conservation and ecological restoration in the borderlands.

Parallel to this, a legal argument played out. Lawyers for the opposition contended in early 2018 that the designation of national nature monument was a political and ecological overreach: the current protection status was adequate, and in general a smaller-scale, more locally specific protected area status was sufficient and more accurately reflected the realities of the ecological patchwork that existed on the ground.[65] In their response, the opposing lawyers, working for the BUND, argued in support of an earlier assessment that had backed the national designation, pointing out that "the 'outstanding importance' [required by the federal nature conservation law for national nature monument designation] can be justified by the fact that the circumstances and phenomena . . . have national, identity-creating meaning for the population.[66]

These debates raged while the draft law lay before decision makers in 2017 and early 2018. The BUND responded by kicking its campaign—and its *Erinnerungsarbeit* (memory work) into higher gear. Goldstein's book and his speaking tour fall temporally into this window, demystifying the project, adding a human dimension, and honoring individual and collective memory. Between September 2017 and December 2018, the law was edited in response to feedback, criticism, and opposition. Comparing the draft and final version of the law is illuminating.[67] A number of points were revised for greater specificity and clarity. The law as passed ensures greater information flow and participation regarding the management of the national nature monument (paragraph 2), and more room was made for considering different types of memorial sites, including razed villages, that should be included in the designation and come under protection (paragraph 3, section 2). Featuring several substantial additions, paragraph 5 regarding "sponsorship, cooperation with border museums, care, development and information plan" was the most heavily revised portion of the law. Section 1 discusses how the national nature monument should be governed, who should be involved, and who bears the financial burdens. Significantly, sections 2 and 3 carve out a more pronounced educational role for border museums and other historical institutions to curate memorial sites in the Green Belt. In contrast to the draft law, the final version of paragraph 5, section 5, requires the creation of a council (*Beirat*) to oversee the development of a management plan that should involve the affected municipalities. Additional caveats and exceptions to land use restrictions were included in the final version that gave hunters, private property owners, and some industries slightly more leeway and freedoms.

The precedent-setting National Nature Monument Law passed by the Thuringian Parliament in the final weeks of 2018 responds to the main concerns of its critics while upholding many, if not most, of the ecological protections sought by the Green Belt's supporters. Since then, neighboring Saxony-Anhalt followed suit with its own designation in 2019, and more will likely occur in subsequent years.

THE NATURE OF MEMORY-WORK

Conservation is always about more than ecological preservation. As historians, geographers, anthropologists, and others have shown, it is also always a question of power and space, and quite often, nation and national identity.[68] From its beginnings, the Green Belt has been discursively closely associated with unity in general and German reunification more specifically.[69] Its origin story is, of course, tied up with the fall of the Berlin Wall along with the collaboration between West and East German environmentalists, and several of the largest protected areas that it connects were created in the last days of the GDR. In the German press, one can hardly find a Green Belt–related story without the tagline "from death strip to lifeline" (*vom Todesstreifen zur Lebenslinie*). Another popular slogan used by Green Belt supporters is "borders separate, nature connects" (*Grenzen trennen, Natur verbindet*), and similarly draws on the death/life, division/union binaries. The landscape art and storytelling described above, and narratives in BUND brochures and signage scattered along the Green Belt, marshal the metaphor of unity and reunification as well. This strategy has unique resonance in Germany because reunification continues to be emotionally fraught and difficult.

The borderlands, now reinvented as a national nature monument, represent a mnemonic landscape in which conservation does the work of an otherwise-troubled reunification: the Green Belt ecological paradise has been tasked with stitching east and west back together in a vision of a green future that draws on traditions from the past. Ecological imperatives—the safeguarding of biodiversity and adaptation to climate change—supersede old divisions; *natural* heritage becomes *national* heritage. The nature represented by the Green Belt—the life that returned to suture this wound in the landscape—becomes the universal healer, the common denominator that all people can learn to love, care for, protect, and take pride in. The many aerial photographs taken of the Green Belt these past decades (figures 2.5–2.6) that show it literally as a green band in the middle of monoculture fields of wheat have the effect of softening and veiling the border, rendering it as an abstract and bizarre form in the landscape.[70] It becomes a curious work of art, stripped of historical detail and obscuring its ecological complexity. The BUND then must restore those meanings with additional information, photographs, and narrative techniques. These Green Belt narratives also push the boundaries of classical conservation: the advocates of the Green Belt present a hybrid imaginary that highlights the inextricably merging and emergent socioecological reality of this layered landscape. In the Green Belt story, ecological resurgence—even an accidental one—was dependent on human intervention, and it continues to be so to this day.

Integral to the BUND's messaging is the notion of Heimat, or homeland. As discussed above, the rural idyll references a particular romantic vision of Heimat, anchored in traditional crafts and ostensibly "sustainable" ecological lifeways. The next chapter will comment on the place of Heimat in ecological discourse, but politically, finding Heimat in the Green Belt is another strategy that responds to a conflict-laden postreunification. The kinds of crafts and lifestyles that are highlighted and portrayed—making felt hats, carving walking sticks, herding sheep, and tending small, organic family farms—all point to a premodern (and prepartition) sensitivity, a nostalgia for a nineteenth-century condition that aligns with the early forms of nature conservation in Germany. This eco-nostalgia harks back to a more "innocent" time where relationships to land and other people were locally anchored as well as seemingly uncomplicated by national and international demands. Even the readily available photographs of the village of Jahrsau show not the 1950s or 1960s but instead the early twentieth century.[71] Doing so allows the Green Belt to project a positive understanding of the national community as a place of togetherness and shared, interdependent existence beyond the East-West problematic.[72]

But the message is not all that clear-cut. National identity in Germany is fraught; "more than any other nation in Europe, Germany has suffered from bouts of anxiety regarding its national identity," and reunification, "rather than settling the question of German identity once and for all, has raised it anew."[73] For some historians of Germany, the country's drive to preserve those dear things "constantly corroded by the ravages of social change, war, love, and neglect, has symbolized a sense of the nation, constantly destabilized by forces beyond its control and therefore promoted again and again, in countless recastings and re-creations, as the key to collective being, the center of gravity of political weight."[74]

5 MNEMONIC ECOLOGIES IN THE MANAGED AND WILD BORDERLANDS

At the end of winter in 2015, the BUND cleared about 8.5 acres of Green Belt land near the town of Dippach in western Thuringia to create open land habitats and corridors. This was the second Green Belt–related clear-cut here; just the year before, such measures had destroyed forests in this community. Local people felt confused and outraged over this perceived assault. The BUND-affiliated staff member supervising the ecological management strategy in this part of Thuringia admitted that it was unfortunately common for landscapes to look "pretty devastated immediately after the measure is taken." Some locals were saddened by the BUND decision since Dippach already lacked forest and it would have been "good for the community" to allow these spaces to develop into "real woods" rather than cutting down the trees, including large oaks, in the name of conservation. Local hunters similarly criticized the clearing, concerned that species of interest to them would now no longer find suitable habitats.[1]

This is, of course, only one small story among many, but it puts into relief how complicated conservation is. In this case, locals were attached to the trees and "naturally developing woods" that many welcomed. The clear-cut clashed with their ecological understanding and also left behind a denuded landscape, ugly now when it had been beautiful. In Dippach and many communities around the world, changes in the land are often resisted because local inhabitants "define themselves in terms of a sense of belonging to a landscape whose message they can understand."[2] This form of placemaking relies on particular, stable landscape formations that remain familiar, and thus represent to people comfort and safety.

The border had already destroyed many of these attachments when it was built decades earlier. It was quite arbitrary in the way that it cut through human and ecological communities, without much regard for terrain and landmarks or the many ties that bound people to each other. Socially, this means that postreunification life remains fractured. Ecologically, this means that the borderlands today represent a rich and sometimes unpredictable combination of established and novel ecosystems, succession and regression, and desirable and undesirable ecological dynamics. Management strategies reflect this complexity—something that requires expertise, secure financing, and much planning. Even so, conservation activities sometimes run up against rooted anger.

This chapter examines how mnemonic ecologies are products of not just human but more-than-human agency as well. Ecosystems both perform memory for human beings and have their own forms of memory. Ecological processes as well as plants and animals therefore become anchors for human remembrance, but themselves also hold the possibilities of return to past landscapes as much as movement toward novel assemblages. This discussion focuses on management approaches in particular places—whether codified as "cultural landscape," "border," or "wilderness"—to demonstrate how notions of both environmental and human pasts, local and national history and homeland, inflect management practices and conservation conflicts, and how other-than-human lives take part therein.

RENATURING, REWILDING, AND THE CULTURAL LANDSCAPE

As explained, the Green Belt is being managed with a dual intention: as floral and faunal habitat and memorial landscape. In many parts of the borderlands, the best locations to realize both these goals are open land or partly open corridors that allow plants and animals the ability to find homes and pathways, and that create accessible spaces for viewing, visiting, and memorializing the border along with any of its remaining structures. Such approaches rest on reinforcing and maintaining the novel ecosystems that the border regime created. In other segments of the Green Belt, the orientation is toward ecological restoration and even rewilding. I draw on research in

Eichsfeld in central Germany, northern Bavaria and southern Thuringia, and along the Elbe River in northern Germany to show how ecologies and ecosystems are made to perform collective and cultural memory, and how people's attachment to places and species relies on anchors of identity located in multiple socioecological histories.

Maintaining Novel Ecosystems as Cultural Landscapes

The imposition of the border was not just a socially violent act but an ecologically violent one as well: while villages were razed, so were forests; while minefields killed people when they came too close to the border, they also killed animals; and while the control strip revealed escapee footsteps, it existed because herbicides had snuffed out all plant life in it. The floral and faunal communities that emerged under such significant human interventions can be called novel ecosystems. Even today, there are portions of the borderlands that show the ecological legacy effects of GDR policies. In some places where the border transected forest, like the Harz mountains in central Germany, the resulting deforestation exposed the topsoil, and much of it was lost to wind and water erosion. Herbicides were then applied on top of this clear-cut, wreaking ecological havoc on the plant communities that had established themselves there long ago. Even more than thirty years after the end of the border regime, regrowth in these areas remains severely stunted: small and languishing spruces stick out of a heathlike landscape. And yet the sickly trees have opened opportunities for better-adapted plants, often ones that are in decline in Germany like club mosses (*Lycopodium clavatum*), to find a foothold.[3]

In other places along the Green Belt, the border takes on the look and feel of a preindustrial, agrarian cultural landscape, generated by centuries of human use. The Green Belt in Eichsfeld, already discussed in the previous chapter, is one such place. In my conversation with one of the ecologists who led the Green Belt project in Eichsfeld for several years, a clear argument was made for this particular vision of the cultural landscape:

> Of course, we could also have said, "We'll promote the wilderness idea." But this valuable composition of species that we had in the Green Belt, those were actually primarily species of the cultural landscape. . . . The best exam-

ples are the beautiful calcareous grasslands that we have, where there are lots of orchids.[4] Following natural succession, those grasslands would become forest, but they have been used by people—for example, as sheep and goat pastures—and they have thus become a special habitat with many specialized species that evolved, which are, however, dependent on future human landscape use.

We want to preserve certain qualities of this cultural landscape. That's what I meant earlier. . . . If you have calcareous grassland and have no manager for it, such as a farmer with whom you work, a shepherd or goat farmer or cattle farmer, and you don't do anything in this area, you leave it to its own dynamics, then these habitats that have the qualities for such highly specialized species. . . . the habitats would just be lost.[5]

Managing for open space—*against* natural dynamics—is the key here, and forms a sharp contrast to some restoration projects elsewhere along the Green Belt where the emphasis is precisely on rehabilitating ecological processes and "rewilding" landscapes. The background screen against which this open land approach is projected is, as explained earlier, the rural idyll, a form of eco-nostalgia of a less industrialized, smaller-scale, and mosaiclike landscape. This did once exist in Germany, prior to the Second World War, or if aligned with the German conservation movement, in the mid- and late nineteenth century when the conservation and Heimat movements first surged. Green Belt conservationists are aware of this temporal baseline, including its strengths and limitations. In my conversation with a Green Belt project supervisor at the Thuringian Ministry for Environment, Energy, and Conservation (Thüringer Ministerium für Umwelt, Energie und Naturschutz), he clearly affirmed that in the open land areas of the Green Belt, restoring an agrarian landscape from the 1700s and 1800s was the goal. With respect to a conservation project near the Thuringian-Bavarian border, at the southern tip of the Green Belt, the staffer explained,

Conservation would like to continue land use as it was in the eighteenth century . . . growth of bogs, sheep farming . . . It would like to turn back the clock a little. In 1850, for example, we had the greatest diversity of plants in Germany. Then fertilization and mechanization began. When it comes to nature conservation, one wants to connect to romantic traditions: the critique of technology, an idyllic world. But at the same time, that landscape romanticism is false: the land was already totally battered back then, even the botanists said then that it couldn't go on like this, the land was totally overused before the switch to coal, all that mining and charcoal production. We know that 1850 as a model doesn't work, but at least we can take a small step toward it.

The GDR borderland clear-cuts, the harsh opening of the landscape from the 1950s through the 1970s, and the arrival of new species communities give conservation today an opportunity to re-create spaces that hark back not only to the German partition but further still to the previous century. The same interviewee felt that connecting to this particular past, and re-creating a landscape as today's conservationists think it used to be, has another purpose: "The borderlands area is characterized by an inhumane past—barbed wire, mines, fatalities, broken family ties, razed homes and forced resettlement, constant surveillance—which calls for healing. A beautifully designed cultural landscape that has largely been spared the ruptures of modern civilization and is mostly accessible to everyone could benefit this healing process."[6] Pastoral beauty, the rural idyll rendered in a carefully tended cultural landscape, and its marked contrast with the machinery and technologies of the border would not only heal ecological wounds but social ones too. And of course, a direct and somatic relationship with nature, where natural spaces can be accessed and enjoyed directly, has been shown to be healing and healthy in all sorts of ways.[7]

The contrast with US conservation could hardly be starker. In Germany, an agrarian cultural landscape has been elevated as one of the guiding ideals for restoration and conservation. Beyond the concerns articulated earlier by my interviewee, though, even the re-creation of nineteenth-century landscapes can spark discomfort with people. Unlike rewilding, which is being attempted along the Elbe River and will be discussed later in this chapter, open land preservation is high maintenance. When I asked the Green Belt supervisor at the Thuringian Ministry for Environment, Energy, and Conservation why conservationists were not simply allowing ecological dynamics to play out on their own as is the case with some rewilding projects, he explained, "If we allow forest succession, then humans can't connect with the landscape. If a place used to be dry meadow, a shepherd needs to be on that land, otherwise it doesn't resonate with the aesthetic ideal. Grassland has support with people. With succession, there's no experiential value: folks don't want to hike through undergrowth or walk their dog there."[8]

Conservation always exists in a political, economic, and cultural context, and must remain sensitive to it in order to succeed. The Green Belt managers understand that access to and the somatic and sensual experience of the landscape are important for locals to support the project. Place attachment, aesthetics, and emotions matter materially, and ecological management in this case can be directed toward them. Landscape aesthetics are formed by individual experiences as well as overarching cultural messages captured in anything from fairy tales to travel magazines, and may be inflected by ideals emanating from ecology. They may be personal memories retained from childhood, or they could be broader and older cultural memories of what a romantic agrarian countryside was and what was lost during modernization. At least in the West, a beautiful landscape is frequently one that reflects human predilections for order and composition—the romantic era's *pittoresque*.[9] Nostalgia, the remembrance of and yearning for an ostensibly simpler and innocent time that informs the "aesthetic ideal" mentioned by my interviewer, has long been a motivator for all kinds of social mobilization. It is interesting to note in this context that the meaning of *landscape* in German popular culture and colloquial discourse has remained surprisingly stable across generations. A study in the 1990s showed that Germans used the word to mean roughly the following: "quiet, beautiful, rural, green, healthy and relaxing, harmonious, diverse and aesthetic. It is also still surrounded by a swarm of Arcadian associations: happiness, love, leisure, peace, freedom, security, home. . . . It symbolizes culture grown and rooted, against false progress and empty civilization."[10] Even in the most recent national survey on nature awareness in Germany, people chose "maintaining beautiful landscapes" as one of the top reasons to establish protected areas.[11]

And so the BUND creates—and must keep re-creating—open land. It accomplishes this in part with machines or by contracting with farmers and shepherds, but in many instances, it is volunteers of all ages who participate in mowing grass, uprooting shrubs, and even felling trees to keep succession at bay. Depending on how radical such measures are, they can cause consternation and even outrage among locals. As the chapter's opening vignette illustrates, the larger issue at play here is the role of emotional attachments to place, often developed over long periods and related to people's pasts and that of their families. People's sense of whether a landscape is "right" or "wrong" is shaped by cultural images that are produced from the meanings people ascribe to them: "These meanings are symbolic expressions of people's understandings of who they are and where they belong—of identities. Landscape reflects a set of ideas and values about how society is or should be organized."[12] Ecological processes, like forest succession in Dippach, are intertwined with deep-seated emotions that are, in turn, constitutive of memory and identity. Hence management policies like clear-cuts can trigger a much larger political debate over a perceived assault on Heimat. Perhaps more than anything else, it is tree death that produces such reactions, given the visibility of this change as well as the importance of trees to personal and cultural memory and identity.

Conservationists along the Green Belt have been learning from their experiences in Dippach and elsewhere. I asked a Green Belt project manager in another part of the borderlands about community reactions to land clearing, and he explained that they "try to get ahead of it through informational leaflets and public relations work. We try not to intervene radically so that a beautiful landscape still remains, like an African savanna. That just goes over better with people than clear-cutting."[13] The evocation of an African landscape, even as casual as it was in our conversation, may seem odd, but as I explain below, it is not altogether surprising.

Ecological Cocreators in the Borderlands

In southern Thuringia and northern Bavaria, across the administrative districts of Sonneberg, Hildburghausen, Coburg, and Kronach, a large-scale Green Belt conservation project has been up and running since 2010. The project bears the somewhat-cumbersome name Rodachtal–Lange Berge–Steinachtal (after two river valleys and a mountain range, hereafter shortened to Rodachtal), and is governed by a broad coalition of municipalities, national and local public and private conservation groups, and other land use groups like farmers, forest owners, and hunters. According to the BfN, which has funded the project since its beginnings, this former border region features a range of critically endangered or priority habitat types including bogs, dystrophic ponds, and alluvial forests as well as dry heath and calcareous grasslands. About 43 percent of the project area is in a "near-natural and natural" state and home to large numbers of Red List species, including 140 endangered species and 12 critically endangered ones.[14] Its habitat mosaic requires different kinds of ecological management, where forests are sometimes left to normal succession, but the same open land policy applies here too. Grasslands and heath, either newly created during the German partition or re-created by it, continue to be maintained as such to protect species that have settled here over the past sixty years, like the scarce large blue (*Phengaris teleius*), a threatened butterfly species that is dependent on wet meadow habitats.[15]

Green Belt conservationists have been creative in their methods to generate and maintain open land. Occasionally succession has progressed so far that bulldozers and chain saws are unavoidable. Young forest might need to be felled, or hazel bushes may need to be dug out by their roots. In some situations, the banks of streams, choked by reeds and willows, may also require the use of machines to facilitate their restoration. More frequently than not, however, more "natural" means are used, and thus nonhuman animals and plants become key collaborators in landscape management. Sheep and goats, for example, have an important role to play in helping to engineer open land. In the Green Belt project near Rodachtal, another animal species has joined them: heck cattle. Starting with twenty animals in a sixty-hectare area in the municipality of Straufhain, the hardy heck cattle are left outside to graze year-round.[16]

Heck cattle (figure 5.1) are a rebreed of the extinct wild aurochs (*Bos primigenius*), a large ruminant that had roamed central Europe since the retreat of the glaciers. The last aurochs died in Poland in 1627, a victim of habitat loss and overhunting. The attempt at de-extincting the species was made in the 1920s by the German brothers Lutz and Heinz Heck, directors of the Berlin and Munich zoos, respectively. By the 1930s, the brothers had aligned

Figure 5.1
Heck cattle, a rebreed of the extinct aurochs, are being used to maintain open land along the Thuringian-Bavarian border. *Source*: Günther Reger, used with permission.

their work with the aspirations of the Nazi leaders who saw in the aurochs a manifestation of ancient Teutonic spirit, and for whom the animals were a crucial element in their schemes to colonize eastern Europe with German settlers.[17] In fact, several animals were introduced into the Bialowieza forest in today's Poland to help rewild the area. Those animals were killed in the confusion of the war, but several individuals survived at the Munich zoo, "where they gained a reputation for being especially hardy, able to withstand cold winters, on poor ground, with little human management."[18] They were rediscovered in the 1980s by Dutch rewilding enthusiasts looking for just such animals, and Heck cattle have been used in a variety of restoration and rewilding initiatives ever since.[19] While the history and original meaning of Heck cattle have become more and more diluted since the end of the Second World War, the use of such "German" livestock on the former borderlands does seem significant beyond just the animals' ecological role. Heck cattle, in their very bodies, signal a resurrection of an extinct, "wild and ancient" forebear and with it a sense of an equally ancient landscape.

Plants can do similar work. In the same Green Belt project near Rodachtal, some farmers are experimenting anew with old crops. They are planting ancient grains like emmer (*Triticum turgidum*) and einkorn wheat (*Triticum monococcum*), albeit still at a small scale. The two cultivars were among the first to be domesticated in the Fertile Crescent and were grown as staple foods in early agricultural societies. Today they exist mainly as relict crops in remote and mountainous areas of Europe. The Green Belt project explains that emmer "is an old and undemanding type of grain. It is suitable for growing on dry and poor soil. It is not very susceptible to disease, especially against fungal diseases. Einkorn is the oldest known grain. It is robust and undemanding and particularly suitable for cultivation in marginal locations."[20]

The histories of these organisms are striking. Both plant and animal bodies, managed and shaped by humans today, are imbued with ancientness, nativeness, place attachment, and belonging. They have been drawn in as cocreators of the borderlands' reinvention as cultural landscape that predates the partition by centuries or even millennia. Their presence also sends messages, whether intended or not, about Heimat, place, and past. I comment in greater detail on this below.

German Wilderness

The third Green Belt project I present in this chapter highlights a different kind of landscape: one that resurrects a purported "wilderness" through the process of "rewilding." This kind of management approach forms part of a larger, more recent conservation paradigm premised on prehuman nature. The "wilderness" imaginary has a long and troubled history, and as the antithesis to modernization it continues to excite affluent publics across the Global North. It functions as an ostensibly scientific umbrella concept for the IUCN, for instance, where wilderness areas are "protected areas that are usually large unmodified or slightly modified areas, retaining their natural character and influence, without permanent or significant human habitation, which are protected and managed so as to preserve their natural condition."[21] Understood this way, wilderness has until recently not been a magnet of mobilization in Germany since it practically does not exist in densely inhabited central Europe. Romantic artists, poets, and writers certainly conjured seemingly untamed places—old-growth forests, mountains, gorges, and waterfalls—but set them out as elements to be feared and respected rather than loved and safeguarded. Despite masquerading as a scientific term, however, wilderness is malleable.[22] As historians and philosophers have pointed out, the form and shape of wilderness is not objective reality but instead responds to specific cultural, political, and psychological needs:

> An area is a wilderness whenever we—consciously or unconsciously—assign it the symbolic meaning of a counterworld to the cultural or civilizational order and emphasize our lack of control over it. . . . For this, it is sufficient that the area is not made or ruled by humans, or at least does not appear to be, in at least *one* way that is relevant to the viewer. . . . The particular symbolic meaning of wilderness depends on the image of humanity or the ideal of society and the concept of freedom, reason and order that is characteristic of it.[23]

Much of the German longing for wilderness is embedded in a desire to escape ordinary life in a highly technocratic, urbanized, and controlled society. Instead of a temporal escape first (say, going back to the Pleistocene), German yearning for wilderness tends to manifest spatially as an ache for faraway places, *Fernweh*. In that sense, until recently at least, wilderness has been anything but German. Karl May, a popular novelist writing in the late nineteenth century, made a career of penning adventure stories of such "wild" places as the US West, North Africa, South America, and the Middle East, and influenced generations of Germans right into the mid-twentieth century, after which television began to substitute for his Orientalist narratives.[24] In this latter category, arguably the most famous is a film by Bernard Grzimek, a zoologist at the Frankfurt zoo, founding member of the BUND in the 1970s, and tireless advocate for African national parks. Grzimek's 1959 Oscar-winning documentary *Serengeti Shall Not Die* painted such an exoticized picture of northern Tanzania that it quickly became the stand-in for all of Africa. Its deeply colonial perspective showcased Edenic habitats for wild animals while blaming Black Africans for trouble in paradise: their population growth and poaching became the core explanations for faunal endangerment and extinction.[25] Not unlike the use of wilderness in US culture, and especially given Germany's colonial ambitions in sub-Saharan Africa, here it also functions as a white escape fantasy, a flight from history and responsibility.

A strange thing has happened, though: in the twenty-first century, the wilderness idea is now being applied to German landscapes. It is happening elsewhere in the Global North too, where it can be understood as an antidote to the despondency in the environmental community, animated by the hope to save our future by looking to the past.[26] In Germany, wilderness and rewilding emerged as conservation priorities in the late twentieth century.[27] By 2007, the German National Strategy for Biodiversity had elevated wilderness as an important component for increasing biodiversity domestically as well as meeting national and international targets: "Today there is hardly any wilderness in Germany. . . . In order to reactivate the natural processes of habitat dynamics, a certain amount of space in Germany must be freed from human influence. This mainly applies to the remnants of natural ecosystems, but can also include areas that are no longer used by humans and can develop in the direction of a 'new wilderness' in the future."[28]

In 2007, the national target for wilderness areas was set at 2 percent of German territory by 2020—a modest number at first glance, but the country has barely managed 0.6 percent, missing its objective and falling significantly behind many of its European neighbors.[29] The National Strategy for Biodiversity, however, makes room for both old and "new wilderness"— where the latter may be crafted by human hands and often reliant on novel ecosystems—that can be included in its policy plan, and federal agencies have been working in public-private partnerships to fund restoration projects aimed at mitigating human damage and re-creating older, preindustrial landscapes.

Currently spearheading the wilderness movement in Germany is a coalition of twenty environmental NGOs, foundations, and federal agencies that calls itself Wir für Wildnis (We for Wilderness) and whose public portal is the website Wildnis in Deutschland. One of the main funders of the initiative, and the group's headquarters, is the Frankfurt Zoological Society, former home of Grzimek. Leaning on national guidelines, the group invites novel ecosystems into its definition of wilderness and gives ecological restoration an important place: "When you think of wilderness, you think of grandiose landscapes without roads and power lines, of impenetrable forests and adventures in distant lands. Is there no more wilderness here in Germany? Yes, there is! Wilderness is also re-emerging in Germany, whether in former military areas, mining landscapes, or in the core zones of some national parks."[30] Compared to its US counterpart, the German version of wilderness is thus much more flexible, permissive, and open-ended. Given population densities and intensive land use here, it must be. In some ways, the German wilderness comes closer to the English term *wildness*, understood as "unbounded, limitless life with incalculable potential for 'creative' complexity."[31]

From Wilderness to Rewilding

In general terms, rewilding is an ecological process–oriented form of conservation that attempts to restore ecosystem dynamics back to a time before human influence. In the United States, where the idea originated, candidate regions for rewilding were mostly located in the country's west, and the emphasis rested on the "three Cs": large and unpeopled core areas, landscape connectivity, and top-level carnivores.[32] Others have advocated for the replacement of extinct Pleistocene megafauna with contemporary taxonomic or ecological neighbors, which may also involve captive breeding and the release of keystone species or ecosystem engineers like beavers or wolves.[33]

Once the concept made its way to Europe, though, conservationists there adapted its meaning, recognizing that European landscapes have been modified extensively and continuously since the Neolithic period. For them, the ecological baseline is not a time and place unpeopled. In Europe, rewilding can occur through ecological restoration practices where the stress is on "the development of self-sustaining ecosystems, protecting native biodiversity and natural ecological processes and providing a range of ecosystem services." In some cases, rewilding can and should occur in landscapes formerly inhabited and used by humans, or even almost destroyed by them, like abandoned fields or old mines—places that according to German conservationists, have wilderness potential. Restoration toward rewilding can establish "novel ecosystems . . . designed to be as similar as possible to some historical baseline in the recent or distant past, but they will often involve the introduction of new biotic elements."[34]

Just as wilderness should not be rendered as a one-size-fits-all concept, rewilding should remain a multidisciplinary and geographically contingent approach. A European definition of rewilding has emerged that is more open and flexible while holding onto the field's core concerns. It sees "rewilding as a subcategory of ecological restoration and define[s] it broadly as a type of ecological restoration aiming to (partially) restore self-sustaining and complex ecosystems via restoring natural ecological processes while minimizing human interventions."[35]

REWILDING ALONG THE ELBE RIVER

The Green Belt has been experimenting with rewilding as well, especially in its treatment of freshwater bodies. River floodplains are among the most dynamic ecological systems on earth and internationally renowned as biodiversity hot spots.[36] In their natural state, "riverine landscapes exemplify the 'new paradigm in ecology,' in which ecological systems are widely recognised as non-deterministic, open systems in continual states of flux, rather than internally regulated, homeostatic systems exhibiting equilibrium conditions."[37] The Elbe, the second-largest German river after the Rhine, is a slow-flowing stream, meandering across a wide floodplain as it approaches the North Sea. In its lower reaches, the river has made a broad, flat bed for itself, splitting across countless smaller arms and streams, constantly moving the sands through which it flows into new configurations, shaping and reshaping its many dunes, beaches, and banks. Prompted by the annual snowmelt, the Elbe tends to flood in late winter and spring, which can drastically change the water levels. Because the Elbe's bed is so shallow and the slope so gentle, even a few feet of flooding can carry water far inland, supplying the surrounding land and forests with nutrient-rich sediment.

Over the centuries, the Elbe has therefore crafted many new branches, oxbow lakes, and small ponds that may be connected episodically to the main river, or they may eventually lose that connection but remain fed by ground- and rainwater. These secondary bodies of water are quite differentiated and offer many species varied ecological niches across space and seasons.[38] Before permanent human settlement started altering the landscape, wildfires, ice, and even beaver dams helped create a mosaic of closed and open spaces, which in turn attracted larger herbivores like deer, elk, aurochs, and horses. The alluvial forests that historically existed along the banks of the Elbe were adapted to its ebb and flow. Softwood forests (including alders, willows, and poplars) grow closer to the water and are more resilient against flooding and ice formation, with hardwood forests (such as oaks, elms, and ash trees) established behind them. The latter are considered to be among the most structurally complex and diverse forest types of central Europe as well as the most endangered. Historical records show that before the expansion of agriculture and industrial development, hardwood alluvial forests existed in large swaths all along the Elbe's floodplains.[39] The river's biodiversity is further enhanced by its role as an important stop on the East Atlantic migratory flyway and an especially popular nesting ground for waterfowl, cranes, and storks.[40] The region's ecological significance was already documented in the Ramsar Wetlands Convention of 1976 and by its designation as a United Nations Educational, Scientific, and Cultural Organization (UNESCO) biosphere reserve in 1997.

Human interventions like dike and jetty construction, channeling, gravel infilling, and bank consolidation have significantly disrupted the river's ancient ecological processes. Dikes and jetties, built as early as the Middle Ages, have narrowed and deepened the river over the centuries, making it more navigable but also dropping groundwater levels along the river and drying out the backwaters that for so long had been an elemental part of the Elbe's ecology (e.g., as spawning grounds for native fish). Today about 80 percent of these surviving habitats, and especially those that are located behind the dikes and have lost all connection to the river, are in their end stages.[41]

This has been the story of many German rivers. The BfN reported in 2012 that about 90 percent of the country's historical floodplains have been destroyed over the past two hundred years. The loss of the full floodplain due to diking and channeling of course has negative implications for human inhabitants and the larger economy as well: during floods, the river's waters are not absorbed by a wide expanse of land or held by the alluvial forests upriver but instead gather force in the narrowed channel and eventually hit populated areas downriver, often with catastrophic consequences. The most recent instance occurred in 2013, when heavy summer rains swelled the Elbe's water levels to a height not seen in five hundred years. Just in Saxony and Saxony-Anhalt alone, the flood cost 4.6 billion euros in damage and displaced tens of thousands of people.[42] When researchers and government agencies studied the patterns of floods along the Elbe, they noticed that they roughly coincided with former alluvial plains.[43] Meanwhile, centuries of deforestation and expanding agriculture particularly along the river's right bank have destroyed the biodiverse alluvial forests, while industrial pollution with chemicals and heavy metals killed off the Elbe's famous fisheries.[44]

The postreunification years, however, led to broad-scale environmental cleanup and remediation. In turn, water quality has improved markedly, and many fish species have recolonized the Elbe. Yet land use is a different story: many of the dikes still exist and have even been reinforced and heightened in some places. Agriculture still pushes up against this delicate and changeable system, and the river still has a ways to go to be considered restored. Nevertheless, its role in the German partition has created a starting point for this.

Along a stretch of about ninety-six kilometers, between the towns of Lauenburg and Boizenburg at the western end, and Schnackenburg and Lenzen at the eastern, the Elbe was integrated into the GDR's highly fortified border system. There was never agreement on where the borderline ran precisely. The GDR insisted on running that line right through the middle of the river, while the West Germans sought to push that border back to its eastern banks.[45] The GDR's border police reinforced the river's work: guards sat in control towers built atop East German dikes, and patrol boats scanned for anyone desperate enough to try to swim or row themselves to the West. West German boats were subject to gunfire if they got too close to the eastern bank. Old villages near the Elbe were either razed to the ground completely and their inhabitants forcibly moved, as in the case of Stresow, or simply swallowed up by the border fortifications, like Rüterberg, to the point that you needed a special passport to reenter your home after a day away at work.

The Elbe also had its share of border fatalities: around thirty people drowned or froze to death in or near the river in their attempts to flee the GDR, while others were killed by spring guns, ripped apart by mines, or shot by border guards.[46] Drownings often happened quietly and unnoticed in the dead of night, and only weeks or even months later the bloated bodies or skeletal remains were pulled out of the Elbe farther downstream. It could take months or years for the families to be informed of the fate of their loved ones. Today, a range of memorial sites dot this landscape. They may be small, such as a wooden cross affixed to a remnant of border fence marking the place someone was killed.[47] Or they may be larger, like the open-air museum of the villages of Konau and Popelau, caught in the midst of the prohibited zone (*Sperrgebiet*), or a memorial site near the "Vockfeyer grave," a former branch of the Elbe into which the GDR border forces dumped the rubble of demolished homes.[48] On the top of the dikes, right alongside remnants of the patrol road and a more recently built bicycle path, a few control towers still cast their shadow.

The Elbe as Protected Area

While the Elbe's delta is located near Hamburg in the former West Germany, most of it flowed through the former Eastern Bloc. The GDR did not have the financial means to significantly reengineer the river in the way that West Germans had, for example, altered the Rhine, and so the Elbe remains today the only major German waterway that still flows free of any dams; even the existing modifications to the Elbe pale in comparison to those of West German rivers.[49] During the partition, economic development came to a standstill, and this already-marginal region became quieter still; the West German district of Lüchow-Dannenberg, on the left side of the Elbe, was the most sparsely settled region in all of West Germany.[50] The flats along the Elbe, so close to the deadly border, were either used infrequently by farmers or reverted back to older ecological processes. The border regime thus left behind a landscape that partly retained or recovered some of its historical, preindustrial features. By the time of reunification and in the final days of the GDR, the middle Elbe near Magdeburg was made a biosphere reserve, joining fourteen other protected areas that were designated as the GDR formally ended.

The biosphere reserve currently stretches along both sides of the Elbe and encompasses riverine landscapes across three of Germany's federal states: Lower Saxony (the former FRG) as well as Mecklenburg-Vorpommern and Berlin-Brandenburg (the former GDR). The Green Belt runs through this ecological corridor and integrates the border remnants with its conservation vision. The BUND has collaborated with the biosphere reserve office and other partners to design and implement a dike relocation and floodplain restoration project. By setting back the dike and once again freeing up space for the river, conservationists are attempting to restore and rewild the landscape to what it might have looked like before deforestation and dike construction. Alongside its conservation goals, the project sought to improve flood control upstream and draw tourists to the region.[51]

Over the years, the Elbe region has acted as the canvas for a range of meanings and nature ideals, ranging from wilderness to cultural landscape. The newest iteration of this discursive and material struggle, the BUND's river rewilding project, has to be seen as part of this back and forth—a politics of meaning and memory that echoes the Elbe's own ebb and flow.[52]

Initially, when the border first opened, conservationists (the BUND among them) demanded strict protection of this "pearl of nature." This land attracts some of the most charismatic animals of central Europe: Eurasian cranes, white and black storks, fish otters, huge flocks of migrating geese, and even sea eagles. The idea to convert the water meadows and alluvial forests along the Elbe River into a national park gained momentum in the 1990s when the effort was picked up by the environmental ministry of Lower Saxony. According to the 1994 IUCN protected area categorization, the designation of a national park requires that "nature" remains "not materially altered by current human occupation or exploitation."[53]

The BUND at first lobbied for such a designation, highlighting the Elbe as one of the "last remaining dynamic riparian landscapes in central Europe" that still exhibits the "natural, landscape-shaping processes" in at least some places. The BUND also pointed out that the task of carving out "wilderness zones" could "not just be demanded of poorer nations after the motto: please protect the rainforest so that we're OK ecologically." The BUND's plans for the Elbe national park focused most on the areas immediately adjacent to the river—a narrow band of floodplain where riparian dynamics would be relatively easy to reestablish. Of great interest from the start were the forests: "Of 1,000 hectares of alluvial forest 150 years ago, only about 40 are left in the areas of the planned national park. We imagine that we'd first stabilize those remainders. Beyond that, of course we want more areas on which softwood and hardwood forests can develop."[54]

In 1998, Lower Saxony's environmental ministry managed to establish just such a park, but local farmers and property owners immediately launched a successful legal challenge that forced a retraction of the designation. Conservationists had argued that a national park could be established in areas modified by humans if those areas could be returned to a more "natural" state once human activity ended. This was not, however, in the spirit of Germany's federal nature conservation law, which insists that only land not materially altered by humans can be designated as a national park. According to court records, the plaintiffs prevailed by contending that the area in question was quite significantly "materially altered" by human inhabitants "because it is in almost all parts a cultural landscape that has been decisively shaped by human hands." For centuries, the park opponents asserted, people have lived along and with the river, shaping the land beside it by building towns and cultivating fields. In more recent memory, local people invested in dikes and higher embankments to safeguard their families and properties. In fact, these park opponents maintained, the Elbe landscape looks the way it does precisely because it has been molded by human hands for so long. The national park would displace those people who had shaped this region. This was a cultural landscape, not a "natural" one. The court's decision to side with the plaintiffs further made it clear that just because an ecosystem (or parts of it) might still behave in ways deemed "natural," it could still be one that is modified by humans, "especially since diverse and natural biotopes can also develop on areas that have been heavily changed by human activity, such as extraction sites. Likewise, nonintensive land use does not necessarily mean that the areas are only slightly influenced by humans."[55] Lower Saxony's court thus denied the application for a national park designation.

Clearly, resistance to the national park was stoked most immediately by the fear of losing control of one's land and a mistrust of the conservationists who were seen as outsiders to the region.[56] The group that emerged in resistance to the national park calls itself the Association for the Protection of the Cultural Landscape and Property in the Elbe Valley (Verein zum Schutz der Kulturlandschaft und des Eigentums im Elbtal, or VSKE). Its members want:

- to live with nature in our landscape, take care of it, and work here;
- to continue to cultivate the landscape, as has happened here for centuries;
- to not allow ourselves to be pushed from our homeland [Heimat];
- to not let our living space be deliberately changed by external forces;
- that the economic developments, which the region urgently needs, are not hindered by wrong decisions.[57]

The cultural landscape here is evoked by dwelling, care, labor, and age-old land use traditions that connect people to place, and grants them legitimate and authentic belonging.[58] This is opposed to the "external forces" that threaten local and regional identity. The mention of Heimat is, of course, a rhetorical strategy aimed at shoring up political support in defense of the status quo, but it also speaks to something deeper. Conservation feels ahistorical to locals. In the locals' oppositional narrative, past land use gives the current residents a claim on this landscape, making them ecological cocreators whose historical influence should not be rendered meaningless or even invisible by conservation. As discussed in chapter 3, Heimat also references a particular kind of past, a nostalgic view of childhood and youth, and an emotive identification with a layered landscape. Here, place equals heritage: elements of the past remain relevant and important to the present and future. The wilderness vision inherent to the BUND's national park idea erases people from place.

In response, the area became (or rather, remained) a biosphere reserve. UNESCO defines biosphere reserves as "learning sites for sustainable development," as testing grounds for "interdisciplinary approaches to understanding and managing changes and interactions between social and ecological systems, including conflict prevention and management of biodiversity."[59] Moreover, it means that with the exception of the reserve's strictly protected core area, there are fewer constraints on land use. The VSKE has a seat on the biosphere reserve administration board and continues to monitor and influence ecological management procedures in the region.

Dike Relocation, Restoration, and Rewilding

Set in this larger context, the dike relocation and floodplain restoration project sought to rewild part of the river's historical reach and revive some of its almost-extinct alluvial forests. At present only about 20 percent of the original Elbe floodplain remains.[60] Similarly, about 90 percent of the original alluvial forests are thought to have been lost, and nationwide, only about 1 percent of the historical alluvial hardwood forest remains.[61] The historical baseline for forest restoration was provided by eighteenth- and nineteenth-century maps that showed the floodplain near Lenzen as a forested region.[62] Here along the Elbe, the project is overseen by the Castle Lenzen Association (Trägerverbund Burg Lenzen). The association brings together the main stakeholders in the region, including local municipalities, farmers, and representatives of the BUND.

The project area consisted of a sixteen-kilometer span of floodplain on ·the eastern bank of the Elbe—that is, former GDR land—making it the largest such project in Germany to date.[63] This area of the floodplain is mostly pastureland, as the last remaining alluvial forests were cut two centuries earlier.[64] After the fall of the wall, local conservationists from the west were able to seize an opportunity for conservation by collaborating with the director of the former agricultural cooperative across the river in the east. Shortly after the collapse of the GDR, it became clear to the cooperative director that agriculture alone would not be able to provide enough jobs in such a structurally weak and impoverished region. In his long-term vision, informed by his work with the biosphere reserve director at the time, the dike relocation project would also supply touristic opportunities, hopefully offering a little boost to the troubled local economy.[65]

According to the accompanying hydrologist, the project sought to "integrate cultural and natural landscapes" too, thereby addressing the fracture that had characterized the earlier conflict between the two.[66] From the outset, it was multifunctional: moving the dike back would not just restore the river, provide floral and faunal habitat, and attract tourists but also act as a flood control, a keen interest expressed to me by local and regional decision makers in the wake of several devastating flood events.[67] The process of relocating the dike was relatively simple: build a new dike farther back, and punch six holes in the old dike, each 200 to 600 meters wide so that the Elbe could reclaim the space in between. In this way, over 420 hectares of historical floodplain were restored (figure 5.2).[68]

Conservationists are now attempting to re-create alluvial forests by enrolling the help of certain plants and animals. Initial cells of native hardwood tree species (oak, ash, and elm) were planted in hopes that they might encourage longer-term regeneration of the alluvial forest.[69] In order to keep

Figure 5.2
The expanded floodplain after the dike relocation with the old dike partly submerged and the new dike clearly visible on the right. The Elbe flows from the bottom edge of the picture toward the top. *Source*: Frank Meyer, used with permission.

competitors like grasses and shrubs to a minimum, the cooperative director and his allies introduced a small herd of "wild" horses. The horses have virtually no contact with humans and live on the floodplain for much of the year. Their low-intensity grazing creates short-grass wet meadows, another ecological element to add to the floodplain's structural complexity.[70] The idea to bring in large herbivores like these was inspired by rewilding experiments in the Netherlands, which pioneered a radical rethinking of Europe's ecological history. Mainstream theory has argued that before human settlement, much of Europe consisted of dense, unbroken forests, and those forests would reestablish themselves the moment that human agriculture and livestock grazing ended. In contrast, Dutch scientists asserted that prehistoric Europe was a diverse mosaic of forests and open lands that was maintained by grazing herds of large herbivores.[71] This vision fits in with the BUND's interest in sustaining ecologically diverse structures along the Green Belt and works with the biosphere reserve's ambition to create a multifunctional landscape that offers habitat to many different species. Allowing large grazers to do the work of farmers and their machines can also be a more cost-effective, less disruptive, and more tourist-friendly way to achieve this goal. The horses used along the Elbe are called "Liebenthaler Wildlinge," which emerged from a crossbreed of Norwegian Fjord horses and the Polish Konik. The horses were originally bred in the 1960s by a German biologist and horse enthusiast who was interested in resuscitating the tarpan (*Equus ferus ferus*), a European wild horse that had gone extinct in the late nineteenth century, and resettling it in Germany. Herds exist today in the Liebenthal region of Brandenburg.[72]

The opinions about this restoration and partial rewilding process are divided, and the project retains an experimental character. When I spoke with a landscape ecologist employed at the biosphere reserve office in Brandenburg, he shared doubts and complications:

> You have to take efforts at "renaturing" with a grain of salt. You cannot simply plant alluvial forest. You have to wait for that kind of forest to colonize areas on its own. One should wait for succession to happen, wait for the first pioneer trees, so that the alluvial forest can establish itself in their wake. But the German conservation movement is impatient. Conservationists are not allowing for pioneer vegetation; it has to be alluvial forest from the get-go. . . .

> Conservation tends to be linked to action: either you prohibit or you manage. Letting nature be and letting it just do its thing, that hasn't arrived yet.

In a way, then, it is wilderness with caveats. Whether the project will succeed in the strict sense (as in go according to plan) remains to be seen. The dike relocation was completed in 2012, but questions linger: Was it misguided to plant hardwood instead of softwood? As we stood on top of the dike and surveyed the newly created floodplain, the landscape ecologist remained worried that "there were too many goals with the dike relocation. The hardwood trees, the oaks, were a mistake, it would have been better to plant softwood species like willow. Those would be forerunners for others."[73]

Conservation goals can sometimes be self-limiting and even contradictory: the endangered alluvial forest is one form of nature deeply valued here, but plant too much forest, and the huge flocks of waterfowl—another desirable form of nature—have no resting grounds, which is something kept available to them by the large herbivores.[74] Whether the horse herd is large enough to actually keep the terrain open, is another question, and neither was it clear what would happen if at some point the herd grows too large. Another concern is how to treat the materials generated by dike demolition and reconstruction, much of which is tainted with heavy metals and even dioxin—legacy effects of the GDR. Cattle used for commercial purposes cannot be grazed on polluted land, but herbivore grazing is needed to maintain the open grasslands that both the Green Belt and biosphere reserve administration consider important ecological elements in this region.[75] In fact, the biosphere reserve plan of 2009 repeatedly refers to local soils as "landscape archives" in terms of their recording of both "natural" and "cultural" history.[76] The use of the term points to a kind of ecological remembrance. All in all, and despite the caveats, recent evaluations of the dike relocation sponsored by regional and national agencies suggest that the project remains generally successful.[77]

In the context of another, much more famous rewilding project—the Oostvaardersplassen in the Netherlands—researchers have commented that the open-ended experiments at rewilding and restoration there "offer a space for wildness without the impossible geography of wilderness." Such an approach avoids a "biopolitics of closure that is associated with orthodox forms of wildlife conservation premised on equilibrium ecology."[78] To the extent that ecological management here can relax enough for the Elbe's dynamics to carve their own paths, the dike relocation project might offer similar lessons to conservation in Germany.

MNEMONIC ECOLOGIES OF RESTORATION AND REWILDING

Throughout the Green Belt, the past looms large. Restoration is predicated on history, both ecological and social. Similarly, rewilding cannot rid itself of it even as it is sometimes seen to do so. To begin with, consider ecological history and ecological memory. We can include here ancient geological and ecological processes that influence landscape patterns today, whether the karst of central Germany or glacial deposits of the Elbe floodplain. These have interacted with past and current human land uses to shape the environments of present-day borderlands. The calcareous grasslands so prized today as rare and endangered habitats along the Green Belt tend to be traces of ancient livestock grazing, renewed now by herds of goats, sheep, and cattle. Toxicants in the sediments of the Elbe and its dikes are reminders of industries that closed decades ago but whose impacts will be felt for decades, if not centuries, to come. They will continue to influence the health and well-being of human and nonhuman inhabitants of the Elbe region, and shape what can and cannot be done in the name of conservation (or industry or agriculture, for that matter).

Science speaks of *ecological memory* to describe "the degree to which an ecological process is shaped by its past modifications of a landscape."[79] The more an ecosystem is shaped by its history, the stronger its ecological memory. This concept has been used in the study of ecosystem resilience to disturbance: How well does a system tolerate abrupt changes (wildfires, for instance) and how well does it return to a similar state? Where disturbances are frequent (though not necessarily predictable), species tend to evolve survival and regeneration strategies, so-called information legacies. These, in turn, are influenced by "material legacies"—in other words, the changing physical realities of the environment (e.g., soil quality). Both information and material legacies that have emerged in response to previous disturbance events will make an ecosystem more or less resistant to future ones.[80] If we think of ecological memory in a slightly broader way, we can consider all ecosystems as holding onto memories and expressing them today. In almost all cases, those systems show the effects of their interactions with human land use and settlement—disturbances to which some species have been able to adapt while others have not. In the Green Belt, herbicide applications along the border continue to stunt the growth of spruces decades after reunification, and calcareous grasslands have attracted plant and animal species that rely on ongoing disturbance (like grazing or mowing) to survive. The ecological past continues to haunt the present.

This is true also for ecological *ghosts*. The meaning of the term is somewhat vague in the scientific literature, where it often refers to the remnant population of a once-thriving species, or a species that has lost much of its habitat or ecosystemic context but continues to survive—more likely languish—in an impoverished landscape.[81] If viewed today, the species may strike us as odd and nonadaptive, but we simply see the leftover, the ecologically marooned, and are not conscious of what was lost. Ghosts thus identify hardy survivors while signaling ecological deterioration. Flipping the script, we can also consider ecosystems as ghostly if they have lost species permanently. The Elbe's ecological recovery has restored much of its fish diversity, but some species remain absent, and it is not clear if they will ever return.[82] Moreover, ghosts can be species that are rare, rarely seen, of liminal presence, or those whose status is unclear: is the species truly extinct or not?[83]

Today's rewilding species—Heck cattle and Liebenthaler horses—are ghosts as well. Aurochs and tarpan are long gone, but some part of their genetic heritage is said to live on in other species that have been used in back-breeding these animal populations. They allow us to guess at what was lost; they give the extinct animal a spectral presence. Despite the media hype, de-extinctions are never truly possible. Even in the unusual circumstance that the entire genome of an extinct species is known to scientists, and even if an individual could be bred and made to live, the resulting animal would still be left without a community, without a culture, bereft of the possibility of learning to behave like its forebears did. A Carolina parakeet or woolly mammoth would exist without an ecosystem to which it was adapted and with which it interacted to help shape and reshape its environment.[84] The most we can hope for are proxies: animals that might look like the lost ones, fulfill their ecological functions, or share some portion of their genetic material. To an extent, grains like emmer and einkorn have spectral qualities as well, for they exist in a current context altogether different from the ecological and cultural circumstances in which they were created. They, too, act as memorial devices for us to remind ourselves of landscapes and people long gone. They, too, however, allow for hope that not all is lost, that some part of the dead can be resurrected yet.

History and memory shape Green Belt landscapes in other ways as well. As in other places along the Green Belt, the memories of state socialism reverberate in the Elbe biosphere reserve, affecting both the practice and place of restoration. In my conversation with an administrator of the Elbe biosphere reserve in Brandenburg, I was told that "the people live here with special historical experience: first the 'red,' then the 'green' expropriation . . . that is immediately equated. The people here are very sensitive regarding their freedom to act and own property."[85] After reunification, management positions were filled with West Germans (derisively called *Besserwessis* by East Germans)—something that happened across East Germany, and caused outrage and resentment among locals who felt displaced and devalued.[86] At the time of our interview in 2016, the reserve administrator had been in her position twelve years, and as a West German working in the former GDR, still had to cope with tensions and prejudices in her professional life. In this part of Germany and this individual's personal experience, people still asked where you were from—to her an expression of regional identity mixed with a persistent East-West dynamic.

The border history also matters ecologically. The fact that Lenzen was chosen as the place for such an ambitious restoration project was in large part because the border regime had curtailed development and river modifications, giving conservationists a much better starting point for their work. The agricultural collectives on the river's right bank owned a series of large properties, which made it easier to negotiate land tenure and land use decisions than in western Germany, where landownership is complicated by the comparatively small agricultural plot size.

Moreover, the dike relocation and floodplain restoration project rests on ideas of certain German pasts: the project developers used maps from the eighteenth and nineteenth centuries to make an argument for hardwood alluvial forests and a river that flows more freely than before the enhancement of the dike system near Lenzen. The horses grazing along the water meadows today are a rebreed of a species that went extinct in the nineteenth century as agricultural expansion and industrialization destroyed its habitat. Altogether, the historical baseline that is both explicitly and implicitly present here gives off the impression that the restoration project is ultimately re-creating a landscape that dates to the first half of the nineteenth century— putting it squarely into the realm of the romantic-nostalgic Heimat conservation movement.

Yet it still clashes with other ideas of Heimat, expressed, for instance, by the VSKE. For the VSKE, Heimat is not a restored wilderness or the rebreeding of extinct species that roamed Germany until the 1870s. It is a historically rooted cultural landscape shaped by human interaction with the environment, a living expression of place identity and regional custom as well as land and property relations. It is deepened by the memory of state socialism and its repeated expropriations, and articulated to some extent against it. Heimat in the context of rewilding and restoration does not simply mean a return, however, since it is codified as a possible future as well—one more sustainable and ecologically sound.

Ecology as Heimat

If we understand Heimat as a form of nostalgic, place-based memory, then it is evident that ecology plays a significant role in anchoring it. Biotic and abiotic forms, brought together in ecosystems and landscapes, give material shape to a sense of the past, and belonging to a place and the communities in that place. Heimat can be expressed through ecologies in a number of ways. One might be by reintroducing formerly native species back into their old home range—as is the case with beavers along the Elbe or lynx in the Harz forest. It can also be expressed by bringing back-bred versions of extinct species into an ecosystem in hope that they help engineer a desirable agrarian or "wild" landscape, like Heck cattle and Liebenthaler horses. Behind all of this is, quite literally, the insistence on providing a Heimat—a place of belonging, origins, reproduction, and habitat—for plants and animals in the Green Belt's borderlands. Germans speak of organisms that are *beheimatet* in particular locations, meaning that they have a home there, are native, and belong there. This contrasts with those that are not: migratory species, or more problematically, exotic and invasive ones. The Elbe biosphere reserve website warns of such creatures, such as the Egyptian goose (*Alopochen aegyptiaca*) and nutria (*Myocastor coypus*), which are spreading quickly or have shown the potential to do so. In the former case, reserve staff are considering systematically hunting and killing the birds to minimize their competition with more desirable, native avifauna.[87] The same fate may also befall the nutria.

There is considerable debate over how to understand invasive species. Within the sciences, prompted by nonequilibrium ecology, a reassessment has been underway these past years. In many cases, invasive species have shown that they do not just wreak havoc (though some do) but rather are valuable to native species and can even enable the survival of endangered populations.[88] Meanwhile, critical histories of science have examined the discourses of invasion and nonnativeness along with their social consequences, including xenophobia.[89]

The Green Belt management documents are relatively silent on the question of invasives, although one can find in the lists of recommended and actual management strategies references to the "removal of nonnative species" and (re)establishment of native ones.[90] More generally, though, the Green Belt, across all of its publications and in the press, aligns with the ideas of nativeness and Heimat. After all, its claim to fame has been its quality as a refuge for Germany's endangered species. It is a place where new communities have formed, but their members have arrived from all over Germany and thus belong together—*naturally*. Here, the Green Belt again resonates with national narratives of an imagined community—all European (German) species, living together in harmony. The Green Belt becomes the great unifier, a corridor that links habitats and species homelands while it signals Heimat for the German nation. Traditional land uses are celebrated (sheep herding and organic agriculture) while others are ignored (industrial agriculture and extractive industry) in the stories that it tells. Native ecology is the healer, a message clearly broadcast by the emblematic photograph of the whinchat perched on an old GDR border post (figure 2.2). Native species, assembled in both old and novel ecosystems along the former borderlands, make Germany more German in a sense. Whether white stork or white-tailed eagle, club moss, heck cattle, or wild horse, beaver or hardwood riparian forest, Green Belt ecology embodies Heimat, memory, and nation, all brought into harmonious union on the lands that once split Germany in half. We do not have here a dualism between a cultural landscape based on Heimat and restored wilderness evacuated of it; both forms of nature draw on Heimat, albeit in different forms.

ANCHORING MEMORY ECOLOGICALLY

Memory, from personal to cultural, emerges from the interaction between the "remembering mind and the reminding object," where the latter is broadly conceived. It can be conveyed in symbols, images, and text as well as behaviors and rituals. Higher-order cultural memory "is not limited to the past that is shared together but also includes a representation of the past embodied in various cultural practices. . . . It is not only what people really remember through their own experience, it also incorporates the constructed past which is constitutive of the collectivity."[91] This is crucial in understanding the Green Belt. The borderlands are a memorial landscape after all, and remembrance occurs through memorials large and small—like wooden crosses, border remnants, landscape art, and ruins—and the practice of writing stories of the past and sharing them with others.

But this chapter shows that that is not all: memorialization can be carried in ecologies too. In this way, a different kind of memorial landscape is crafted, not reliant on buildings or structures, nor on rituals and collective gatherings. Instead, memories are materially instantiated in the bodies and genes of plants and animals as well as in ecological processes. Reliance on these gives considerable mnemonic ecological agency to other-than-human actors whose influences may yet surprise conservationists.

We also see that changing the landscape in the name of conservation, restoration, and rewilding means bumping up against the environment's meaning to local people and their decades- or even generations-old place attachments. Restoration along the Green Belt is necessarily multifunctional, and not just in terms of providing multiple ecosystem services. In addition to, say, flood control or biodiversity, cultural functions may matter in conservation, and practitioners need to think broadly about multiple uses, multiple values, and multiple meanings. These borderlands are sensitive spaces, marked by the loss of human life, community, and land.

Based on the experiences so far, conservation actors are still learning to make greater room for the need many border communities have for remembering and honoring a difficult past. Lack of participation and information, and lack of attention to people's senses of the past along with their place histories, nature aesthetics, and emotional investment in all of these, will sink a conservation project—a lesson painfully learned by Green Belt advocates all along the borderlands. The complex ties between memory and belonging are put into relief again and again by these conservation efforts. Not only does this nexus matter ecologically—in terms of informational or material legacies, say—but it matters socially. The suggestion of Heimat, German homeland, is in many ways an effective tool for conservationists. It can soften ecological changes by building in elements that are culturally meaningful and fit, however awkwardly, within a system of representations of the past: if we clear-cut forest, then at least maintaining the resulting open land with animals that read as "German" might smooth out the ecological rupture. Cast this way, the Green Belt does indeed become an ecological corridor and connector—not just across space, but across time, and not just for plants and animals, but for people.

Under certain circumstances, however, the discourse of Heimat and its ecological translation can also become narrow and rigid, rather like the dikes that continue to constrain the Elbe. In its preservationist bent, it is a conservative reaction to change and expresses a desire to return to a past that was somehow simpler. Heimat elevates elements of the past as desirable goals for the future. At best, this can be a critical and forward-looking agrarian ideal, searching and visionary as well as sensitive to ecological limits, regional cultures, and people's senses of place, history, and memory. At worst, it can produce parochial and exclusionary blood-and-soil identity politics. Where Heimat lands today is a matter of how it is coded, by whom, and toward which audience. If conservation writ large wants to speak to more audiences, should Heimat discourse be a consideration at all? If so, is it possible to redefine the term in a more generous way to speak to everyone's Heimat, not as a synonym for nation, but as a container for much more: roots, family, connection, validation, place, cultural traditions, and memory?[92] The Green Belt will need to confront these questions explicitly in the coming years if it wishes to remain relevant to a rapidly changing Germany. The BUND's 2019 Lenzen Declaration is one step in that direction.

As of now, the Green Belt attempts to act as an ecological and national unifier. Its attentiveness to memory and sense of place speaks to many Germans in the West and East. Its ability to not just reflect national anxieties about identity but also partly respond to them puts this project in an interesting and potentially game-changing position. The conservation approaches pioneered in the borderlands have the potential to be pathbreaking for conservation and German politics more broadly. And, I would argue, there is clear global relevance for the Green Belt's mnemonic ecologies—a topic to which the next chapter turns.

6 GLOBAL MNEMONIC ECOLOGIES

Mapping areas of the highest biodiversity against the locations of the world's major armed conflicts over the past fifty years reveals a shocking convergence: 90 percent of wars occurred in regions known to be extremely species rich.[1] Some of the globe's most iconic landscapes—savannas, high mountains, and rain forests—have been ravaged by violence, devastating flora and fauna, and forever changing the human communities that call these places home: scorched-earth campaigns wipe entire ecosystems off the map and destroy the livelihoods of millions; militias and militaries slaughter animals indiscriminately for food; and warlords and cartels traffic in endangered species to raise funds for weapons and equipment. Moreover, war's corrosion of traditional environmental governance institutions as well as its tendency to produce massive human displacement and migration, and the chemical or atomic legacy effects of military technologies, often create widespread and lasting ecological impacts, even after peace has been reestablished.[2] Mnemonic ecologies are created in these cases by brutal human actions that have environmental effects that may be partly anticipated but are frequently accidental, random, or open-ended. Much of the scholarship on war and ecology so far suggests that conservation and restoration are needed more urgently than ever in these areas. What is less clear is what kinds of social obligations should flow from doing this work in former killing fields, where the memories of death and destruction might still haunt local people, and where ecosystems still bear the scars of past violence. Any consideration here must therefore not simply include the ecological consequences but also the past and present human activities and human suffering that are entangled with the fate of biodiverse landscapes.

A focus on memory helps mediate the relationship between ecosystems, the people who live there, and international conservation interests. The study of the German Green Belt offers important lessons on how to lean into history when conserving and restoring wounded land and establishing the conditions for an ecologically sustainable and socially just future. As we begin to draw concentric circles beyond the German case, the need for a mnemonic ecological approach becomes evident here too. From the European Green Belt's Balkan region to the Korean demilitarized zone (DMZ), borderlands are contested spaces that force questions of history and memory like few others, but taking a more capacious view allows us to see that this is true for many other scarred places, including megabiodiverse countries that have seen some of the worst violence of the twentieth and twenty-first centuries: Cambodia and Colombia. I briefly summarize these cases to highlight the convergence of biodiversity and war, point out the ways in which memory considerations are still largely absent from ecological work, and consider why they matter. I end by bringing mnemonic ecological matters back to the United States. My intention here is not to simplify and reduce these places to violence, or their inhabitants to their traumas. Conservation has tended to erase people and their pasts from the land, however, even though most species-rich regions are inhabited and the effects of war form part of the terrain. If we want to craft a post-2020 biodiversity agenda that ensures the survival of the ecosystems supporting human life, then attending to memory will be an unavoidable and necessary component of the work.

THE EUROPEAN GREEN BELT

Borderlands are among the most contested spaces in the world. They are often sites of symbolic accretion—instances where meanings and commemorations are appended to already existing locations—and where national and local politics crystallize in unique ways.[3] This is evident in the German case, and it is also at the heart of an initiative, launched in 2004, to re-create the Green Belt model along the entire former Iron Curtain. In other words, the former dividing line between two economic and political orders, capitalist and Communist, would become the green "backbone" of an ecological revival. The Iron Curtain runs from the extreme north of Europe, where Finland and Russia meet north of the Arctic Circle, along the Baltic coast, through the middle of Germany, past Austria and the Czech Republic, then south into the Balkans, ending in the Mediterranean and Black Sea (figure 6.1).

*in accordance with UNSCR 1244 and opinion of ICJ.

© European Green Belt Association

Figure 6.1
The European Green Belt runs along the entire reach of the former Iron Curtain. It is shown here in its four different administrative segments. *Source*: European Green Belt Association, used with permission.

The border between West and East was nowhere as stark and militarized as in Germany, nor did it split any other country in two the way it did here. The European Green Belt does, though, delineate the old European Union from the new, and it is no coincidence that the impulse to create a European Green Belt occurred at the time of the broader-scale political integration of Europe. And while some borders, such as between Finland and Russia or the Baltic coasts, were not quite as contested, the European Green Belt does include sections, like the Balkans, that were deeply mired in conflict—not so much of the Cold War itself, but in its turbulent aftermath.

In 2002, Gorbachev attended the inauguration of the German Green Belt's West-East gate and helped mark the official launch of the European Green Belt. Formal discussions began at an international workshop in Bonn in 2003 that brought together representatives from most of the Iron Curtain countries. An international working group was formed under the aegis of the IUCN, which began meeting in 2004. By 2010, the IUCN had stepped back as coordinator and transferred its functions to a newly reconfigured steering committee comprised of regional coordinators for each of the four Green Belt sections and financially supported by the German government.[4] Yet by 2014, it was clear that a higher-level and more formal body was needed to ensure stability, representation, and long-term funding, which led to the establishment of the European Green Belt Association in 2015.[5] Regional coordinators still oversee the work in each of the four Green Belt sections, with the central European one administered by the German BUND.

The European Green Belt is 12,500 kilometers long and acts as a corridor for 3,272 protected areas, including 40 partly transboundary national parks. It connects 24 countries (including EU member states, EU candidates, and non-EU countries) and travels through a diverse set of European landscapes ranging from arctic tundra and boreal forests to seacoasts, bogs, floodplains, alpine peaks, and grasslands.[6] While the original thrust of the initiative was an ecological one—where the Iron Curtain would become a cross-continental ecological corridor—it later acquired additional dimensions. In an echo of the German original, the lands that the former Iron Curtain cut through were mostly isolated and rural. Those same regions, however, were considered to be important for the continent's cultural heritage, not just its ecological one. The European Green Belt, it was hoped, would draw attention to the border areas, take advantage of already existing forms of "natural and historical heritage," and thus become the staging ground for sustainable regional development predicated on "soft tourism."[7]

Like the German experience, where the drive to protect land for ecological reasons preceded any deeper reflection on the many meanings and layers of that land and their historical implications, the European Green Belt initiative seems keen on developing the ecological corridor first. What appears so far as only a slowly emerging consideration is the memorial component of conservation and restoration. This comparative silence on memory amid all the excited biodiversity-related discussions is particularly noticeable in the places that have been scarred by violence, such as the Balkans, site of the 1991–2001 Yugoslav Wars. These ethnic and religious conflicts, which dissolved Yugoslavia, killed 140,000 people and displaced 4 million more.[8]

Little mention of this history is made on the European Green Belt website, which gestures vaguely at the Green Belt's ability to "bring people together from countries once hostile to one another."[9] The European Green Belt moves across the former sites of a brutal war and ethnic cleansing campaign that occurred within living memory. For instance, sections of the European Green Belt pass through the region of Slavonia in northeast Croatia near the border with Serbia, a highly contested space fought over in the early 1990s by the Yugoslav army, Croatian independence movement, and Serbian paramilitaries. While not currently a part of the European Green Belt, just a few miles south of the Croatian border lies the town of Vukovar, reduced to rubble by shelling, and near where, in November 1991, Serb forces violently beat and then executed over 260 Croatians in what would become one of the worst massacres of the war. Official memorialization of the war has been uneven, state centered, and concentrated in urban areas, leaving rural communities without a real sense of justice as they continue to hold onto their own forms of commemoration.[10] Decades after the 1995 Dayton peace agreement formally ended the conflict, the ongoing attempts to reckon with the war as well as rebuild, reintegrate, and coexist remain difficult and painful.

One of the Balkan European Green Belt's big projects featured on the front page of its website, the restoration of the Sava River, does not speak of the war or its consequences once, even as the initiative seeks to "create unique recreational sites that are within the city of Zagreb"—a city that saw some of the worst fighting of the Balkan Wars.[11] The table summarizing the project's benefits mostly lists ecological ones, and among the social benefits are "jobs," "recreation," "tourism," and "regional welfare." Again, no mention of the possibilities that a more historically attentive approach could offer to deepen engagement with the landscape's and people's pasts along with the memories they hold. Healing from trauma takes time, and it has been shown again and again that societies require generational distance from the events to be able to process them; the broader-scale societal reckoning with the Nazi atrocities did not begin in Germany until the 1970s and 1980s.[12] We are approaching that generational mark in the Balkans, and thus the ecological restoration projects launched here are prime opportunities to contribute to a larger, collective process of remembering and problematizing the past.

Beyond the wounded lands of the Balkans lie larger questions about the meaning of these cross-continental borderlands that the European Green Belt comprises. The recent push to designate the European Green Belt as a UNESCO world heritage site is a case in point. The 2014 feasibility study (written by an all-German team and sponsored by two German federal environmental agencies) seeks to make a case for why the former Iron Curtain borderlands possess both extraordinary cultural and ecological value. The authors developed two possible paths to the Green Belt's UNESCO nomination: as a "relic landscape" (*Reliktlandschaft*) or "associative cultural landscape" (*assoziative Kulturlandschaft*). Whereas the former relies on relics of the partition and Cold War to curate and memorialize certain histories, the latter is a more open-ended treatment of the borderlands, relying on "cultural links to nature" rather than material traces. The borderlands would therefore survive predominantly as a symbol instead of a more concrete, museum-like set of artifacts. The "risk of forgetting" is greater in this latter scenario, the authors explain, because "intensive awareness-building processes are necessary to maintain the memory of the Cold War and its border system." There is a risk that the major value of the European Green Belt is "perceived as detached from the Cold War border system."[13] The greening of the borderlands once again becomes an avenue for dehistoricization. In the end, conservationists are confronted with the problem of whether to curate or not curate. Should meanings be fixed as much as possible? The landscape art along the German Green Belt has tended toward the associative scenario, but there are clear arguments for "closing" meanings rather than leaving open a broad interpretative space that may or may not fill in as intended or hoped. It is conceivable that the borderlands, without intensive curation to work against it, are reinterpreted to support exclusionary and violent politics, this time cast in the light of post-Communism or a vexing relationship to the European Union.

Lastly, elevating the European Green Belt to a world heritage site raises another, until now somewhat-dormant question: If the Green Belt is thought of not simply as an ecological corridor but also a pan-European memorial landscape—which is the assertion that has been made from the beginning and that motivates the reach for UNESCO—then that implies something akin to a "European memory." Is there such a thing as a "European experience"? And can one therefore speak of Europe as a mnemonic community? The question of a European identity has been in the air for at least two hundred years, but has been especially debated in the wake of the twentieth century's devastating world wars. It continues to hover over every single EU summit, and remains a controversial and unsettled scholarly debate.[14] The European Green Belt initiative will need to confront it sooner or later.

The Korean DMZ

There are few instances in the world today that resemble the postwar inter-German partition and border fortifications. The most well-known is the Korean Peninsula, cut in half since the cease-fire and armistice agreement that ended the Korean War in 1953—a conflict that killed at least three million people, including over fifty-eight thousand US soldiers. Despite its name, the demilitarized zone separating North and South Korea is, in fact, the opposite: a fortress of land mines, armed guards, fences, observation posts, and more. The North Korean army sits to the north, and six hundred thousand South Korean and seventeen thousand US soldiers are stationed to the south.[15]

Until Korea's partition, the lands of the DMZ, like the regions surrounding it, had been inhabited and farmed by local people. In that sense, the region along the thirty-eighth parallel was unremarkable, resembling the landscapes to the north and south. The DMZ, however, ended all human settlement, and farms reverted to grasslands and forest. Today there are distinct land use patterns on each side of the border: in North Korea, lands adjacent to the DMZ were reopened for farming, leading to deforestation; in the South, a US-created civilian control zone severely restricted development.[16] With the gradual expansion of human settlement, agriculture, and industrial extraction and production elsewhere in Korea, the 2.5-mile-wide and 155-mile-long DMZ has become ecologically important.[17]

As mentioned, the lands of the DMZ are not "pristine"—they were formerly inhabited, cultural landscapes devastated by warfare, depopulated, and then cordoned off—and so the ecologies of the DMZ are emergent and novel in some places, while in others, older ecological relationships are forming again. While Korea's internal borderlands represent a cross-section of peninsular habitats, and with them significant ecological diversity, a full accounting of the DMZ's flora and fauna does not exist.[18] Inferences can be made from data gathered nearby, however, which show at least sixty-five hundred plant and animal species present, two dozen of which have protected status in South Korea, and some appear on the IUCN's Red List of endangered species as well.[19] Among them are symbolically freighted and charismatic animals such as the crested ibis (*Nipponia nippon*), and perhaps of greatest interest, the red-crowned crane (*Grus japonensis*)—with less than three thousand individuals left, among the rarest birds in the world.[20]

Korean ecologists expect that once a peace agreement is signed and the DMZ is decommissioned, the development pressures on this strip of land will be severe. In anticipation of an eventual reunification, the Korean conservation community has been keenly interested in the German experiment. In February 2012, the German and South Korean governments signed a Joint Declaration of Intent that broadly spelled out the logistical and scientific support Germany could provide in helping Korea develop conservation and restoration activities in the DMZ.[21] Across the past decade, Korean delegations have visited Germany repeatedly to learn more about the Green

Belt project and have followed the BUND's successes and setbacks. BUND staff, including Frobel himself, have also traveled to Korea to help advise local agencies on how to best proceed. For a top administrator at Korea's National Institute of Ecology, "the German Green Belt holds great implications for the direction of the DMZ's preservation and use, in that it was a well-harmonized mixture of preservation and restoration with a tourism model that increased its symbolic value as a space for sustainable development."[22] Tourism, especially ecotourism, seems to be another key element of South Korean government plans, emphasizing the DMZ's ecological wonders as well as the contrast with their violent and militarized context (the Korea Tourism Organization even offers "Peace and Life Zone" tours).[23]

By now, the DMZ has also made it into Korea's national biodiversity strategy, the document detailing the country's efforts to meet its commitments under the UN Convention on Biological Diversity. Here, the DMZ is mentioned over a dozen times, forming the core part of a postpartition vision that sees the two Koreas working together in "building a natural ecosystem cooperation system" that would "designate DMZ areas with superior biodiversity as a biosphere reserve."[24] The DMZ still stands, and so the work of *Aufarbeitung*, reckoning with the past, must wait for now. But once it begins, ecological and human memories will need to be part of the labor to reimagine and transform this landscape.

BEYOND BORDERLANDS: LANDSCAPES OF POSTVIOLENCE

Moving outward from the German Green Belt, we find that its model reverberates in other places that bear some similarity to the German case. The image of former "death zones" becoming "lifelines" is a potent one that translates well to other former and current borderlands. Here, the BUND's approach to the layered landscapes of war and partition seems to make good sense, and places as different as Croatia and Korea are drawing their own insights from it. But the Green Belt can carry us further, holding bigger and more foundational lessons for conservation and restoration on troubled land. The BUND has been discovering in fits and starts how to move from an ecological project to one that leans into history and story, attempts to merge a consideration of the past and its traces with their remembrance and memorialization, and connects scientific perspectives with local input. The basic, elemental need to make conservation and restoration not just eco-logically effective but also meaningful for local people and sensitive to their realities, however, is a global one. A few more examples will illustrate this.

Cambodia

Since the beginning of the twentieth century, Cambodia has been governed by seven distinct colonial and postcolonial regimes, of which those of Lon Nol (1970–1975) and Pol Pot (1975–1979) are the most infamous. The violent 1970s began with a coup that installed the right-wing, US-backed, military-led Khmer Republic. The Communist opposition soon congealed in the form of the Khmer Rouge, which took control of Cambodia despite heavy US military action against it. Under Pol Pot's leadership, the Khmer Rouge attempted to liberate Cambodia from foreign influences and aimed to craft a self-sufficient, socialist agrarian society called the Democratic Repub-lic of Kampuchea. Forced to clear land and build dams, canals, dikes, and reservoirs, hundreds of thousands of people toiled and died in horrible con-ditions, while famine caused hunger and mass starvation. Together with Pol Pot's widespread and brutal campaigns against actual and perceived oppo-nents, his five-year rule of terror killed between one and three million people, only ending with the invasion of Vietnamese forces that toppled the Khmer Rouge regime in 1979.[25] Local skirmishes between remnant Khmer Rouge and the government continued well into the 1990s.[26]

The haunting reminders of the war and its infamous killing fields are scattered across the country, and efforts are still underway to find more. By combining on-the-ground fieldwork with global position systems, the Documentation Center of Cambodia has identified over 390 killing sites containing more than 19,000 mass graves, clustered mostly in the more densely populated south and central parts of the country, but with some reaching far into the northeast. Moreover, the center lists 197 prisons and 81 memorials to the genocide.[27] As recently as 2018, Khmer Rouge leaders have been tried and convicted of crimes against humanity.[28] The landscapes of such violence are being selectively memorialized by postwar Cambodian governments, and at least according to some critics, often negate more local, lived experiences of millions of people.[29]

At the same time, Cambodia is one of the most biodiverse countries in Southeast Asia, boasting over 8,000 different plant species, more than 870 fish species, and over 500 bird species.[30] Together with Thailand, Laos, Myanmar, Vietnam, and southern China, Cambodia forms part of the Greater Mekong River watershed. It thus ranks among Conservation International's "biodiversity hot spots," meaning there is both a high level of biodiversity and significant loss of habitat, and is included in the World Wildlife Fund's "global 200 ecoregions," so labeled due to their irreplaceability or distinctiveness.[31]

The impact of Cambodia's war on its wildlife has been significant, with species numbers declining most rapidly in the 1970s. Meanwhile, the legacy effects of war—especially the proliferation of weapons, profound shift in livelihood strategies prompted by the conflict, and lingering weaknesses in protected area governance institutions—continue to trouble biodiversity recovery in the country.[32] Cambodia still maintains high levels of forest cover relative to its neighbors, but even here, deforestation is proceeding at astonishing rates; between 2000 and 2013, researchers noted a nearly 40 percent forest decline.[33] Many large and charismatic mammals, like the tiger, are nearly extinct here; Asian elephants and wild buffalo persist, although in ever-shrinking numbers.

Conservation imperatives lie uneasily on top of a landscape of trauma. To highlight just one particular space, Cambodia's Cardamom Mountains (a one-million-acre national park near the border with Thailand that was created in 2016) are a biodiversity hot spot within a biodiversity hot spot. Major international conservation NGOs—including the World Wildlife Fund, Conservation International, and Wildlife Conservation Society—flag this region as being of special interest to their work. Yet these mountains were also one of the strongholds of the Khmer Rouge, which killed, raped, pillaged, and drove thousands of locals from their homes and into Thai border camps. While militia members were slowly reintegrated into Cambodian society after 1999, many former Khmer Rouge members—and their former targets—still live in these mountain villages.[34] The landscape is deeply marked by this past—more than anything in the minds of its people:

> There is a mountain named after one of the Khmer heroes of the war, a pond named after the killing of Thai soldiers, a mountain said to be made of Thai ammunition, and, of course, the Thai footprint. People . . . show these places to their children and tell them the story that is connected to them. In this manner, the story is cast into the landscape, where it becomes a feature of the moral order. That is, the historical event has been morally resolved in a manner that constitutes the ancestral past as exemplary and potent, an achievement resolved in landscape through the social act of making that past into part of the landscape.[35]

Ponds, rivers, mountains, and forests become signifiers for local people as they craft meaning from past violence and re-create for themselves a sense of equilibrium. These meanings, in turn, are passed on to descendants in a form of collective memory of trauma and survival, guilt and atonement.

Conservationists working in Cambodia have suggested that "conservation investments in post-conflict societies should be integrated within and support broader peace-building efforts targeting combatants, noncombatants, civil society organizations, and the state."[36] Given that the ongoing memorialization of the past in the vernacular landscapes of Cambodia is so central to living and surviving there, one should not conceive of conservation without it.

Colombia

Like Cambodia, Colombia has also seen atrocious violence. The country endured an over fifty-yearlong civil war, a triangulated conflict between the central government, various leftist guerrilla groups, and paramilitaries.[37] The war began in 1964, but was itself an outgrowth of an earlier, decade-long conflict known as La Violencia that had pitted liberal and conservative elites against one another. Peasant farmers had begun organizing to protect themselves from the violence—something that the governing elites considered a threat and sought to eliminate. The local resistance movement congealed into the Fuerzas Armadas Revolucionarias de Colombia. Around the same time, influenced by Marxist ideology too, another guerrilla group formed, led by students naming themselves the Ejército de Liberación Nacional and aiming to topple the country's oligarchy.

The low-intensity conflict got more and more heated until, in the 1980s, paramilitary groups formed from segments of the Colombian army, business interests, and large landowners, supposedly independent from government but seeking to maintain elite power. The paramilitary factions merged in 1997 to form the Autodefensas Unidas de Colombia, ushering in another period of heightened violence and killings, which controversially also involved the US government and its attempts at reducing cocaine production at the source. The civilian population was caught in the cross fire as the warring factions killed, abducted, and tortured thousands of mostly poor and rural people in their struggle for territory and power.

Across the decades, the Colombian conflict has left as many as 450,000 dead, 25,000 disappeared, and over 7 million displaced.[38] Investigations by Colombia's National Center for Historic Memory (CNMH) show that 82 percent of the casualties were civilians rather than combatants, and paramilitaries killed 100,000 people, while guerrillas were responsible for the deaths of another 35,000. The center warns, however, that these numbers are likely a low estimate.[39] A milestone peace agreement between the Colombian government and the Fuerzas Armadas Revolucionarias de Colombia was signed in 2016, bringing a modicum of calm to the country.

Colombia is enormously rich in species, hosting close to 10 percent of the entire planet's biodiversity. Globally it ranks first in bird and orchid species diversity, and second (after Brazil) in plants, amphibians, freshwater fish, and butterflies.[40] Its many ecological zones, from coastal plains—both Pacific and Caribbean—to the Andes, to the Amazon rain forest, are home to practically every habitat type known in South America. Half of them are under threat.[41] The decades-long war had an ambivalent effect on these ecosystems. Persistent violence in many rural, forested areas kept resource extraction relatively low. At the same time, though, the conflict did have serious environmental impacts: guerrillas bombed government infrastructure, including pipelines, spilling 4.1 million barrels of oil into local waterways and soils. The breakdown of both communal and governmental resource governance regimes also opened up opportunities for unregulated and illegal gold mining, the latter a practice with enormous ecological ramifications due to cyanide and mercury pollution.[42] Moreover, the entanglement of the drug trade in Colombia's civil war meant that over 5 million acres of tropical forest were cut to grow illicit crops, chemicals used in cocaine production were dumped into fragile ecosystems, and US-funded aerial spraying poisoned not only coca fields but nearby farms, fields, and forests too.[43]

As is true for other biodiverse landscapes of postviolence, war exacts an ecological toll, but peace can as well. The 2016 peace agreement has raised concerns by conservationists that areas previously inaccessible to agribusiness and the mining, oil, and lumber industries will now become the new frontier of accumulation.[44] Across Colombia's protected areas, deforestation has already increased by a dramatic 177 percent since 2016.[45] Pushing against this are the government's attempts at expanding protected areas—since 2010, it has doubled the area of national park lands to almost 110,000 square miles, but in areas scarred by the legacy effects of war, both in their landscapes and the memories of local people. Survivors talk of hundred-year-old ceiba trees riddled with bullet holes and a large tamarind tree to which twelve men were tied and then decapitated. Witnesses say that the tree dried up after that, only to bloom again after the peace deal was brokered. Memorialized fear continues to shape Colombia's postwar landscapes, and local people insist that "without environmental restoration there can be no social reparation."[46]

These few examples highlight the inevitability of mnemonic ecologies—the inseparability of violence, history, memory, and nature. The world's most biodiverse regions are often also inhabited by people whose current and past land uses are still apparent. In some cases, as in Europe, past land use has actually increased biodiversity.[47] Places as different as Cambodia and Colombia are joined by the tragedy of violence and loss. Survivors of a traumatic past still call many of these landscapes home as they try to make their way into an uncertain future. International conservation interests frequently add to that precariousness with the threat of yet more displacement and changes in local livelihood that have been the historical pattern as conservation expanded into the Global South. I argue that attending more explicitly to people's memories—of places, events, family and kin, and ecological relationships—can make conservation more sensitive to local people's needs and thus help heal the wounds they still carry. Ecological restoration and social reparation become two sides of the same coin, two mutually dependent elements to successful conservation. Unfortunately, this ideal goes against much of the current thrust of conservation, made apparent in the ongoing negotiations for a post-2020 global biodiversity vision.

BIODIVERSITY AND THE QUESTION OF COMMUNITIES

The state of biodiversity today can only be described as grim. The World Wildlife Fund's bombshell 2020 *Living Planet Report* revealed that between 1970 and 2016, in a span of less than fifty years (decades during which the human population doubled), we have lost more than two-thirds of all vertebrate life on earth, with the most precipitous declines happening in the most biodiverse regions.[48] More than one million species will disappear forever in the coming decades, according to the sweeping global biodiversity assessment by the United Nations.[49] This mass annihilation is pitching species that have evolved over eons into the abyss at rates a thousand to ten thousand times higher than the natural background rate of extinction.[50] Loss of diversity on this scale will dramatically curtail the evolutionary possibilities for life on this planet for millions of years into the future. What makes the situation worse is our uncertainty around the depth of this crisis: we do not know how many species exist on the planet, so we cannot know how fast we are losing organisms of whose presence or ecological importance we remain ignorant. Our cataloging of extinction is woefully inadequate for the task, although the IUCN's Red List is making valiant efforts at rendering threat levels and loss visible. It is likely that we are losing life at the rate of anywhere from two hundred up to one hundred thousand species a year—a huge potential range—but we will ever only know of some small number of those disappearances. Humanity's destruction of its own conditions for existence will not only cause many more such losses—too many to count, too many to mourn—but also threaten the lives of billions of people worldwide, starting with those most directly dependent on functioning ecosystems yet ultimately ricocheting upward to reach even the wealthiest.

One of the newest initiatives to address this galloping crisis is the "30x30" movement that seeks to protect 30 percent of the earth's land and oceans by 2030. Promoted by powerful conservation interests, most of them located in the Global North, this essentially requires more than a doubling of protected areas, which in 2020 covered about 17 percent of earth's terrestrial surface and 8 percent of the world's oceans.[51] The proposal was first published in 2020 as part of the negotiations surrounding the UN Convention on Biological Diversity and represents an attempt to develop a post-2020 policy vision that can effectively rally governments worldwide to halt biodiversity loss.[52] While an important step forward, it is in some ways also a significant retreat from the more ambitious "half-earth" vision, put forth by the likes of Edward O. Wilson, according to which 50 percent of the world's terrestrial and marine systems should be protected, thus safeguarding 80 percent of the world's nonhuman life.[53] The 30x30 plan, in contrast, is estimated to cut extinction only by about half, but is widely seen as a more politically feasible target.

The proposal has garnered a lot of attention, especially from the "high-ambition coalition" of seventy-plus countries (including the United States) aligning in support of the idea.[54] In October 2021, the Convention on Biological Diversity's conference of the parties issued the Kunming Declaration, setting out 30x30 as the policy touchstone.[55] The 30x30 idea is instantly appealing: it is easy to understand, seems realistic, and relies on an old and familiar area-based strategy (like national parks or marine reserves), and its goals and hoped-for outcomes can be expressed through the dominant, economistic discourse of ecosystem services and natural capital, thereby offering a counterargument to business interests that for decades have insisted that conservation destroys the economy.

In the run-up to the UN proposal, the Wyss Foundation in partnership with *National Geographic* (which together have formed the Campaign for Nature) commissioned a report to explore and disseminate information about the economic benefits of the 30x30 approach. The August 2020 document was authored by a large group of conservation scientists and environmental economists (almost all of them from the United States and western Europe) to demonstrate that nature conservation would be a "good investment." Thomas Lovejoy, a biologist known as the "godfather of bio-diversity" for having introduced the concept to the scientific community in 1980, speaks of a "large financial return if we protect 30% of terrestrial and marine nature." Stephen Woodley of the IUCN's World Commission on Protected Areas states that "the report shows we can gain financially and economically by implementing this policy."[56]

The increasingly frequent tendency to frame environmental concerns in the language of economics, finance, and accounting has been roundly cri-tiqued elsewhere, but the report was attacked for another reason: its apparent obliviousness to the needs of local communities on whose lands much of this conservation work would need to happen.[57] Within weeks, Indigenous organizations and their Global North allies issued a letter expressing concern that a 30x30 plan would affect over three hundred million people worldwide and that Indigenous land rights and livelihoods would once again be put at risk for the sake of conservation.[58] This letter was followed by another in August 2021, signed by representatives from nearly fifty charitable founda-tions, making similar points and warning of a likely increase in militarized conservation in the attempt to cordon off areas from human incursions.[59]

Around the same time, a group of academics and conservation prac-titioners (most of them social scientists, and many of them from Global South institutions or with Indigenous affiliations) published an open letter in response to the 30x30 initiative and, more specifically, Campaign for Nature's report. According to the letter's authors, the Campaign for Nature document ignores the political contexts in which conservation is embed-ded. It does not adequately recognize the losses that local people can suffer from conservation that simply cannot be priced. The report also computes gains and losses at the national scale, thus erasing the local level at which all protected area conservation literally takes place. Ultimately for the letter's authors, the Campaign for Nature's report—and the 30x30 approach it attempts to delineate and defend—"reads to us like a proposal for a new model of colonialism."[60]

Conservation has been controversial in this way for well over a century. The global model for protected areas has been the national park pioneered in the United States, but the Yosemite and Yellowstone parks emerged in the context of the country's westward expansion, and as such, are inextricably tied to settler colonialism along with the genocide and land theft on which it is predicated.[61] The "Yellowstone model" found favor with the British, who then exported and implemented it in their African colonies, with similarly disastrous effects for local people, who found themselves dispossessed of and displaced from their ancestral lands.[62] Until the late twentieth century, conservation in the Global South mostly proceeded via militarily enforced protected areas, and what we would now call human rights violations were the order of the day. Local people were framed as the problem while white intervention was considered necessary, and white presence (like trophy hunting and tourism) was defined as benign or even helpful.[63] Conservation was anchored in the colonial (and later postcolonial) state and imposed from the top down with little that local communities could do to shape it, let alone prevent it.

Under the influence of the human rights movement and global mobilization of Indigenous peoples in the 1970s and 1980s, things began to change. Managers of conservation projects designed the first prototype "integrated conservation and development" projects in the mid- to late 1970s as they sought ways to work with people in and around protected areas. In the 1980s, the World Conservation Strategy was drafted and became the document legitimizing what is now known as community-based conservation. By 1985, the World Wildlife Fund (deeply implicated in African conservation) had taken up the baton and developed a new and more socially sensitive approach called "Wildlands and Human Needs." Other conservation organizations followed suit, also influenced by the new buzzword in environmental circles: sustainable development. Community-based natural resource management emerged as an approach that sought to create conservation processes that would simultaneously provide financial and livelihood benefits for locals while giving them a sense of "empowerment."[64] But community-based approaches did not end up being the magic bullet many had hoped, and biodiversity loss has continued, despite localized successes. By the early 2000s, a backlash against the socially oriented projects had developed, resulting in a retrenchment of an ostensibly apolitical, science-based approach that sees nature conservation as separate from social concerns.[65]

The debate highlights the divergent assumptions about nature and people that shape conservation imaginaries in the Global North and South. This becomes clear when one compares the discourses and practices of conservation in Europe with those in sub-Saharan Africa: whereas for policy makers in Europe, "biodiversity is humanized and incorporated into narratives of culture and history," those same conservation agents "naturalize" biodiversity in the South and "incorporate it into a narrative of an undiscovered primordial wilderness."[66] This is particularly odd since the archaeological record shows that Africa was inhabited by humans much earlier and for much longer than Europe, and hence one should consider African environments, like European ones, as landscapes that have been used and shaped by human cultures for millennia. The same is true for tropical forests, including those in Latin America as well as South and Southeast Asia.[67]

The question this comparison raises is what a European biodiversity narrative, based on the notion of cultural landscapes, might offer when applied more consistently to the Global South. If conservation policy reconsiders those Global South landscapes so often defined as wilderness instead (or also) as sites of human pasts, presences, and futures, then what can a mnemonic ecological approach contribute? It begins by asking questions about the protected area paradigm, not to dismantle it so much as to reimagine it to make it work better, longer, and more synergistically with the needs of the people who have lived, labored, and lost in these places, and who know their environments best.

THE POSSIBILITIES OF MNEMONIC ECOLOGIES

Looking to memory in this context opens up greater awareness and appreciation for local knowledge and points to the need to include local people in conservation, even letting them drive it. There is by now a voluminous literature on the importance of local knowledge to environmental management. Whether in the form of community-based conservation, community-based natural resource management, integrated conservation and development projects, or Indigenous people's protected areas, the arguments for involving communities in conservation projects are compelling for many reasons, beyond simply the need to meet UN biodiversity targets. Involving local people in conservation projects on the lands they inhabit adds important socioecological memory—knowledge gained and passed down across generations of how plants, animals, ecosystems, and anthropogenic landscapes behave and function—and makes those conservation initiatives more acceptable, resilient, effective, and sustainable over the long term. Socioecological memory is place based and empirical, subject to constant experimentation and fine-tuning, and is carried in people and the institutions they form, including rituals, stories, teachings, and usage rules. In this way, individuals and communities develop a "collective memory of resource use," a reservoir of past (even ancestral) experience that can be accessed in times of disturbance and crisis, allowing for both community and ecosystem adaptation and renewal.[68] Conservation cannot continue to count on ecological stability (inherent to the protected area paradigm) but instead must find ways to effectively confront chaos and flux as we move into an increasingly climate-changed future. Seeking to understand local people's socioecological memories is one important way to do so.

Indigenous approaches have enriched this discussion by insisting that truly decolonized conservation must center Indigenous knowledge, practices, and cosmology—in other words, Indigenous lifeways understood as a totality.[69] Merely seeking to "integrate" a detached domain of "traditional ecological knowledge" into the epistemologically dominant scientific framework quickly runs into difficulty, with Indigenous knowledge becoming either another data point or a quaint anecdote easily sidelined by, and without much relevance to, Western (read "real") conservation praxis.[70] Paying closer attention to Indigenous-*led* conservation efforts helps us foreground the importance of stories and memories to any land-based intervention, and allows us to see the potential for reconciliation and land healing as inherent to restoration. Given histories of settler colonialism, war, militarization, strategic violence, or forced displacement, "restoration" can easily sound like turning back the clock to more oppressive earlier states or replicating ecological conditions that erase people's lives from their old or new home places.[71] Restoration approaches that treat memory seriously can recognize this risk better and reorient themselves. To take one example, Māori in New Zealand are developing their own approach to river restoration that rejects the common historical baseline of 1840 (the year marking the formal beginning of British colonialism) since it implies that no history happened prior to the arrival of Europeans. Instead, a looser concept is used, focused on healing, reconciliation, and cultural resurgence that elevates Māori ways of knowing and doing ecological work.[72] The river restoration project's

> physical actions of growing and planting, of removing weeds and sowing seeds helped [Māori] rebuild the relationships (with one another, their ancestors, and the non-human worlds) that were/are disrupted by colonialism. The practices of tending to a plant, replanting a riverbank, and restoring a wetland, also allowed for restoration practitioners to maintain and enhance their connections to their ancestors, their knowledge, and their ethics.[73]

Restoration, on Indigenous terms, can help reverse the identity-crushing effects of colonialism and help support Indigenous revitalization as well as social and ecological resilience. In the connections to ancestral presence, restoration is also an enactment of memory in the landscape, a way to keep the ties to material and spiritual pasts alive. From the perspective of Indigenous and traditional peoples the world over, species loss was and still is "the loss of kin, of culture, of knowledge, of relationships, and of modes of living."[74] Restoration is a way to address that grief by shaping the land, giving back, and healing its wounds along with one's own. Acting on the landscape in this way, then, is a form of restitution and setting things right. For Māori, working to restore the local river is wrapped up in intergenerational obligations to both their ancestors and descendants. It is also, however, a question of intragenerational responsibility toward other human and nonhuman beings.

Mnemonic Ecologies of Justice

Conservationists may balk at the suggestion that on top of saving the world's biodiversity, on top of being tasked with eradicating poverty (as community-based natural resource management seemed to suggest to them), they are now being asked to engage in broad-scale projects of decolonization or reconciliation too. This book illustrates, though, that one has never been easily separable from any of the others, and it was a pretense to think so. The impulse to sever science from politics is not unique to conservation, but it is particularly understandable here since biodiversity loss is so overwhelming in its speed, scope, and emotional impact. It seems easier, more efficient, and perhaps more appropriate to the problem to seek quicker, scientific solutions, and not bother with the complicated and time-consuming social and emotional dimensions of conservation. Yet the ability for those not living in the landscapes of such loss to segregate the world into discrete compartments (science versus everything else) is a sign of material detachment and preference for conceptual order rather than a reflection of people's lived reality. By integrating a consideration of memory—both ecological and social—into the work of conservation, it becomes easier to understand the connections between human beings and their environments as well as harder to ignore them. And seeing such connections is at the center of the environmental justice paradigm.

As both a scholarly field and arena of social activism, environmental justice grew from the refusal of Black and Brown communities in the United States to continue to be subjected to toxic waste and pollution. Structures of power including settler colonialism and white supremacy entrench poverty as well as urban and rural segregation, drive land theft, deepen health disparities, and put communities of color in harm's way while allowing white people to avoid these forms of violence. The environmental justice movement initially focused on the distribution of locally unwanted land uses as the problem. Since then, however, environmental justice activists and their allies have expanded their critiques of power and fine-tuned their demands for justice. A sole emphasis on distribution may identify the unfair outcomes, but it does not address the structural causes of inequity, nor can it ensure rights and opportunities or ultimately shift power, because those are deeply lodged in social relationships.[75] Procedural and compensatory justice frameworks add nuance to environmental justice claims, but in cases of trauma from war, human and ecological death, loss of land and livelihood connected to conservation projects, and loss of culture due to the loss of species, they are also limited.

More recent articulations of restorative and transitional justice that are based on a relational understanding of power, and Indigenous-led calls for reconciliatory justice, offer opportunities for longer-term healing and deeper resolution. Restorative justice seeks to redress harm and rebuild relationships by engaging offenders, victims, and the larger community in a structured dialogue. A crime, in this view, is not just a violation of the law but of people and relationships as well, and it entails an obligation to make things right by repairing victims and communities through truth telling and apology, recognition, restitution, or compensation.[76] At the center of this form of justice is the felt experience of the victim, and at the heart of this experience, in turn, is the memory of harm and suffering. Having one's testimony be heard offers the person who suffered the assault, crime, or violence a way to reclaim some measure of balance, dignity, and safety. Restorative approaches are common in truth and reconciliation commissions, and form part of the transitional justice paradigm that concentrates on the aftermath of violent conflict or repressive or dictatorial regimes.[77] Increasingly, scholars and practitioners are realizing that restorative approaches can also be applied productively to situations of environmental crime. Accountability for ecological destruction through a restorative approach would not just involve retribution (fines and imprisonment) and compensation (payment for damages) but also direct, face-to-face dialogue between perpetrators and victims, giving the latter much-needed voice, recognition, and a sense of dignity.[78] In the wake of ecological devastation, listening to local people's memories and interpretations of how their environments changed, and who is to blame, can create the scaffolding for just futures. Attending to people's positive memories of the way things used to be, despite or even because of their nostalgic inflections, can similarly offer outsiders a glimpse of people's ideas of a better life, and may provide restorationists and conservationists with an ecological vision worth realizing.[79]

The Center for Native Peoples and the Environment under the leadership of Dr. Robin Wall Kimmerer defines biocultural restoration as "the science and practice of restoring not only ecosystems, but human and cultural relationships to place, so that cultures are strengthened and revitalized along with the lands to which they are inextricably linked."[80] Conservationists seeking to reestablish and protect ecological communities after significant and often violent change may want to consider their work in the light of this doubly understood restoration: drawing on local socioecological memories to better imagine the landscape as it once was or should have been, and better imagine ways in which communities today can drive the vision and direction of conservation as a path toward healing and justice. In the context of environmental justice, "one should not simply remediate the soil, but remediate that sense of place that has been lost over time, and to take seriously the rupture created by absence."[81] Almost all landscapes in the United States are scarred by violent pasts, including genocide, dispossession, and slavery. Conservationists and restoration ecologists working here should look to Indigenous, Black, Latinx, and Asian American scholars, activists, poets, and writers to gain a deeper appreciation of these histories, the ways in which diverse communities have imagined and shaped these spaces, and the manner in which (often painful) memory suffuses human-environment relationships throughout.[82]

It should be said that there is no necessary or imperative connection between memory and justice, but rather it is "contingent and open-ended, and rooted in personal, situated and embodied experience. Similarly, our understandings of [ecological] justice must be rooted not only in formal notions of 'ideal type' justice (such as distributional and procedural justice), but also in the affective, experiential, and embodied nature" of local and lived socioecologies.[83] The link between memory and justice cannot be assumed but instead must always be made and remade. In some Indigenous frameworks, this must occur in "ethical space" where "knowledge systems interact with mutual respect, kindness, generosity."[84] Important work is already being done, and much can be gained from searching for synergies between conservation groups (both domestic and international), local communities, and the wisdom accumulated through existing initiatives. Just a cursory view suggests the need to acknowledge the diverse strategies worldwide to peacefully deal with the legacies of war, violence, and ecological destruction.

Let us look back at the cases discussed earlier. In Cambodia, for instance, disarmament, demobilization, and reintegration left local communities struggling with how to achieve reconciliation between perceived perpetrators, collaborators, and victims. The Documentation Center of Cambodia (also known as DC-Cam) has sought to create a more nuanced approach to the past as part of its interest in transitional justice based on education and remembrance.[85] One of its projects focuses on Anlong Veng, a town in the country's remote northwest near the Thai border, known as the last stronghold of the Khmer Rouge and the place where Pol Pot died. Even today, about 85 percent of the population are former Khmer Rouge, most of whom eke out a meager living from slash-and-burn agriculture, which has contributed to significant deforestation in the region. DC-Cam is collaborating with the London-based firm DaeWha Kang Design to develop a memorial and educational landscape across the entire district. Ecological restoration forms an integral part of this effort, guided by the philosophy of "heal the landscape, heal the society." Anlong Veng is being reimagined as a region of "peace, reconciliation, and regeneration," where ribbons of reforestation are linked to sustainable agricultural production. The built environment, too, is being recast through the lens of healing: a warehouse for land mines will be transformed into a manufacturing plant for crutches and wheelchairs, and a site where women were tortured is being reimagined as a women's center for those escaping gender-based violence. While much of this is in the draft or initial implementation stages, and it remains to be seen how attuned the project will be to local needs and interests, ecology and memory are clearly already tied together in a transitional justice frame.

In Colombia, state-led ecological restoration has been happening since at least the 1950s, even if still largely lacking a social component.[86] Colombians are, however, deeply involved in postconflict peacemaking and have been refining ideas around restitution, reconciliation, and reparation. Remembrance is part of these processes, and Colombia's National Center for Historic Memory has been leading traveling workshops across the country to help local people heal their trauma, validate their grief and anger, honor their resilience and strength, and let them speak their stories to others who will listen.[87] Meanwhile, civil society organizations like Sembrando Paz (Sowing Peace), whose members are all conflict survivors, see their work as both healing people and healing the environments on which they depend. Their focus is on land access and land reform given the numbers of internally displaced people barely eking out a living. It means creating "restorative spaces" through "education based on nonviolent coexistence, spirituality, solidarity, dialogue, democracy, and respect toward the environment" that allow for integrated development, and through it, "a more just and happy society."[88] Colombia's peace agreement, at least in principle, recognizes the centrality of land management and rural development to a successful and sustainable peace process. Their careful implementation will have lasting consequences for both the biophysical and sociopolitical climate in the country.

Mnemonic ecological work is also important in the United States. Unlike the lengthy collective processing in Germany decades after the Holocaust—the result of a painful and often shame-inducing *Aufarbeitung* (reckoning with the past) and *Erinnerungsarbeit* (memory work)—a similar broad-scale reappraisal of the country's violent past is still missing. It is urgent and overdue, expressed for instance by the recent movement to take down Confederate statues or reconsider the histories of some of the United States' most exalted institutions of higher education.[89] Conservation areas, along with the national parks that occupy a cherished place in the country's self-image, would be quite literally a natural place to extend this work, drawing connections between land, loss, pain, and ecological renewal through a well-considered collective process of remembrance, debate, critique, listening, learning, and reconciliation.

The changes have already begun. By naming sites such as the Stonewall, Bears Ears, or César E. Chávez National Monuments, the National Park Service over the past decade has made strides to broaden what it considers to be a past worthy of marking, all the while having to confront its own racist origins.[90] Working within and beyond the US national park system, some organizations are finding additional creative ways to merge collective memory, history, and conservation. The Center for Native Peoples and the Environment, mentioned earlier, is currently collaborating with the Nature Conservancy in New York on a "re-story-ation" project that is built on the recognition that all land under environmental protection is Native land. The center's work will not only increase Indigenous access to lost territories but also aim to "restore Indigenous Peoples' engagement with their ancestral homelands and give voices to their perspectives in interpretation, education, and stewardship practices."[91] As another example, the Conservation Fund, a nonprofit organization focused on the dual objectives of land conservation and economic development, has been working with federal, state, and local partners across the country to acquire historically significant land for what it calls "cultural conservation" purposes.[92] One of the projects in the fund's portfolio is the Harriet Tubman Rural Legacy Area. Launched by the state of Maryland, this 28,300-acre natural, cultural, and historic landscape on the state's Eastern Shore has been prioritized for conservation. The Conservation Fund land acquisitions and conservation easements safeguarded important wildlife habitat in the Chesapeake Bay alongside key historical sites that mark Tubman's life as an enslaved person, her escape, and her courageous work as a member of the Underground Railroad. The landscape-level conservation approach increases the visibility of the already-existing Harriet Tubman Underground Railroad National Monument, created by President Obama in 2013 and itself made possible by a 480-acre land donation by the Conservation Fund. The Harriet Tubman Rural Legacy Area consists of the same mix of forests, farms, fields, and waterways that characterized the nineteenth-century spaces through which Tubman moved. For the Conservation Fund, this project allows visitors an embodied experience of the past, all while it extends the habitat protections of adjacent conservation areas like the Blackwater National Wildlife Refuge. As this book argues, land preservation must also be an inherently storied process. How exactly Tubman's legacy will be narrated, who will do so, and what other socioecological layers might be excavated and elevated from this landscape are questions for the coming decades.

RESTOR(Y)ING CONSERVATION

As we circle outward from the German Green Belt, we recognize the life- and landscape-altering potential that a mnemonic ecological approach holds. Germany, the Balkans, and Korea are by far not the only places where we witness the challenging convergence of war, violence, and ecological and human trauma. Many of the landscapes so treasured by conservationists for their biodiversity are not only inhabited by people but have been staging grounds for brutal and long-lasting conflicts too. Ecological and social memory are important elements to understanding these landscapes; they should be the starting point for biocultural restoration. The need for healing is great, and mnemonic ecological connections have the potential to seed more just futures around the globe. Each will merit its own book.

We must remain aware, of course, that not all people remember the same way; that experience is fissured by race, class, gender, age, religion, and other factors, and memory will be as well; that remembrance is neither always appropriate nor desirable for everyone; that it is deeply context and culture dependent; that it is fragile and changeable; that it has its own peculiar temporality and partiality; that remembrance too soon may worsen trauma rather than soften it; and that collective memory has intricate connections with individual memory. Memory is not a "thing" that can be easily split from other human domains but rather is entangled with them. Memory, collective and individual, is in essence a shifting, complex relationship—with time and place, with oneself and others. Enacting an approach that takes memory more seriously, conservation and restoration practitioners will need to think in creative and interdisciplinary ways, and in terms of collaborations, connections, and coalitions.

Moreover, conservation and restoration are not the same, though especially in the context of postviolence they can overlap so considerably that they become almost indistinguishable. Restoration cannot substitute for conservation. In a world of accelerating disturbance and broader-scale human impacts, however, we will find conservation and restoration coming ever closer. The two fields both involve and invoke the past—with one crucial difference: conservation has generally excluded consideration of human needs and human-environment relationships (and as discussed, even today it remains a highly contested idea), whereas restoration, in its very definition, always has been based on a consideration of human impact, and envisioned a role for humans in ecological rehabilitation and repair.

Rather than thinking of restoration as a small subfield of conservation, I hold that it is restoration that has much to teach conservation. It is restoration, not conservation, that has defined itself from the start as a necessarily interdisciplinary field that must overcome the entrenched divisions between the natural and social sciences. It is restoration that has had to wrestle with historical questions much more explicitly than conservation, which is often aimed at erasing human histories. It is restoration that has had to reckon with the complexities of layered landscapes—multiple socioecological histories frequently still traceable in a landscape—more so than conservation. And it has been restoration that explicitly keeps confronting the ethical and moral questions that conservation, in its reliance on science, has frequently sidestepped. As policy makers attempt to craft a more effective post-2020 biodiversity framework, conservation needs local communities more than ever, and the calls are getting louder for a much more diverse panoply of conservation approaches. Contending with memory in place-, context-, and culturally specific ways is an indispensable component of twenty-first-century ecological work.

CONCLUSION

Mnemonic Ecologies delineates a new field of inquiry and practice: the merging of ecology with a textured and sensitive understanding of memory. Its task is overdue, substantial, and urgent. The learning that has happened along the inter-German border and the ways in which conservationists are continuing to refine and adapt their approaches hold promise for not just Germany but other wounded places worldwide as well. Mnemonic ecologies is an effective framework to investigate the qualities of layered landscapes, an analytic gaze honed by the sciences, humanities, and social sciences. Places are seen here not simply as a series of ecological assemblages, biotic and abiotic relationships, or energy and material flows. They carry within them the emotions, meanings, and memories that human beings ascribe to them, which in turn produce diverse kinds of natures—wilderness, cultural landscapes, novel ecosystems, and more. Memories are bound up in stories that are told about these places. It is through stories that human beings craft order in this world, but "if our goal is to tell tales that make the past meaningful, then we cannot escape struggling over the values that define what meaning is."[1]

Conservation in Germany is not easy; as one of Europe's most industrialized countries, where any and all space is at a premium, making any kind of room for nonhuman needs is ever an uphill battle. And as the examples from the Green Belt show, memory and ecology along the former Iron Curtain are a potent mix. The trauma of SED rule and violent border enforcement runs deep for many former East Germans. Land, especially, has emerged as one of the pivot points on which conservation outcomes turn. The BUND has recognized that thoughtful memorialization matters here, and its approach has proceeded by trial and error. Emerging memorial sites along the Green Belt in some form or another attempt to address lingering trauma and honor memories, all the while projecting visions of a different, healing future. Ecology thus becomes a metaphor for making the best of things, enduring and even flourishing despite setbacks, and healing despite the hurt. The lead BUND staffer for Thuringia remarked that the time for all of this was right:

> It's now about thirty years after the fall of the wall, and we've seen that the reckoning with the Second World War also happened in certain waves, so to speak. And I believe that now is another point in time when you look differently at German history and at the situation after the fall of the wall. And especially with this topic of the Green Belt you can somehow access that quite well, because it's ultimately about, well, history. It's not just something big and abstract, with numbers and data and whatever. History lives through the individual stories of people, and they can be told really well this way.[2]

The BUND has used different strategies to develop the Green Belt as a memorial landscape. The borderlands in their materiality—whether in terms of art, monuments, or ruins—are open-ended sites. Full of meaning, yes, but not directive in any way. This leaves the sense making almost entirely up to the viewer. There are merits to this, as discussed in earlier chapters, but there is also at least one significant shortcoming: with time, meanings will shift and perhaps disappear entirely. For the generation that experienced the GDR and fall of the wall, these monuments have a particular kind of valence based on personal witnessing and embodied memory. Over thirty years on from reunification, however—as remnants of the border decay and ecological processes scramble once-extant categories, and as former East Germans age and new generations born in a reunified country view the borderlands with no immediate connection to the past—these sites are not explicit enough. What should be their message to the future? We see here a conflation of personal memory with history—where the former stands in for the latter. Yet as time goes on and personal memory is incrementally lost, the sites are left with little else.

Figure 7.1
A former GDR border surveillance tower, now overgrown and abandoned in the Green Belt. *Author*: Niteshift, July 29, 2014. *Source*: Wikimedia Commons, https://commons.wikimedia .org/wiki/File:Pötenitz_BT6_Führungsstelle_Grenztruppen_2014-07-29.JPG, Creative Commons License CC-BY-SA 3.0. Reprinted by permission.

In response to the criticism that conservation was erasing the border-lands' troubled layers, the BUND's efforts have focused on memory, often relying on oral histories and testimonies to convey a sense of the past. This is a compelling tool in many ways as information flows from one person to another directly and immediately. Some German historians, though, are demanding a "departure from memory" in favor of a more concrete, "museal-ized," and meticulously documented presentation of the past. Central to this project are sites of ethicohistorical remembrance where the affective connects with the cognitive to produce and intensify learning. In this framework, remembrance of the kind that informs responsible and ethical citizenship presupposes knowledge. At the point at which time robs the present gener-ations of eyewitnesses and survivors who actually knew the past, something lasting must be there to take on that burden.[3]

Green Belt conservationists have acknowledged this in the 2019 Lenzen Declaration, explored in chapter 2, but it is not yet apparent how precisely that should be done and who should do it. *Which* histories should the Green Belt make apparent? *Whose* memories of the past should it language? And while it may be a truism that "memory complements history, and history corrects memory," less has been said about who is allowed or encouraged to remember, who listens to them when writing history, and who governs the narratives and imaginings that result.[4] The conflicts along the former inter-German borderlands arise in response to these unsettled questions. History, in my view, should not be stripped clean of memory as an objective thing that somehow stands apart and above it; the Green Belt must recognize and present their interdependence. In this case especially, there is another silence: How does ecology come to matter to both history and memory? Both are rooted in ecological matter, and it will become important to attend to how this relationship intertwines with both the material past and people's felt, experienced, and narrated sense of it.

In the German borderlands, a space layered with painful memories, ecology and memory are inseparable. How that indelible connection is nar-rated and curated depends largely on particular human goals and visions—I say largely, because nature itself is yet another actor in this ensemble. Trees, moss, lichen, animals, soil, wind, air, and water all help comprise these socioecological communities knotted together in webs of life and death. Landscape art and ruins, de-extinced animals, ancient plants, and newly restored rivers can tell this story in ways that shift our insides and force our bodies to experience memory physically and sensually. At its simplest, "to perceive landscape is to carry out an act of remembrance, and remembering is not so much a matter of calling up an internal image, stored in the mind, as of engaging perceptually with an environment that is itself pregnant with the past."[5] Creating opportunities for such engagement is crucial for conservation praxis that wishes to be lasting and meaningful.

ETHICAL AND PRACTICAL MNEMONIC ECOLOGIES

As we enter the UN Decade on Ecosystem Restoration, mnemonic approaches will have context-specific relevance for the way ecological work is conducted in scarred landscapes. I offer a series of considerations—let me call them ethical commitments—that are inspired by the Green Belt and other postviolent places worldwide, and that can provide broad principles for a reinvigorated practice of conservation and restoration.

In general terms, attending to memory means, first, *taking nature seriously*. By this I mean that we should assume that what we call "nature" (based on a problematic dualism not shared by all societies) has agency, it operates according to its own logic—though one responsive to human presence—and ecological legacies in soil, water, bedrock, atmosphere, ecosystems, and plant and animal bodies shape what will be possible for human beings. We need to assume that disturbance, and the ecological memory that exists to cope with it, matters to human and nonhuman beings in real, consequential ways. We need to allow for wildness and remain attuned to the emergent qualities of ecological relationships, even as we need not uncritically accept all of them. Emergence describes a process that can change the existing order, "contain the promise of supplanting deeply rooted structures . . . , that materialize in interstitial spaces, between divided forces," and "through detours and happy accidents generate a novel sense of order."[6] Novel ecosystems cannot substitute for old and established ones—shrubs growing in the space of clear-cut old growth forests cannot replace the former—but neither should they be declared useless, for shrubs will grow into secondary forests, which in at least some contexts have been found to hold an astonishing amount of biodiversity.[7]

Mnemonic ecologies also means *taking people seriously* by recognizing that their present lives and pasts count. Their past experiences, and that of their ancestors, influence their collectively held memories and in turn how they see themselves along with their environments, communities, and relationships to each. Their hurt and pain, their longings and yearnings, their hopes and dreams, their inventiveness and ideas matter to conservation and restoration anywhere, but more so in places of past and present violence. It requires paying attention not simply to the official forms of memorialization but also to the informal, ordinary, and common ones: the manner in which local people relate to place and use elements of the landscape to remember pieces of themselves or their communities. A focus on socioecological memory can help here, as outlined in the previous chapter, where we accept that local people (even those in urban areas) enact and reenact their relationships with their environments in ways that tie them to the past.

Part of taking people seriously means *taking socioecologies seriously* as well: we take time to understand the ways in which landscapes are the result of both anthropogenic and nonanthropogenic effects and the ways in which landscapes shape what is possible for human communities living there. This means that despite the evidence for human destruction, we must acknowledge the possibility that human cultures are not necessarily always damaging to local ecologies and have in some cases, over many generations, cocreated the landscapes that so many of us outsiders consider worth saving. As part of this work, the "European" view of the cultural landscape should be considered applicable to many Global South contexts that continue to be imagined in ahistorical, romanticized, and simplistic "wilderness" terms that can reproduce quasi-colonial situations.

Closely related to this is *taking the local seriously*. As described in the previous chapter, there is a pull toward abstraction in many environmental policy circles. We often speak of "net-zero carbon emissions" or "global" biodiversity loss, and UN conventions are anchored in country-level commitments. But climate change mitigation projects or protected areas literally "take place" and have discrete local impacts and implications for plant, animal, and human life. I do not mean to imply that "the local" is a unified, singular thing; all communities are multiple, all landscapes are complex, and most human societies are fissured by all manner of differences. In the context of postviolence especially, those differences may consist of deep cuts that must be understood. Moreover, defining local "participation" or "involvement" is deeply complicated, as decades of failed or fraught programs worldwide have shown. Participation can be tokenistic and exploitative or empowering and rights affirming, and even then, its effects might not be felt equally by everyone in a community.[8] Merely calling for local involvement offers no guarantees, but much can be learned from conservation failures and local critique since they, too, form part of the mosaic of memory in a particular place. Practitioners should be prepared to lean into people's place stories and understand their attachments to landscape as much as possible through their eyes. It may mean honoring different—and perhaps even contradictory—versions of a remembered past, or letting local people debate the version that is most true to them. What matters to whom, how, and why? What memories are anchored here, and how do places express past human and more-than-human lives? How can nonlocals learn to read a landscape for the things that matter? It may also mean having to do the hard work of articulating plurivocal narratives of a place rather than a singular one (however participatory the process was to create it), and highlighting diverse ways of knowing, feeling, and remembering.

As part of a commitment to local realities, we need to query existing, state-centered forms of memorialization in postviolent landscapes—whether in the German borderlands, Cambodia, or Yosemite National Park. Across the globe, scholars have documented the sometimes-yawning gaps between state-sanctioned monuments, on the one hand, and the frequently invisible, informal processes of remembrance and commemorative landscape rituals, on the other; villagers in Croatia return annually to plow a bare field, thus keeping alive the memory of a massacre that occurred here during the Yugoslav Wars, while a Colombian community tells stories of the tamarind tree that, in its death and rebirth, mirrors the country's transition from war to peace.

Critical local histories offer indispensable moral guidelines for inclusive, accountable, and responsible interventions in part because they can "expand the capacities for acknowledgement and response to harmful human-environment relationships and their social and cultural legacies. The wider role of history in ecological restoration is to ensure that it does not become a project of re-engineering and domination, unmoored from ethical considerations at local scales."[9] Centering memory accomplishes a subtle but important shift here: it is not simply significant as a means to an end—though it is unequivocally that; it becomes also an end in and of itself. A focus on social and ecological memory returns to local communities a sense of themselves and their dignity, and grants nonhuman actors and their ecological relationships a form of agency all too often erased.

Thinking through the nexus of memory and ecology also means *taking emotions seriously*. Grief, loss, and anger are universal human experiences, as are joy, gratitude, hope, and love. Doing ecological work requires us to be open to the emotional realities of both conservation practitioners and the people whom they encounter. Such emotional openness is not unprofessional; it is the only way that reconciliation and restoration of any kind—human and ecological—even becomes possible. Some practitioners have admitted to the role that emotions play in their work, even as science's insistence on dualism and objectivity negates it.[10] A grappling with one's own feelings of loss, hurt, anxiety, and so forth can enable a more authentic presence and build strong, normative foundations for one's work. It similarly allows for the recognition that the human communities inhabiting biodiverse corners of the world are not simply "stakeholders" or "victims" but instead fully fleshed-out people with their own needs, wants, desires, and emotional lives that they may or may not choose to bring to the table.

Working the terrain of grief need not be the sole responsibility of the conservationist but rather should be facilitated by broader coalitions than usual. Science-based conservation NGOs are used to working with local partner organizations, but especially in landscapes of postviolence, it is time to draw in new allies such as historians, postwar documentation centers, mental health professionals, pastoral care workers, victims' organizations, museums, artists, theater groups, storytellers, poets, and peacemakers—in other words, those who understand how to care for the living by honoring their dead. In the wake of bloodshed or environmental loss and destruction, there may be a profound need for healing prior to any talk of conservation or restoration. Yet complete healing will likely be unattainable: the need is too great, too complex, too old, and too diverse. It will thus remain an aspiration, though an important one. In these ways, restoration and conservation in the spaces of postviolence become a form of socioecological *Aufarbeitung*, a critical interrogation of the past as well as a reckoning with its lingering effects on the present and possible futures. Land and community healing become mutually reinforcing endeavors.

At their heart is the challenging work of caring about, for, and with the world. The Greek root of the word memory—*mermēra*—means "to care."[11] Deriving from the Indo-European *(s)mer*, which also gave rise to the English phrase *to mourn*, memory is also related to "anguish" and "concern."[12] The elisions are poignantly significant and carry over into other languages. In German, *sich kümmern um* means "to care for." Yet the word is related to others that draw in something else: the noun *Kummer* means "sorrow," while something that is *kümmerlich* is "wretched" or "pitiable." We hear the same in the English word *encumbered*, meaning "weighed down" or "burdened." The millennia-old linguistic ties between memory, care, anguish, and mourning are not coincidental. Grief is birthed from the loss of something we cared about, and remembrance is our way to hold close our beloved, be they distant or deceased. Grief "both acknowledges what has been lost and ensures that we don't forget what must be remembered. . . . Some grief is not meant to be resolved and set aside. . . . In this way, we may be able to honor the losses and live our lives as carriers of their unfinished stories. This is an ancient thought—how we tend the dead is as important as how we tend the living."[13] Almost anyone in mourning will say that grief is a hallmark of care and the price one pays for the joy of love.

Care is a power with a finely honed double edge. In the social and political contexts of conservation and restoration, care represents a basic concern for the treatment and well-being of others. Its practice can be kind and supportive, but given extant structures of power, it can also be suffocating and controlling.[14] Separating the former from the latter are moral principles based on awareness, respect, compassion, and empathy. An *environmental* ethics of care thus highlights "the inevitability of dependence and interdependence" along with the importance of our concern for the welfare of "all kinds of others."[15] It lives from the basic recognition that the ties that bind us are metabolic and molecular, material and emotional. That distributed and generous interest in the lives of others, however, is stifled by the West's hyperseparation of humans from the rest of life. It is "our inability to *really get*—to comprehend at any meaningful level—the multiple connections and dependencies between ourselves and these disappearing others: a failure to appreciate all the ways in which we are at stake in one another, all the ways in which we share a world."[16]

I see the Green Belt's work increasingly moving into this more networked, multiplied labor of care—for land, for plants and animals, but also increasingly for people and their haunted pasts. This is, on the one hand, a pragmatic shift in response to the exigencies of doing conservation and restoration work in cramped quarters. On the other hand, it is—and ought to be—a moral and ethical move to create foundations of empathy, compassion, curiosity, and accountability, tied to a critical awareness of how the past can be more expansively woven into the social fabric. If we follow this path, we may yet find that it leads us to a planetary future committed to life, joy, and love.

Acknowledgments

As is true for many creative endeavors, this book could not have been generated without the labor and love of many. My reasons for gratitude are therefore numerous.

My thanks, first, go to the many people in Germany who helped me understand and see the layers of the borderlands again and again in new and intriguing ways. So many individuals all along the former inter-German border and beyond took time out of their busy days to speak with me, sometimes more than once, about their past experiences, current work, and future hopes and dreams. They included staff at the BUND project office as well as several BUND field offices overseeing Green Belt projects, federal and state conservation agencies, biosphere reserves, educational institutions, and environmental NGOs along with members of farmers' unions, municipal officials, and local mayors. They all held a diversity of views—supportive or critical—of this massive conservation project. Sometimes our conversations were easy and sometimes they were harder, but I am grateful for the unflinching ways in which so many shared their insights with me. In some cases, people's expert guidance helped me walk the borderlands differently by paying more careful attention to earth, grass, and forest, listening for the lives both present and absent, and tracing the border's remains even in the locations where they had almost vanished. So many clearly care about this land, even if for different reasons and even if that puts them at considerable odds with each other. Out of respect for their privacy, throughout the book I rarely name these individuals in connection with their comments unless they have a public persona or a role as well-known spokespeople. I want to especially thank Kai Frobel, Liana Geidezis, and the rest of the BUND staff in Nuremberg who welcomed me multiple times for stimulating conversation and allowed me access to their archives. Their unceasing work to make their vision a reality is deeply inspiring.

I also wish to thank my academic community at Bates College in Maine: my generous, smart, and dedicated colleagues in the Environmental Studies Program who make me excited to show up for work every day, and my terrific students whose intellectual curiosity always keeps me engaged and on my toes. Faculty colleagues Jane Costlow, Jim Richter, Tom Tracy, and Stephanie Wade were early readers of my work, and I remain thankful to them for their sage advice. Research for this book began in 2014, and was supported by two Bates College Faculty Development grants and two sabbaticals, one funded by a Phillips Fellowship and another by the college's enhanced sabbatical program. Together they enabled my travels and granted me the time to write about them.

Intellectual partners beyond my home institution include Astrid Eckert, Carol Hager, David Havlick, Thomas Lekan, Frank Wolff, and the attendees and discussants at different conferences, including the 2017 and 2018 annual meetings of the Association of American Geographers, 2017 European Rural Geographies Conference at the von Thünen Institute, 2021 meeting of the International Association for the Study of Environment, Space and Place, and 2021 German Studies Association conference. All offered new angles and ideas, asked thoughtful and constructive questions, and suggested new sources worth exploring.

In addition, I remain grateful to the many individuals in Germany and the United States who helped support my research logistically. The library staff at the Bundesamt für Naturschutz in Bonn unfailingly helped me find the sources I needed for my work. Hubert Becker of Beckers Blockhaus, Klaus Leidorf, Frank Meyer, Günther Reger, Thomas Stephan, the European Green Belt Association, and the BUND kindly allowed me to use their photographs for this book. At Bates College, I could not have functioned without the crucial assistance of Jeanne Beliveau, Zach Handlen, Perrin Lumbert, and Camille Parrish, and the transcription help of Bates students

Angel Echipue, Kate Blandford, and Anjali Thomke. I thank Sage Press and Taylor and Francis for permission to reuse parts of already-published articles in this book. Big thanks to my wonderful editor at MIT Press, Beth Clevenger, who championed my ideas and perspectives from the beginning and made this book a reality. Anthony Zannino at the press reliably helped me navigate the ins and outs of the publication process, and Ginny Crossman and Cindy Milstein guided me through copyediting. Multiple reviewers provided invaluable commentary on the initial proposal as well as a later draft of this manuscript, and the book is considerably improved for it. Special thanks to Eric Higgs for engaging with depth and encouragement in that role.

Much closer to home, I have felt held and supported by friends and family. Suzanne Blackburn, Gallit Cavendish, Susanne Gaul, Monique Hoeflinger, Jennifer Hoopes, Jan Kernis, Nancy Koven, Joanie Kunian, Hali Lebsanft, Carleen Mandolfo, Julia Metger, Sandra Moog, Amy Nelson, Andrea Pieck, Monika Schneider-Garbe, Timo Schol, Betsy Smith, Paul Susman, and Peter and Nora Urban—along with a marvelous and tight-knit group of neighbors here in Maine—remained engaged and interested in my ideas, and provided important community for me during the research and writing process. Lisa Arellano introduced me to the art of book proposals and plowed through my manuscript undaunted by a cross-continental life transition. Rebecca Herzig's sage advice and steadfast encouragement kept me buoyed, and our many rich conversations about this book and beyond it helped shape my thinking and writing.

Long before any book at all, my parents, Werner and Irene Pieck, created a home filled with gentle love, reminded me to always search out beauty, and taught me to cherish the living world. And for over twenty years, my spouse, Ariel Kernis, has provided the unshakable bedrock of my life. Her keen intellect, indefatigable sense of humor, and deep well of kindness helped bring this project—and many before it—to fruition. To them all, my profound gratitude.

* * *

I cannot end, though, without acknowledging the one who has had perhaps the greatest influence of all on this book, however unintended. During my first trip to the Green Belt in June 2014, I discovered that after years of trying, I was finally pregnant. Alongside the new and unfamiliar landscapes of the inter-German border, I found new emotional and physiological terrain in me, and experienced pregnancy as a borderland of sorts too: a blissfully liminal place of deep knowing, anxious hope, wonder, love, and intense connection to life. Yet when I finally went into labor in March 2015, things quickly descended into nightmare. Complications from an unplanned, chaotic C-section nearly killed me, while my daughter died just a day and a half after she was born. I am forever thankful to my spouse, my friends, my family, and the many skillful helpers who saw me through this excruciatingly difficult time. And although I never saw it coming, writing this book became a vital part of my healing. My child is in every page. During every trip to the field, with every walk in the woods, every document I pulled from an archive, every research-related conversation, and throughout this entire past year of writing, I have held my daughter close. This book has allowed us both to touch the earth—together—and I dedicate it to her in loving memory.

Notes

INTRODUCTION

1. I use the term *borderlands* throughout this book in a different way than it often appears in the scholarship. Borderlands studies is its own field, where the US-Mexico border features prominently. There, the term is used to not simply evoke contested territory but also the borders of identity, gender, race, ethnicity, and politics. In this book, *borderlands* refers more directly to the land itself, both the narrow strips of territory that materially constituted the inter-German border, slightly wider ribbon that formed the East German restricted zone, and lands adjacent to it that conservationists want to integrate into the Green Belt protected area.

2. The Red List is a comprehensive inventory of endangered species. First introduced globally in 1965 by the International Union for Conservation of Nature (IUCN), Red Lists today exist not just at the global scale but at the country level as well.

3. Marion Hourdequin and David Havlick, eds., *Restoring Layered Landscapes* (New York: Oxford University Press, 2016).

4. Interview with the author, June 27, 2014.

5. Arvid Nelson, *Cold War Ecology: Forests, Farms, and People in the East German Landscape, 1945–1989* (New Haven, CT: Yale University Press, 2005); Sagi Schaefer, *States of Division: Borders and Boundary Formation in Cold War Rural Germany* (New York: Oxford University Press, 2014).

CHAPTER 1

1. Tabatha J. Wallington, Richard J. Hobbs, and Susan A. Moore, "Implications of Current Ecological Thinking for Biodiversity Conservation: A Review of the Salient Issues," *Ecology and Society* 10, no. 1 (June 2005): 14. On nonequilibrium ecology, see Daniel Botkin, *The Moon in the Nautilus Shell: Discordant Harmonies Reconsidered* (Oxford: Oxford University Press, 2012).

2. Saleem H. Ali, ed., *Peace Parks: Conservation and Conflict Resolution* (Cambridge, MA: MIT Press, 2007); Rob H. G. Jongman and Gloria Pungetti, eds., *Ecological Networks and*

Greenways: Concept, Design, Implementation (Cambridge: University of Cambridge, 2009); Karl Zimmerer, ed., *Globalization and New Geographies of Conservation* (Chicago: University of Chicago Press, 2006).

3.   Richard J. Hobbs, Eric Higgs, Carol M. Hall, Peter Bridgewater, F. Stuart Chapin III, Erle C. Ellis, John J. Ewel, et al., "Managing the Whole Landscape: Historical, Hybrid, and Novel Ecosystems," *Frontiers in Ecology and the Environment* 121, no. 10 (December 2014): 557.

4.   Margaret A. Palmer, Joy B. Zedler, and Donald A. Falk, "Ecological Theory and Restoration Ecology," in *Foundations of Restoration Ecology*, ed. Margaret A. Palmer, Joy B. Zedler, and Donald A. Falk (Washington, DC: Island Press, 2016), 3–4. Understood more broadly, restoration is as old as humanity: for millennia, people all over the world have had an interest in maintaining or restoring ecological conditions to maximize their survival. I speak here, however, of the Western, institutionalized form of restoration.

5.   William R. Jordan, *The Sunflower Forest: Ecological Restoration and the New Communion with Nature* (Berkeley: University of California Press, 2012), 13.

6.   Eric Higgs, *Nature by Design: People, Natural Process, and Ecological Restoration* (Cambridge, MA: MIT Press, 2003).

7.   Society for Ecological Restoration, *The SER International Primer on Ecological Restoration* (Tucson: Society for Ecological Restoration International, 2004), 1, 3.

8.   George D. Gann, Tein McDonald, Bethanie Walder, James Aronson, Cara R. Nelson, Justin Jonson, James G. Hallett, et al., "International Principles and Standards for the Practice of Ecological Restoration," *Restoration Ecology* 27, no. S1 (September 2019): S1–S46S3.

9.   Karen Keenleyside, Nigel Dudley, Stephanie Cairns, Carol Hall, and Sue Stolton, *Ecological Restoration for Protected Areas* (Gland, Switzerland: International Union for Conservation of Nature, 2012), 5, 16.

10. I thank Eric Higgs for this point.

11. Stefan Zerbe, *Renaturierung von Ökosystemen im Spannungsfeld von Mensch und Umwelt* (Berlin: Springer, 2019), 8, 11. Zerbe includes a long list of texts in chronological order that have shaped the field of restoration. At least two-thirds of them are from US-based scholars.

12. Richard J. Hobbs, Eric S. Higgs, and Carol M. Hall, "Defining Novel Ecosystems," in *Novel Ecosystems: Intervening in the New Ecological World Order*, ed. Richard J. Hobbs, Eric S. Higgs, and Carol M. Hall (New York: John Wiley and Sons, 2013), 58.

13. Julia-Maria Hermann, Kathrin Kiehl, Anita Kirmer, Sabine Tischew, and Johannes Kollmann, "Renaturierungsökologie im Spannungsfeld zwischen Naturschutz und neuartigen Ökosystemen," *Natur und Landschaft* 88, no. 4 (2013): 150.

14. Zerbe, *Renaturierung von Ökosystemen*, 26–27.

15. Katherine J. Willis and Harry John Birks, "What Is Natural? The Need for a Long-Term Perspective in Biodiversity Conservation," *Science* 314, no. 5803 (November 2006): 1261–1265.

16. Joseph Mascaro, James A. Harris, Lori Lach, Allen Thompson, Michael P. Perring, David M. Richardson, and Erle C. Ellis, "Origins of the Novel Ecosystem Concept," in *Novel Ecosystems: Intervening in the New Ecological World Order*, ed. Richard J. Hobbs, Eric S. Higgs, and Carol M. Hall (New York: John Wiley and Sons, 2013), 55.

17. Sonja K. Pieck and David G. Havlick, "From Iron Curtain to Green Belt: Considering Central Europe as a Mnemonic Ecosystem," *Society and Natural Resources* 32, no. 11 (2019): 1312–1329.

18. Eric Katz, "The Big Lie: Human Restoration of Nature," in *Environmental Ethics: An Anthology*, ed. Andrew Light and Holmes Rolston (Malden, MA: Blackwell, 2003), 390–397; Eric Katz, "Further Adventures in the Case against Restoration," *Environmental Ethics* 34 (March 2012): 67–97.

19. Andre F. Clewell, "Restoration for Natural Authenticity," *Ecological Restoration* 18, no. 4 (Winter 2000): 217.

20. Eric Higgs, Donald A. Falk, Anita Guerrini, Marcus Hall, Jim Harris, Richard J. Hobbs, Stephen T. Jackson, et al., "The Changing Role of History in Restoration Ecology," *Frontiers in Ecology and the Environment* 12, no. 9 (November 2014): 499–506.

21. Higgs et al., "The Changing Role of History," 503–504.

22. Stuart K. Allison, *Ecological Restoration and Environmental Change: Renewing Damaged Ecosystems* (London: Routledge, 2012).

23. Restoration ecologist quoted in Yasha Rohwer and Emma Marris, "Renaming Restoration: Conceptualizing and Justifying the Activity as a Restoration of Lost Moral Value rather than a Return to a Previous State," *Restoration Ecology* 24, no. 5 (September 2016): 676.

24. Restoration ecology, and specifically the insistence on novel ecosystems, has generated debate among ecologists, some of whom see it as the "Trojan horse of conservation" that could lead to an anything goes conceptualization of what is natural and of conservation value. See Carolina Murcia, James Aronson, Gustavo H. Kattan, David Moreno-Mateos, Kingsley Dixon, and Daniel Simberloff, "A Critique of the 'Novel Ecosystem' Concept," *Trends in Ecology and Evolution* 29, no. 10 (October 2014): 548–553. See also Rachel J. Standish, Allen Thompson, Eric S. Higgs, and Stephen Murphy, "Concerns about Novel Ecosystems," in *Novel Ecosystems: Intervening in the New Ecological World Order*, ed. Richard J. Hobbs, Eric S. Higgs, and Carol M. Hall (New York: John Wiley and Sons, 2013), 296–309.

25. Robyn Fivush and Catherine A. Haden, *Autobiographical Memory and the Construction of a Narrative Self: Developmental and Cultural Perspectives* (Mahwah, NJ: Lawrence Erlbaum and Associates, 2003); Anne Wilson and Michael Ross, "The Identity Function of Autobiographical Memory: Time Is on Our Side," *Memory* 11, no. 2 (March 2003): 137–149.

26. J. David Sweatt, *Mechanisms of Memory* (London: Elsevier, 2010). For a social science treatment, see Hamzah Muzaini, "On the Matter of Forgetting and 'Memory Returns,'" *Transactions of the Institute of British Geographers* 40, no. 1 (January 2015): 102–112.

27. The literature on post-traumatic stress syndrome, which includes intrusive memories and flashbacks, is large. For an introduction, see Bessel van der Kolk, *The Body Keeps the Score: Brain, Mind, and Body in the Healing of Trauma* (New York: Viking, 2014); Rachel Yehuda, "Post-Traumatic Stress Disorder," *New England Journal of Medicine* 346 (January 2002): 108–114.

28. Aleida Assmann, *Shadows of Trauma: Memory and the Politics of Postwar Identity* (New York: Fordham University Press, 2016), 12–13.

29. Maurice Halbwachs, *On Collective Memory*, 48, quoted in Astrid Erll, *Memory in Culture* (London: Palgrave Macmillan, 2011), 16.

30. Barbara A. Misztal, *Theories of Social Remembering* (Philadelphia: Open University Press, 2003), 15–19.

31. James W. Pennebaker and Becky L. Banasik, "On the Creation and Maintenance of Collective Memories: History as Social Psychology," in *Collective Memory of Political Events: Social Psychological Perspectives*, ed. James W. Pennebaker, Dario Paez, and Bernard Rimé (Mahwah, NJ: Lawrence Erlbaum Associates, 1997), 3–20. For Germany, see Sabine Bode, *Die vergessene Generation: Die Kriegskinder brechen ihr Schweigen* (Stuttgart: Klett Cotta Verlag, 2015) and Harald Jähner, *Aftermath: Life in the Fallout of the Third Reich, 1945–1955* (New York: Alfred Knopf, 2022).

32. Jan Assmann, "Communicative and Cultural Memory," in *Cultural Memories: The Geographical Point of View*, ed. Peter Meusburger, Michael Heffernan, and Edgar Wunder (Dordrecht: Springer, 2011), 17–18.

33. Assmann, *Shadows of Trauma*, 41.

34. Simon Schama, *Landscape and Memory* (New York: Alfred Knopf, 1995), 61. See also Tim Edensor, "National Identity and the Politics of Memory: Remembering Bruce and Wallace in Symbolic Space," *Environment and Planning D* 29 (1997): 175–194; David Harvey, "Monument and Myth," *Annals of the Association of American Geographers* 69, no. 3 (September 1979): 362–381.

35. Karen Till, *The New Berlin: Memory, Politics, Place* (Minneapolis: University of Minnesota Press, 2005), 8. See also Brian Ladd, *The Ghosts of Berlin: Confronting German History in the Urban Landscape* (Chicago: University of Chicago Press, 2008).

36. Adam Searle, "Spectral Ecologies: De/extinction in the Pyrenees," *Transactions of the Institute of British Geographers* 47 (2022):167–183.

37. Gordon F. Avery, *Ghostly Matters: Haunting and the Sociological Imagination* (Minneapolis: University of Minnesota Press, 2008), xvi, 8.

38. "Trauma," American Psychological Association, accessed July 31, 2019, https://www.apa.org/topics/trauma/.

39. Assmann, *Shadows of Trauma*, 74.

40. The Holocaust has been studied as such a collective trauma. See, for example, Martin S. Bergmann and Milton E. Jucovy, eds., *Generations of the Holocaust* (New York: Columbia University Press, 1990); Hadas Wiseman and Jacques P. Barber, *Echoes of the Trauma: Relational Themes and Emotions in Children of Holocaust Survivors* (Cambridge: Cambridge University Press, 2008).

41. Dominick LaCapra, *Writing History, Writing Trauma* (Baltimore: Johns Hopkins University Press, 2014), 144.

42. Janet Donohue, "The Betweenness of Monuments," in *Interpreting Nature: The Emerging Field of Environmental Hermeneutics*, ed. Forrest Clingerman, Brian Treanor, Martin Drenthen, and David Utsler (New York: Fordham University Press, 2013), 265, 266.

43. Marion Hourdequin and David Havlick, eds., *Restoring Layered Landscapes* (New York: Oxford University Press, 2016).

44. Tim Ingold, *The Perception of the Environment: Essays on Livelihood, Dwelling and Skill* (New York: Routledge, 2000), 189.

45. James Feldman, *Storied Wilderness: Rewilding the Apostle Islands* (Seattle: University of Washington Press, 2013), 123. See also Laura Alice Watt, *The Paradox of Preservation: Wilderness and Working Landscapes at Point Reyes National Seashore* (Oakland: University of California Press, 2016).

46. Chris Pearson, Peter Coates, and Tim Cole, "Introduction: Beneath the Camouflage: Revealing Militarized Landscapes," in *Militarized Landscapes: From Gettysburg to Salisbury Plain*, ed. Chris Pearson, Peter Coates, and Tim Cole (London: Bloomsbury, 2010), 1–18.

47. Götz Ellwanger, Axel Ssymank, and Mareike Vischer-Leopold, *Erhaltung von Offenlandlebensräumen auf aktiven und ehemaligen militärischen Übungsflächen* (Bonn: BfN, 2012); David G. Havlick, *Bombs Away: Militarization, Conservation, and Ecological Restoration* (Chicago: University of Chicago Press, 2018).

48. Julia Adeney Thomas, "The Exquisite Corpses of Nature and History: The Case of the Korean DMZ," in *Militarized Landscapes: From Gettysburg to Salisbury Plain*, ed. Chris Pearson, Peter Coates, and Tim Cole (London: Bloomsbury, 2010), 161.

49. Caitlin DeSilvey, *Curated Decay: Heritage beyond Saving* (Minneapolis: University of Minnesota Press, 2017), 35–36.

50. David Foster, Frederick Swanson, John Aber, Ingrid Burke, Nicholas Brokaw, David Tilman, and Alan Knapp, "The Importance of Land-Use Legacies to Ecology and Conservation," *BioScience* 53, no. 1 (January 2003): 77–88; Stephen Pyne, *Fire: A Brief History* (Seattle: University of Washington Press, 2019).

51. Monica Gagliano, Michael Renton, Martial Depczynski, and Stefano Mancuso, "Experience Teaches Plants to Learn Faster and Forget Slower in Environments Where It Matters," *Oecologia* 175, no. 1 (May 2014): 63–72; Yuehui He and Zicong Li, "Epigenetic Environmental Memories in Plants: Establishment, Maintenance, and Reprogramming," *Trends in Genetics* 34, no. 11 (November 2018): 856–866.

52. Cecile Rohwedder, "Deep in the Forest, Bambi Remains the Cold War's Last Prisoner," *Wall Street Journal*, November 4, 2009, https://www.wsj.com/articles/SB125729481234926717. See also interviews with Pavel Sustr, lead biologist of the study, such as "For Red Deer, Iron Curtain Habits Die Hard," NPR, March 1, 2014, https://www.npr.org/2014/05/01/3087 37872/for-red-deer-iron-curtain-habits-die-hard.

53. Chris Pearson, "Remembering Resistance: The 'More-Than-Human' Memorial Landscapes at the Vercors and Larzac, France," *Cultural History* 2, no. 2 (2013): 199–212.

54. James McGaugh, *Memory and Emotion: The Making of Lasting Memories* (New York: Columbia University Press, 2006).

55. Misztal, *Theories of Social Remembering*, 80.

56. Phyllis Windle, "The Ecology of Grief," *BioScience* 42, no. 5 (May 1992): 365.

57. Glenn Albrecht, Gina-Maree Sartore, Linda Connor, Nick Higginbotham, Sonia Freeman, Brian Kelly, and Helen Stain, et al., "Solastalgia: The Distress Caused by Environmental Change," *Australasian Psychiatry* 15, suppl. 1 (February 2007): S95–S98.

58. Ashlee Cunsolo and Neville R. Ellis, "Ecological Grief as a Mental Health Response to Climate Change-Related Loss," *Nature Climate Change* 8 (April 2018): 275–281.

59. Olivia Angé and David Berliner, eds., *Ecological Nostalgias: Memory, Affect and Creativity in Times of Ecological Upheavals* (New York: Berghahn Books, 2021).

60. Erich Fromm, *The Anatomy of Human Destructiveness* (New York: Holt, Rinehart and Winston, 1973), 366; Edward O. Wilson, *Biophilia* (Cambridge, MA: Harvard University Press, 1984). For an anthropological perspective, see also Kay Milton, *Loving Nature: Towards an Ecology of Emotion* (New York: Routledge, 2003).

CHAPTER 2

1. Klaus Schroeder and Jochen Staadt, *Die Todesopfer des DDR-Grenzregimes an der innerdeutschen Grenze 1949–1989: Ein biographisches Handbuch* (Berlin: Forschungsverbund SED-Staat, 2017).

2. Bernd Eisenfeld and Roger Engelmann, *13.8.1961: Mauerbau—Fluchtbewegung und Machtsicherung* (Bremen: Edition Temmen, 2001). These two historians put the number of border-related deaths at 809, of which 250 occurred at the Berlin Wall, 370 along the border dividing East and West Germany, and 189 due to drownings in the Baltic Sea.

3. Peter Joachim Lapp, *Grenzregime der DDR* (Aachen: Helios, 2013). For a more oral history-based understanding of life along the border, see Andreas Hartmann and Sabine Künsting, *Grenzgeschichten: Berichte aus dem deutschen Niemandsland* (Frankfurt am Main: Fischer, 1990).

4. Inge Bennewitz and Rainer Potratz, *Zwangsaussiedlungen an der innerdeutschen Grenze: Analysen und Dokumente* (Berlin: Ch. Links, 2012).

5. Edith Sheffer, *Burned Bridge: How East and West Germans Made the Iron Curtain* (New York: Oxford University Press, 2011), 102–103.

6. Sagi Schaefer, *States of Division: Borders and Boundary Formation in Cold War Rural Germany* (New York: Oxford University Press, 2014), 63.

7. Astrid Eckert, *West Germany and the Iron Curtain: Environment, Economy, and Culture in the Borderlands* (New York: Oxford University Press, 2019).

8. Schaefer, *States of Division*, 83–84, 138, 118, 152.

9. Arvid Nelson, *Cold War Ecology: Forests, Farms, and People in the East German Landscape, 1945–1989* (New Haven, CT: Yale University Press, 2005), 110.

10. Quoted in Nelson, *Cold War Ecology*, 111.

11. Nelson, *Cold War Ecology*, 112.

12. The German word *Aufarbeitung* has no equivalent in English. It means something close to "reckoning with" or "processing" the past: a critical and self-interrogating engagement with complicated histories. It is used frequently in the context of the German approach to its Nazi past as well as the Sozialistische Einheitspartei Deutschland (SED) regime of the GDR.

13. Ruth Ebbinghaus, "Psychische Langzeitfolgen und Probleme in der Kausalitätsbegutachtung nach politischer Verfolgung in der ehemaligen SBZ und DDR," in *Übersicht über Beratungsangebote für Opfer politischer Verfolgung in der SBZ/DDR*, 7th ed. (Berlin: Bundesstiftung zur Aufarbeitung der SED-Diktatur, 2020), 23–32. Multiple studies have shown that trauma remains prevalent among survivors of the SED persecution tactics. See Andreas Maercker, Ira Gäbler, and Matthias Schützwohl, "Verläufe von Traumafolgen bei ehemaligen politisch Inhaftierten der DDR," *Nervenarzt* 84, no. 1 (2013): 72–78.

14. Ebbinghaus, "Psychische Langzeitfolgen," 25–26.

15. Peter Wensierski, "Wir haben Angst um unsere Kinder," *Der Spiegel* 29 (1985): 62–68; Schaefer, *States of Division*, 151–152.

16. Andreas Grohmann, W. Winter, and H. Ottenwälder, "Kurzbericht der Fachkommission Soforthilfe Trinkwasser (FKST) über mögliche Beeinträchtigungen des Trinkwassers durch Pestizide aus dem ehemaligen Grenzstreifen," *NNA Mitteilungen* 5, no. 3 (1994): 30–33; Norbert Litz, "Zur Kenntnis der Belastungssituation durch Herbizide im Bereich ehemaliger Grenzstreifen," *Nachrichtenblatt des Deutschen Pflanzenschutzdienstes* 43, no. 12 (1991): 257–261.

17. Quoted in Eckert, *West Germany and the Iron Curtain*, 166.

18. Aaron D. Flesch, Clinton W. Epps, James W. Cain III, Matt Clark, Paul R. Krausman, and John R. Morgart, "Potential Effects of the United States–Mexico Border Fence on Wildlife," *Conservation Biology* 24, no. 1 (February 2010): 171–181; Lesley Evans Ogden, "Border Walls and Biodiversity: New Barriers, New Horizons," *BioScience* 67 no. 6 (June 2017): 498–505.

19. Trevor Wild and Philip Jones, "From Peripherality to New Centrality? Transformation of Germany's Zonenrandgebiet," *Geography* 78, no. 3 (1993): 281–294.

20. Eckert, *West Germany and the Iron Curtain*, chapter 5; William E. Stacy, *US Army Border Operations in Germany, 1945–1983* (Heidelberg: Military History Office, 1984), https://history.army.mil/documents/BorderOps/content.htm.

21. Norbert Theiss, "Lebensraum Grenzstreifen," *Ornithologischer Anzeiger* 32 (1993): 6.

22. Eckert, *West Germany and the Iron Curtain*, 169–171.

23. David Blackbourn, *The Conquest of Nature: Water, Landscape, and the Making of Modern Germany* (New York: W. W. Norton and Company, 2007).

24. Frank Spundflasch, "Renaturierung des Fließgewässers Föritz: Ein Beitrag zur Umsetzung der Europäischen Wasserrahmenrichtlinie," in *Bericht zur Landentwicklung 2005* (Erfurt: Thüringer Ministerium für Landwirtschaft, Naturschutz und Umwelt, 2005), 45–49.

25. The species is an indicator of a healthy stream. It has disappeared from 90 percent of its former range, and is classified as endangered across Europe and especially in Germany. See IUCN, "Thick Shelled River Mussel (Unio crassus)," accessed June 5, 2020, https://www.iucnredlist.org/species/22736/42465628#habitat-ecology.

26. Interview with the author, September 29, 2021.

27. Heinz Sielmann, dir., *Expeditionen ins Tierreich: Tiere im Schatten der Grenze*, 1988, https://www.ndr.de/fernsehen/sendungen/expeditionen_ins_tierreich/expeditionen249.html.

28. Interview with the author, September 29, 2021.

29. As part of political engagement around forest die-offs (*Waldsterben*) in the late 1980s, West German politicians from Bavaria traveled to the GDR to encourage cross-border action against air pollution. One of the delegates on this trip was Weiger, who used the time to make connections with East German environmentalists. Thirty new names were included on the invitee list to the meeting in Hof. See Martin Geilhufe, "Ökologische Erinnerungsorte: Das Grüne Band," October 2012, http://www.umweltunderinnerung.de/index.php/kapitelseiten/oekologische-zeiten/96-das-gruene-band.

30. Hubert Weiger, letter to concerned environmentalists, November 30, 1989. Copy with BUND Green Belt office in Nuremberg.

31. Weiger, letter to concerned environmentalists.

32. Phil McKenna, "The Boys Who Loved Birds," Medium, February 16, 2015, https://medium.com/thebigroundtable/the-boys-who-loved-birds-cd6e117a608.

33. "Resolution," Bund Naturschutz in Bayern, December 9, 1989. Copy with BUND Green Belt office in Nuremberg.

34. Grenzstreifenkartierung, 234. Copy with Zweckverband Grünes Band Rodachtal–Lange Berge–Steinachtal, Coburg.

35. BUND, *Das Grüne Band—Dauereinsatz für eine Vision* (Nuremberg: BUND Projektbüro Grünes Band, 2019), 18–19.

36. BUND, *Das Grüne Band*, 14.

37. More precisely the finance ministry along with the Land Utilization and Administration Agency (Bodenverwertungs und -verwaltungs GmbH), which specialized in the privatization of former GDR land.

38. BUND, *Das Grüne Band*, 20.

39. "Grünes Band: Entscheidender Meilenstein für den Naturschutz in Deutschland erreicht?," Bundesamt für Naturschutz (BfN) press release, March 25, 2003, https://www.bund-natur schutz.de/pressemitteilungen/gruenes-band-8211-entscheidender-meilenstein-fuer-den -naturschutz-in-deutschland-erreicht-1.html.

40. BUND, *Das Grüne Band*, 20.

41. BfN, "Erlebnis Grünes Band," BfN, accessed March 2, 2011, https://www.bfn.de/foerderung /e-e-vorhaben/liste-abgeschlossener-vorhaben/e-e-abgschl-steckbriefe-biotopschutz/erlebni -gruenes-band.html; Liana Geidezis, Thomas Bausch, and Helmut Schlumprecht, "Erlebnis Grünes Band: Entwicklung und Nutzung von Synergien zwischen Naturschutz und Touris-mus," *Natur und Landschaft* 86, no. 12 (2011): 539–542.

42. Geidezis, Bausch, and Schlumprecht, "Erlebnis Grünes Band," 539.

43. Nils M. Franke, *40 Jahre BUND: Die Geschichte des Bund für Umwelt und Naturschutz Deutschland e.V. 1975–2015* (Berlin: BUND, 2015), 49.

44. Geidezis, Bausch, and Schlumprecht, "Erlebnis Grünes Band," 540.

45. See, for example, Thuringian forest, https://www.thueringer-wald.com/urlaub-wandern-win ter/erlebnis-gruenes-band-111700.html; Franconian forest, https://www.frankenwald-tour ismus.de/de/bei-uns/gastgeber/arrangements/erlebnis-gruenes-band.html; Harz mountains, https://www.harzinfo.de/natur-pur/gruenes-band.html.

46. Ulrich Harteisen, Silke Neumeyer, Susanne Schlagbauer, Kilian Bizer, Stephan Hensel, and Lukas Krüger, *Grünes Band: Modellregion für Nachhaltigkeit* (Göttingen: Universitätsverlag, 2010), 243.

47. BUND, "Aktuelle Projekte am Grünen Band," accessed August 27, 2019, https://www.bund .net/themen/gruenes-band/aktuelle-projekte/#c1196.

48. Bundesumweltministerin Hendricks: "Das Grüne Band kann Vorbildcharakter für gutes Zusammenwirken von der Landwirtschaft mit Naturschutz entfalten," BUND press release, August 15, 2017, https://www.bund-niedersachsen.de/fileadmin/niedersachsen/publika tionen/pressemitteilungen/2017/2017-08-15_BUND_PM_Bundesumweltministerin-Hen dricks_Gruenes_Band.pdf.

49. BfN, "Lückenschluss Grünes Band: Sicherung der Biologischen Vielfalt durch Weiter-entwicklung des Grünen Bandes als zentrale Achse des nationalen Biotopverbunds," accessed October 10, 2020, https://biologischevielfalt.bfn.de/bundesprogramm/projekte/projekt beschreibungen/lueckenschluss-gruenes-band-sicherung-der-biologischen-vielfalt-durch -weiterentwicklung-des-gruenen-bandes-als-zentrale-achse-des-nationalen-biotopverbunds .html.

50. "Viele Lücken am Grünen Band erfolgreich geschlossen und Artenvielfalt gestärkt: Bilanz des achtjährigen Projekts 'Lückenschluss Grünes Band,'" BUND press release, December 8, 2020, https://www.bund.net/service/presse/pressemitteilungen/detail/news/viele-lue cken-am-gruenen-band-erfolgreich-geschlossen-und-artenvielfalt-gestaerkt-bilanz-des-acht jaehrigen-projekts-lueckenschluss-gruenes-band.

51. BfN, "Lückenschluss Grünes Band."

52. BUND staff members, interviews with the author, June 14, 2016, and June 22, 2016.

53. Liana Geidezis, Daniela Leitzbach, and Helmut Schlumprecht, *Aktualisierung der Bestandsaufnahme Grünes Band mit Schwerpunkt auf den Veränderungen in den Offenlandbereichen* (Bonn: BfN, 2015).

54. BUND, *Das Grüne Band: Ein Handlungsleitfaden* (Bonn: BfN, 2001), 43.

55. Kersten Hänel and Heinrich Reck, *Nationwide Priorities for Re-Linking Ecosystems* (Bonn: BfN, 2010). There is considerable uncertainty among scientists regarding ecological networks, however, since their effectiveness varies hugely based on species or taxonomic order. And corridors crafted in the interest of one species may fragment the habitat of another, leading to its decline or extinction. This raises ethical and biopolitical questions about which species ought to be saved and which species should bear the cost.

56. Markus Leibenath, "Biotopverbund und räumliche Koordination: Chancen, Risiken und Nebenwirkungen des Metaphernpaares 'Fragmentierung—Biotopverbund,'" *Raumforschung und Raumordnung* 68 (2010): 91–101; Henny van der Windt and J. A. A. Swart, "Ecological Corridors, Connecting Science and Politics: The Case of the Green River in the Netherlands," *Journal of Applied Ecology* 45 (2008): 124–132.

57. H. Strauss, "Zur Diskussion über Biotopverbundsysteme: Versuch einer kritischen Bestandsaufnahme," *Natur und Landschaft* 63, no. 9 (1988): 374–378; quoted in Leibenath, "Biotopverbund und räumliche Koordination," 98.

58. Geidezis, Leitzbach, and Schlumprecht, *Aktualisierung*, 4.

59. Thorsten Aßmann, Estève Boutaud, Peter Finck, Werner Härdtle, Diethart Matthies, Dorothea Nolte, Goddert von Oheimb, et al., *Halboffene Verbundkorridore: Ökologische Funktion, Leitbilder und Praxis-Leitfaden* (Bonn: BfN, 2016), 29.

60. BUND, *Biotopmanagement im Grünen Band* (Nuremberg: BUND Projektbüro Grünes Band, 2012), 10.

61. Bund Naturschutz in Bayern, e.V., "Das Grüne Band: Lebenslinie Todesstreifen." Copy with BUND Green Belt office in Nuremberg.

62. Interview with the author, September 29, 2021.

63. "Stasi" is short for "Ministerium für Staatssicherheit," the GDR Ministry for State Security, which was involved in surveilling much of the East German population. It resembled the Russian KGB with which it had liaisons.

64. Maren Ullrich, *Geteilte Ansichten: Erinnerungslandschaft deutsch-deutsche Grenze* (Berlin: Aufbau, 2006), 198–208.

65. Melanie Kreutz, "Ein lebendiges Denkmal für Freiheit und Demokratie," *Politik und Kultur* 6, no. 20 (2020): 23, https://www.kulturrat.de/wp-content/uploads/2020/05/puk06-20.pdf.

66. See, for example, Union der Opferverbände kommunistischer Gewaltherrschaft, "Mahnmal gegen das Vergessen: Am Grünen Band zwischen Mechau und Bockleben wird an getöteten Grenzflüchtling erinnert," August 2018, https://www.uokg.de/2018/08/rainer-burgis-wird -mit-mahnmal-geehrt/.

67. Kreutz, "Ein lebendiges Denkmal." See also Karin Kowol, "Grenzen trennen—Natur verbin-det: Jugendbegegnungen am Grünen Band," 2020, https://www.bund-thueringen.de/service /presse/detail/news/grenzen-trennen-natur-verbindet-jugendbegegnungen-am-gruenen-band/.

68. BUND, "Lenzener Erklärung zum Grünen Band," September 29, 2019, https://www.bund .net/service/publikationen/detail/publication/lenzener-erklaerung-zum-gruenen-band/.

69. SED is known in English as the East German Communist Party, which ruled the GDR throughout the country's existence.

70. BUND, "Lenzener Erklärung," 3.

71. Stolpersteine, literally "stumbling stones" (the word also carries over into the English figure of speech "stumbling blocks"), were developed by the German artist Gunter Demming in the early 1990s. They are small brass cobblestones that are placed in the pavement in front of the last-known residence of Holocaust victims, detailing their date of birth, date of deportation, and if known, date and location of their death. Family members, communities, and even local schoolchildren can apply to have a Stolperstein placed at an address if research supports its installation there.

72. Frank Uekötter, *The Greenest Nation? A New History of German Environmentalism* (Cambridge, MA: MIT Press, 2015), 9.

73. BfN, *Naturbewusstsein 2017* (Bonn: BfN, 2017), 37–38, 49.

74. BfN, *Die Lage der Natur in Deutschland: Ergebnisse von EU-Vogelschutz- und FFH-Bericht* (Bonn: BfN, 2014).

75. Nelson, *Cold War Ecology.*

76. Arnd Bauernkämper, "The Industrialization of Agriculture and Its Consequences for the Natural Environment: An Inter-German Comparative Perspective," *Historical Social Research* 29, no. 3 (2004): 124–149; Frank Uekötter, *Die Wahrheit ist auf dem Feld: Eine Wissensgeschichte der deutschen Landwirtschaft* (Göttingen: Vandenhoeck und Ruprecht, 2012), chapters 6–7.

77. Caspar A. Hallmann, Martin Sorg, Eelke Jongejans, Henk Siepel, Nick Hofland, Heinz Schwan, Werner Stenmans, et al., "More Than 75 Percent Decline over 27 Years in Total Flying Insect Biomass in Protected Areas," *PLoS ONE* 12, no. 10 (October 2017): e0185809.

78. "NABU bestätigt Vogelsterben in der Agrarlandschaft," Deutschlandfunk, https://www .deutschlandfunk.de/artenschwund-nabu-bestaetigt-vogelsterben-in-der.697.de.html

?dram:article_id=448355; Pan-European Common Bird Monitoring Scheme (PECBMS), "The State of Common European Birds," accessed July 15, 2019, https://pecbms.info/wp-content/uploads/2019/03/sate-of-common-european-birds-2018-download.pdf.

79. PECBMS, "The State of Common European Birds"; Monika C. M. Müller, ed., *Viele Vögel sind schon weg: Vogelsterben und Biodiversität—Ursachen und Gegenmassnahmen* (Rudolstadt: Harfe Verlag, 2018).

80. Dieter Kirschke, Astrid Häger, and Julia Christiane Schmid, "New Trends and Drivers for Agricultural Land Use in Germany," in *Sustainable Land Management in a European Context: A Co-Design Approach*, ed. Thomas Weith, Tim Barkmann, Nadin Gaasch, Sebastian Rogga, Christian Strauß, and Jana Zscheischler (Cham, Switzerland: Springer 2021), 39–61.

81. BfN, *Die Lage der Natur*, 15.

82. According to one source, over 250,000 wild animals are killed in traffic each year in Germany. See Bundesministerium für Umwelt, Naturschutz und Reaktorsicherheit (BMU), *Bundesprogramm Wiedervernetzung: Grundlagen, Aktionsfelder, Zusammenarbeit* (Berlin: BMVI, 2012), 6.

83. Sebastian Knauer, "Die Endlos-Debatte über den Todesstreifen," *Der Spiegel*, November 4, 2005, https://www.spiegel.de/wissenschaft/natur/gruenes-band-die-endlos-debatte-ueber-den-todesstreifen-a-383228.html.

84. Phil McKenna, "The Boys Who Loved Birds," Medium, February 16, 2015, https://medium.com/thebigroundtable/the-boys-who-loved-birds-cd6e117a608.

85. Bundesministerium für Umwelt, Naturschutz, nukleare Sicherheit und Verbraucherschutz (BMUV), "Das Bundesprogramm Wiedervernetzung," accessed January 13, 2022, https://www.bmuv.de/download/das-bundesprogramm-wiedervernetzung.

CHAPTER 3

1. Reinhard Piechocki, Konrad Ott, Thomas Potthast, and Norbert Wiersbinski, eds., *Vilmer Thesen zu Grundsatzfragen des Naturschutzes* (Bonn: BfN, 2010), 41.

2. Thomas M. Lekan and Thomas M. Zeller, introduction to *Imagining the Nation in Nature: Landscape Preservation and German Identity, 1885–1945*, ed. Thomas M. Lekan and Thomas M. Zeller (Cambridge, MA: Harvard University Press, 2009), 3.

3. Thomas Kirchhoff and Ludwig Trepl, eds., *Vieldeutige Natur: Landschaft, Wildnis und Ökosystem als kulturgeschichtliche Phänomene* (Bielefeld: Transcript, 2009), 28; Frank Uekötter, *Die Wahrheit ist auf dem Feld: Eine Wissensgeschichte der deutschen Landwirtschaft* (Göttingen: Vandenhoeck und Ruprecht, 2012), 54–63.

4. Thomas Lekan, "A 'Noble Prospect': Tourism, Heimat, and Conservation on the Rhine, 1880–1914," *Journal of Modern History* 81, no. 4 (December 2009): 824–858.

5. Reinhard Piechocki, *Landschaft, Heimat, Wildnis: Schutz der Natur—aber welcher und warum?* (Munich: C. H. Beck, 2010), 134; Thomas Lekan and Thomas Zeller, "The Landscape of

German Environmental History," in *Germany's Nature: Cultural Landscapes and Environmental History*, ed. Thomas Zeller and Thomas Lekan (New Brunswick, NJ: Rutgers University Press), 4.

6. Piechocki, *Landschaft, Heimat, Wildnis*, 138.

7. Quoted in Piechocki, *Landschaft, Heimat, Wildnis*, 138.

8. Piechocki, *Landschaft, Heimat, Wildnis*, 138.

9. Susanne Scharnowski, *Heimat: Geschichte eines Missverständnisses* (Darmstadt: WBG, 2019), 35–36.

10. Peter Blickle, *Heimat: A Critical Theory of the German Idea of Homeland* (Rochester, NY: Camden House, 2002), 28.

11. Roderick Nash, *Wilderness and the American Mind* (New Haven, CT: Yale University Press, 2001); Max Oelschlaeger, *The Idea of Wilderness: From Prehistory to the Age of Ecology* (New Haven, CT: Yale University Press, 1993).

12. Blickle, *Heimat*, 121–122.

13. Frank Uekötter, *The Green and the Brown: A History of Conservation in Nazi Germany* (New York: Cambridge University Press, 2006).

14. Thomas Adam, "Die Verteidigung des Vertrauten: Zur Geschichte der Natur- und Umweltschutzbewegung in Deutschland seit Ende des 19. Jahrhunderts," *Zeitschrift für Politik* 45, no. 1 (1998): 24–26; Ute Hasenöhrl, *Zivilgesellschaft und Protest: Eine Geschichte der Naturschutz- und Umweltbewegung in Bayern 1945–1980* (Göttingen: Vandenhoeck und Ruprecht, 2011), 74.

15. Stefan Bargheer, "Apocalypse Adjourned: The Rise and Decline of Cold War Environmentalism in Germany," *Environmental Politics* 27, no. 6 (2018): 973–993.

16. Jens Ivo Engels, *Naturpolitik in der Bundesrepublik: Ideenwelt und politische Verhaltensstile in Naturschutz und Umweltbewegung 1950–1980* (Paderborn: Ferdinand Schöningh, 2006), 210.

17. Adam, "Die Verteidigung des Vertrauten," 39–40.

18. A complete accounting of the German environmental movement is beyond the scope of this book. Good summaries include William T. Markham, *Environmental Organizations in Modern Germany: Hardy Survivors in the Twentieth Century and Beyond* (New York: Berghahn Books, 2008); Roland Roth and Dieter Rucht, eds., *Die sozialen Bewegungen in Deutschland seit 1945: Ein Handbuch* (Frankfurt am Main: Campus, 2008); Dieter Rucht and Jochen Roose, "Zur Institutionalisierung von Bewegungen: Umweltverbände und Umweltprotest in der Bundesrepublik," in *Verbände und Demokratie in Deutschland*, ed. Annette Zimmer and Bernhard Weßels (Opladen: Leske+Budrich, 2001), 261–290.

19. The BN is the main pillar of the BUND, but was aided in its efforts by at least two other, smaller and less powerful West German organizations: Gruppe Ökologie and the Bund Natur- und Umweltschutz Baden-Württemberg. See Engels, *Naturpolitik*, 312.

20. Engels, *Naturpolitik*, 312. Among the luminaries who helped found the BUND are zoologist and documentary filmmaker Bernhard Grzimek and animal behaviorist Konrad Lorenz.

21. Adam, "Die Verteidigung des Vertrauten," 38.

22. Reinhard Piechocki, Konrad Ott, Thomas Potthast, and Norbert Wiersbinski, eds., *Vilmer Thesen zu Grundsatzfragen des Naturschutzes* (Bonn: BfN, 2010).

23. Hans-Werner Frohn, "Naturschutz und Staat 1880–1976: Von naturalen Memorialinseln zur Landschaftsökologie," in *Jetzt ist die Landschaft ein Katalog voller Wörter: Beiträge zur Sprache der Ökologie*, ed. Bernd Busch (Göttingen: Wallstein, 2007), 40.

24. Even more recent surveys in Germany show how widespread this belief still is. See Fritz Reusswig, "Lebensstile und Naturorientierungen: Gesellschaftliche Naturbilder und Einstellungen zum Naturschutz," in *Lebensstile und Nachhaltigkeit: Konzepte, Befunde und Potentiale*, ed. Dieter Rink (Wiesbaden: Springer, 2002), 156–180.

25. Eli Rubin, "The Greens, the Left, and the GDR: A Critical Reassessment," in *Ecologies of Socialisms: Germany, Nature, and the Left in History, Politics, and Culture*, ed. Sabine Mödersheim, Scott Moranda, and Eli Rubin (New York: Peter Lang, 2019), 190, 189.

26. Geography played a nontrivial factor here. For instance, West Germany had more rivers, and they had greater flow rates, making waste evacuation easier, while more mountainous terrain also gave West Germany more hydroelectric potential than its eastern neighbor. See Raymond Dominick, "Capitalism, Communism, and Environmental Protection: Lessons from the German Experience," *Environmental History* 3, no. 3 (July 1998): 324. For a longer discussion, see Friedhelm Naujoks, *Ökologische Erneuerung der ehemaligen DDR: Begrenzungsfaktor oder Impulsgeber für eine gesamtdeutsche Entwicklung?* (Bonn: JHW Dietz, 1991).

27. Rubin, "The Greens, the Left, and the GDR," 190. During the 1970s, the SED government briefly saw environmental policy as a way to gain recognition in the West and legitimize its centrally planned economy. The creation of the environmental ministry predated that of the FRG by sixteen years. The first oil crisis in 1974 abruptly ended this environmental period. See Joachim Radkau, *The Age of Ecology* (Malden, MA: Polity Press, 2013), 367.

28. Merrill E. Jones, "Origins of the East German Environmental Movement," *German Studies Review* 16, no. 2 (May 1993): 235–264; Mary Fulbrook, "The Limits of Totalitarianism: God, State and Society in the GDR," *Transactions of the Royal Historical Society* 7, no. 43 (1997): 25–52. The relationship between the church and East German state was tense and complicated, starting with the fact that socialism, as a stepping-stone to Communism, is supposedly atheist. At the time of German partition, over 90 percent of East Germans identified as Christian, however. The church had also been an important recourse for traumatized Germans recovering from Nazism, the war, and displacement.

29. Jones, "Origins of the East German Environmental Movement," 258.

30. On November 16, 1982, the GDR Council of Ministers announced the Directive for the Classification of Environmental Data, which made any information on ecological problems

a state secret. See Peter Wensierski, *Von oben nach unten wächts gar nichts: Umweltzerstörung und Protest in der DDR* (Reinbek: Fischer Verlag, 1986).

31. Jones, "Origins of the East German Environmental Movement," 243, 259.

32. Sandra Chaney, "Protecting Nature in a Divided Nation: Conservation in the Two Germanys, 1945–1972," in *Germany's Nature: Cultural Landscapes and Environmental History*, ed. Thomas Lekan and Thomas Zeller (New Brunswick, NJ: Rutgers University Press, 2005), 222.

33. Chaney, "Protecting Nature in a Divided Nation," 224.

34. This reinterpretation must be understood in the postwar context where millions of ethnic Germans, expulsed from the eastern provinces and pushed into a now much smaller German territory, needed to be settled and housed. Rather than having these populations long for their old homes, now in Soviet territory, the authorities attempted to reeducate them to loosen their ties with their old homelands and ease their transition to the GDR. See Heike Amos, *Die Vertriebenenpolitik der SED 1949 bis 1990* (Munich: Oldenbourg Wissenschaftsverlag, 2009).

35. While the Berlin Wall came down on November 9, 1989, the GDR continued to exist until its official dissolution on October 3, 1990, celebrated today in Germany as the Day of Reunification.

36. Tobias Huff, "Environmental Policy in the GDR: Principles, Restrictions Failure, and Legacy," in *Ecologies of Socialisms: Germany, Nature, and the Left in History, Politics, and Culture*, ed. Sabine Mödersheim, Scott Moranda, and Eli Rubin (New York: Peter Lang, 2019), 56; Michael Succow, Lebrecht Jeschke, and Hans Dieter Knapp, *Naturschutz in Deutschland: Rückblicke—Einblicke—Ausblicke* (Munich: Ch. Links, 2013). The protected areas comprised five national parks (Vorpommersche Boddenlandschaft, Jasmund, Müritz, Sächsische Schweiz, and Hochharz), six biosphere reserves (Südost-Rügen, Schorfheide-Chorin, Spreewald, Mittlere Elbe, Rhön, and Vessertal), and three nature parks (Drömling, Schaalsee, and Märkische Schweiz).

37. Radkau, *The Age of Ecology*, 371.

38. Markham, *Environmental Organizations in Modern Germany*, 142–147.

39. Reinhard Falter, "Rettet die Natur vor den Umweltschützern," *Garten und Landschaft* 7 (1994): 4–6.

40. Quoted in Sandra Chaney, *Nature of the Miracle Years: Conservation in West Germany 1945–1975* (New York: Berghahn, 2012), 185.

41. Reusswig, "Lebensstile und Naturorientierungen," 173.

42. German filmmaker Edgar Reitz, quoted in David Morley and Kevin Robins, *Spaces of Identity* (London: Routledge, 1995), 10.

43. Blickle, *Heimat*, 149.

44. Naika Foroutan and Jana Hensel, *Die Gesellschaft der Anderen* (Berlin: Aufbau Verlag, 2020); Fritz Reusswig, "Heimat und politische Parteien," in *Heimat: Ein vielfältiges Konstrukt*, ed. Martina Hülz, Olaf Kühne, and Florian Weber (Wiesbaden: Springer, 2019), 371–390.

CHAPTER 4

1. Ralf-Uwe Beck, "Baumkreuz: Erinnerungsort. Denkmal. Skulptur," accessed September 20, 2021, https://www.bund-thueringen.de/fileadmin/thueringen/Gruenes_Band/BAUM KREUZ_Info.pdf.

2. Rhea Thönges-Stringaris, "Joseph Beuys: 7000 Eichen—Eine unsichtbare Skulptur," Stiftung 7000 Eichen, accessed October 14, 2021, http://www.7000eichen.de/?id=32.

3. Omnibus für Direkte Demokratie, "30 Jahre friedliche Revolution: Baumkreuz—Ein Ort, an dem die Seele nachkommen kann," accessed September 19, 2021, https://www.youtube .com/watch?v=w30ZlZAKB7I.

4. Lynn Meskell, "An Anthropology of Absence: Commentary," in *An Anthropology of Absence: Materializations of Transcendence and Loss*, ed. Bille Mikkel, Frida Hastrup, and Tim Flohr Soerensen (New York: Springer, 2010), 213.

5. CABI Invasive Species Compendium, "Chalara fraxinea," accessed October 16, 2021, https:// www.cabi.org/isc/datasheet/108083#tosummaryOfInvasiveness.

6. Norman Meißner, "Ifta: Neue Bäume am früheren Todesstreifen," *Thüringer Allgemeine Zeitung*, November 4, 2019, https://www.thueringer-allgemeine.de/regionen/eisenach/ifta-neue -baeume-am-frueheren-todesstreifen-id227541765.html.

7. Annette Kaminsky, ed., *Orte des Erinnerns: Gedenkzeichen, Gedenkstätten und Museen zur Diktatur in SBZ und DDR* (Berlin: Ch. Links, 2016), 342.

8. Maren Ullrich, *Geteilte Ansichten: Erinnerungslandschaft deutsch-deutsche Grenze* (Berlin: Aufbau, 2006), 275.

9. BUND, *Das Grüne Band: Ein Handlungsleitfaden* (Bonn: BfN, 2001), 67.

10. Ullrich, *Geteilte Ansichten*, 278.

11. Paul Cloke and Owain Jones, *Tree Cultures: The Place of Trees and Trees in Their Place* (Oxford: Routledge, 2002).

12. Ursula Breymayer and Bernd Ulrich, *Unter Bäumen: Die Deutschen und der Wald* (Dresden: Sandstein, 2011); Simon Schama, *Landscape and Memory* (New York: Alfred Knopf, 1995), chapter 2.

13. Douglas Davies, "The Evocative Symbolism of Trees," in *The Iconography of Landscape: Essays on the Symbolic Representation, Design and Use of Past Environments*, ed. David Cosgrove and Stephen Daniels (Cambridge: Cambridge University Press, 1989), 34.

14. Michael Perlman, *The Power of Trees: The Reforesting of the Soul* (Woodstock, CT: Spring Publications, 1994).

15. Paul Cloke and Eric Pawson, "Memorial Trees and Treescape Memories," *Environment and Planning D* 26 (2008): 107.

16. Caitlin DeSilvey, *Curated Decay: Heritage beyond Saving* (Minneapolis: University of Minnesota Press, 2017), 29.

17. Robert Ginsberg, *The Aesthetics of Ruins* (Amsterdam: Rodopi, 2004), 201.

18. Mikkel Bille, Frida Hastrup, and Tim Flohr Sørensen, "Introduction: An Anthropology of Absence," in *An Anthropology of Absence: Materializations of Transcendence and Loss*, ed. Mikkel Bille, Frida Hastrup, and Tim Flohr Soerensen (New York: Springer, 2010), 3–4.

19. Bille et al., "Introduction," 13.

20. Alexander Rekow, "Ein Dorf als stummer Zeuge," *Volksstimme*, January 25, 2018, https://www.volksstimme.de/lokal/salzwedel/ein-dorf-als-stummer-zeuge-872962.

21. Ginsberg, *The Aesthetics of Ruins*, 1.

22. Mario Goldstein, *Abenteuer Grünes Band: 100 Tage zu Fuss entlang der ehemaligen deutsch-deutschen Grenze* (Munich: Knesebeck, 2019).

23. For fuller biographies, see Klaus Schroeder and Jochen Staadt, *Die Todesopfer des DDR-Grenzregimes an der innerdeutschen Grenze 1949–1989: Ein biographisches Handbuch* (Berlin: Forschungsverbund SED-Staat, 2017).

24. Goldstein, *Abenteuer Grünes Band*, 37.

25. Goldstein, *Abenteuer Grünes Band*, 79.

26. Interview with the author, August 15, 2018.

27. Martin Hoondert, Paul Mutsaers, and William Arfman, eds., *Cultural Practices of Victimhood* (New York: Routledge, 2019); Christiane Wilke, "Recognizing Victimhood: Politics and Narratives of Rehabilitation in Germany," *Journal of Human Rights* 6, no. 4 (2007): 479–496.

28. There is already considerable debate in Germany over how to count border deaths and who is deserving of victimhood. See, for example, the discussion between border scholars in the online magazine *Deutschland Archiv* (published by the Bundeszentrale für politische Bildung, or Federal Agency for Civic Education), under the heading "Wer war Opfer des DDR-Grenzregimes? Ansichten zu einem umstrittenen Thema" (Who was a victim of the border regime? Perspectives on a controversial topic"), accessed July 15, 2021, https://www.bpb.de/themen/deutschlandarchiv/295078/wer-war-opfer-des-ddr-grenzregimes.

29. Neera M. Singh, "Introduction: Affective Ecologies and Conservation," *Conservation and Society* 16, no. 1 (2018): 1–7. On human and ecological relationships to/with/of/through matter, see Jane Bennett, *Vibrant Matter: A Political Ecology of Things* (Durham, NC: Duke University Press, 2010).

30. The following section draws heavily from Sonja K. Pieck, "What Stories Should a National Nature Monument Tell? Lessons from the German Green Belt," *Cultural Geographies* 26, no. 2 (2018): 195–210.

31. Marion Hourdequin, "Ecological Restoration, Continuity and Change: Negotiating History and Meaning in Layered Landscapes," in *Restoring Layered Landscapes: History, Ecology, and Culture*, ed. Marion Hourdequin and David Havlick (New York: Oxford University Press, 2016), 25. See also Martin Drenthen, "New Nature Narratives: Landscape Hermeneutics and Environmental Ethics," in *Interpreting Nature: The Emerging Field of Environmental Hermeneutics*, ed. Forrest Clingerman, Brian Treanor, Martin Drenthen, and David Utsler (New York: Fordham University Press, 2013), 225–241.

32. IUCN, "Category III: Natural Monument or Feature," accessed July 10, 2021, https://www.iucn.org/theme/protected-areas/about/protected-areas-categories/category-iii-natural-monument-or-feature.

33. The originating idea of a natural monument goes back to the American Antiquities Act of 1906.

34. Bundesministerium für Umwelt, Naturschutz und Nukleare Sicherheit (BMUV), "Kleine Nationalparks oder große Naturdenmäler?," accessed January 7, 2018, https://www.bmub.bund.de/themen/natur-biologische-vielfalt-arten/naturschutz-biologische-vielfalt/gebietsschutz-und-vernetzung/nationale-naturlandschaften/nationale-naturmonumente.

35. Nature conservation in Germany is federalized and thus a matter of the states (*Länder*) rather than the national government. Somewhat contradictorily, then, the designation of a national nature monument must proceed state by state and cannot be accomplished by a singular, national edict.

36. BUND, "Monumental: Das Grüne Band auf dem Weg zum nationalen Naturmonument: Thüringen hat den Anfang gemacht," accessed August 26, 2021, http://www.grünes-band-monumental.de.

37. *Monumental: Das Grüne Band ist auf dem Weg Nationales Naturmonument zu werden*, https://www.youtube.com/watch?v=nP4YF8aYt9Q.

38. BUND, *Spur in der Landschaft* (Erfurt: BUND Thüringen, 2012), 3–6, https://www.bund.net/fileadmin/user_upload_bund/publikationen/gruenes_band/gruenes_band_spur_in_der_landschaft.pdf.

39. Liana Geidezis, Daniela Leitzbach, and Helmut Schlumprecht, *Aktualisierung der Bestandsaufnahme Grünes Band mit Schwerpunkt auf den Veränderungen in den Offenlandbereichen* (Bonn: BfN Skripten, 2015), 4, https://www.bfn.de/fileadmin/BfN/service/Dokumente/skripten/Skript392.pdf

40. BUND, *Spur in der Landschaft*, 5.

41. For discussions of West Germany's relationship to the border, see Astrid Eckert, *West Germany and the Iron Curtain: Environment, Economy, and Culture in the Borderlands* (New York: Oxford University Press, 2019); Edith Scheffer, *Burned Bridge: How East and West Germans Made the Iron Curtain* (New York: Oxford University Press, 2011); Ullrich, *Geteilte Ansichten*. For commentary on the primacy of the West German gaze in Berlin Wall memorials, see Pertti Ahonen, *Death at the Berlin Wall* (Oxford: Oxford University Press, 2011), chapter 8; Carola

Rudnick, *Die andere Hälfte der Erinnerung: Die DDR in der deutschen Geschichtspolitik nach 1989* (Bielefeld: Transcript, 2011), chapter 3.

42. Alisdair Rogers, Noel Castree, and Rob Kitchin, *A Dictionary of Human Geography* (Oxford: Oxford University Press, 2013).

43. Wolfgang Haber, *Landwirtschaft und Naturschutz* (Weinheim: Wiley-VCH, 2014).

44. Peter Aufgebauer, Dietrich Denecke, Klaus Grote, Markus Krüsemann, Eckart Schröder, and Hans-Georg Wehling, *Das Eichsfeld: Ein deutscher Grenzraum* (Duderstadt: Mecke Druck und Verlag, 2002).

45. Thüringer Landesanstalt für Umwelt und Geologie, "Landkreis Eichsfeld: Landwirtschaftliche Standorbedingungen," accessed October 27, 2020, http://www.tlug-jena.de/uw_raum/umweltregional/eic/eic06.html.

46. This is the foundation created by Heinz Sielmann, the nature documentary filmmaker introduced in in chapter 2. Sielmann was among the first to articulate the vision of a protected area along the former border. He passed away in 2006, after which his wife, Inge, took the foundation's helm until her death in 2019.

47. Heinz Sielmann Stiftung, "Übersichts- und Detailkarten," accessed December 9, 2022, https://naturschutzgrossprojekt-eichsfeld-werratal.de/de/service/projektinfos/Detailkarten/index.php.

48. Christian Mühlhausen, "Gegen 'Grünes Band': Landwirte demonstrierten in Duderstadt," *HNA*, April 9, 2013, http://www.hna.de/lokales/goettingen/landwirte-demonstrierten-duderstadt-2846597.html; Kuno Mahnkopf, "Grünes Band Eichsfeld-Werratal: Landvolk bekräftigt Protest," *Göttinger Tageblatt*, April 14, 2014, http://www.goettinger-tageblatt.de/Duderstadt/Uebersicht/Gruenes-Band-Eichsfeld-Werratal-Landvolk-bekraeftigt-Protest.

49. Sagi Schaefer, *States of Division: Borders and Boundary Formation in Cold War Rural Germany* (New York: Oxford University Press, 2014), 59.

50. Interviews with the author, May 19, 2016, and May 24, 2016.

51. Interview with the author, May 24, 2016.

52. Claus Christian Mahlzahn, "Der Traum vom Leben in der Provinz," *Die Welt*, July 20, 2014, https://www.welt.de/print/wams/politik/article130348888/Der-Traum-vom-Leben-in-der-Provinz.html.

53. Interview with the author, May 19, 2016. Natura 2000, adopted in 1992, is an EU-wide policy aimed at increasing protected areas in Europe through ecological networks. See the European Commission, "The Habitats Directive," September 3, 2020, http://ec.europa.eu/environment/nature/legislation/habitatsdirective/index_en.htm.

54. Interview with the author, May 24, 2016.

55. Interview with the author, July 12, 2018.

56. Interview with the author, May 24, 2016.

57. The ThLG is an organization with ties to the Thuringian federal state focused on the sustainable development of rural areas and their agrarian structures. The work of its 130 staff members ranges broadly from land tenure and water management over to conservation and village development.

58. Interview with the author, July 13, 2018.

59. Interview with the author, July 13, 2018.

60. For these position statements, see Thüringer Landtag, "Diskussionsforum: Nationales Naturmonument und Grünes Band Thüringen," accessed October 22, 2021, http://forum-landtag .thueringen.de/dokument/nationales-naturmonument-und-gruenes-band-thueringen.

61. "Stellungnahme des Landesbeauftragen zur Aufarbeitung der SED-Diktatur zum Gesetzesentwurf Nationales Naturmonument 'Grünes Band Thüringen,'" June 13, 2018, especially 7–8, http://www.thla-thueringen.de/images/Stellungnahme_Umweltausschuss.pdf.

62. Christian Dietrich, "Einer Ökologisierung der Zeitgeschichte muss widerstanden werden," *Thüringer Landtagskurier* 10 (2016): 8, https://www.tlfdi.de/fileadmin/tlfdi/presse/landtags kurier_10_2016_internet.pdf.

63. Martin Henkel, mayor of Geisa, position statement, March 6, 2018, http://forum-landtag .thueringen.de/sites/default/files/downloads/Zuschrift%20Stadt%20Geisa.pdf. This point was echoed by officials of several other municipalities in their respective statements.

64. Jürgen Köpper, mayor of Frankenblick, position statement, February 13, 2018, http:// forum-landtag.thueringen.de/sites/default/files/downloads/Gemeinde%20Frankenblick .pdf.

65. Klaus Füßer and Katharina Nowak, "Rechtsprobleme bei der Unterschutzstellung des Grünen Bandes Thüringen," *Thüringer Verwaltungsblätter* 3 (2018).

66. Andreas Lukas, Thomas Jäger, and Franziska Heß, *Rechtsgutachten zur Unterschutzstellung des Grünen Bandes Thüringen als Nationales Naturmonument*, June 10, 2018, https://www .bund-thueringen.de/fileadmin/thueringen/Verfahrensbeteiligung/Baumann_Rechtsan waelte_-___Rechtsgutachten_Gruenes_Band_Thueringen_fuer_BUND_2018.pdf.

67. For the text of the 2017 draft law, see Thüringer Landtag, "Gesetzentwurf der Landesregierung: Thüringer Gesetz über das Nationale Naturmonument Grünes Band Thüringen," September 13, 2017, https://parldok.thueringer-landtag.de/ParlDok/dokument/64115 /thueringer_gesetz_ueber_das_nationale_naturmonument_gruenes_band_thueringen _thueringer_gruenes_band_gesetz_thuergbg.pdf. For the final version, see Thüringer Landtag, "Thüringer Gesetz über das Nationale Naturmonument Grünes Band Thüringen," December 18, 2018, https://umwelt.thueringen.de/fileadmin/001_TMUEN/Unsere_The men/Natur_Artenschutz/Gruenes_Band/thueringer_Gesetz_12.18_thurgbg.pdf.

68. This is most true for state-sponsored or state-supported nature conservation. There are certainly much older forms of conservation that are not connected to the state but rather anchored in communities, and I discuss some of these in chapter 6.

69. The logo of the Green Belt already signals this clearly: a green line running through reunified Germany.

70. See Ullrich, *Geteilte Ansichten*, 207–208.

71. See Grünes Band Deutschland, "Durch eine Errinerungslandschaft in der Altmark," October 28, 2019, https://www.30-jahre-gruenes-band.de/2019/10/28/durch-eine-erinnerungsland schaft-in-der-altmark/.

72. For more on this in another European country, see Katrina Z. S. Schwartz, *Nature and National Identity after Communism: Globalizing the Ethnoscape* (Pittsburgh: University of Pittsburgh Press, 2006).

73. Hans-Georg Betz, "Perplexed Normalcy: German Identity after Reunification," in *Rewriting the German Past: History and Identity in the New Germany*, ed. Reinhard Alter and Peter Monteath (Atlantic Highlands, NJ: Humanities Press, 1997), 41, 57.

74. Rudy J. Koshar, *Germany's Transient Pasts: Preservation and National Memory in the Twentieth Century* (Chapel Hill: University of North Carolina Press, 1998), 330. For a more recent perspective, see Katrin Bennhold, "Germany Has Been Unified for 30 Years. Its Identity Still Is Not," *New York Times*, November 8, 2019, https://www.nytimes.com/2019/11/08/world /europe/germany-identity.html.

CHAPTER 5

1. Norman Meißner, "Grünes Band: Protest gegen Fällarbeiten bei Dippach," *Thüringische Landeszeitung*, February 22, 2015, https://www.tlz.de/leben/natur-umwelt/gruenes-band -protest-gegen-faellarbeiten-bei-dippach-id220729703.html.

2. Martin Drenthen, "Developing Nature along Dutch Rivers: Place or Non-Place," in *New Visions of Nature: Complexity and Authenticity*, ed. Martin Drenthen, Joseph Keulartz, and James Proctor (Heidelberg: Springer, 2009), 216.

3. *Die Wildnis meldet sich zurück*, directed by Vincent Perazio (ARTE, 2019), streaming, https:// www.arte.tv/de/videos/079386-003-A/die-wildnis-meldet-sich-zurueck/; Stefan Huck, *Artensteckbrief: Keulen-Bärlapp (Lycopodium clavatum)* (Giessen: Hessen Forst, 2009); Thorsten Aßmann, Estève Boutaud, Peter Finck, Werner Härdtle, Diethart Matthies, Dorothea Nolte, Goddert von Oheimb, et al., *Halboffene Verbundkorridore: Ökologische Funktion, Leitbilder und Praxis-Leitfaden* (Bonn: BfN, 2016).

4. Calcareous grasslands develop on nutrient-poor, chalky soils. From the Middle Ages to the nineteenth century, grazing, especially overgrazing, created hundreds of calcareous grassland corridors in Germany as people moved their animals from summer to winter pastures. These grasslands are almost extinct today and house similarly vulnerable plant species. See Ingo Grass, Péter Batáry, and Teja Tscharntke, "Combining Land-Sparing and Land-Sharing in European Landscapes," *Advances in Ecological Research* 64 (2021): 251–303.

5. Green Belt ecologist, Eichsfeld, interview with the author, July 18, 2017.

6. Interview with the author, July 13, 2018.

7. The scholarship on this is large and growing. Just one recent book is indicative of the general tenor of this field: Florence Williams, *The Nature Fix: Why Nature Makes Us Happier, Healthier, and More Creative* (New York: W. W. Norton and Company, 2017).

8. Interview with the author, July 13, 2018.

9. Allen Carlson, *Nature and Landscape: An Introduction to Environmental Aesthetics* (New York: Columbia University Press, 2009).

10. Quoted in Martin Prominski, "Dilemma Landschaft?," *Stadt + Grün* 3 (2004): 34–39.

11. BfN, *Naturbewusstseinsstudie 2019* (Bonn: BfN, 2019), https://www.bmu.de/fileadmin/Daten_BMU/Pools/Broschueren/naturbewusstsein_2019_bf.pdf.

12. Martin Müller, "How Natural Disturbance Triggers Political Conflict: Bark Beetles and the Meaning of Landscape in the Bavarian Forest," *Global Environmental Change* 21, no. 3 (August 2011): 937.

13. Interview with the author, June 6, 2017.

14. BfN, "Rodachtal–Lange Berge–Steinachtal Green Belt," https://www.bfn.de/en/project/rodachtal-lange-berge-steinachtal-green-belt.

15. In some cases, grasslands may have been created by livestock grazing thousands of years earlier, but were lost to succession until the midcentury border-clearing policies reopened them.

16. Katja Wollschläger, "Neue Heimat: Heckrinder beziehen Bischofsaue," *Südthüringen*, November 28, 2018, https://www.insuedthueringen.de/inhalt.hildburghausen-neue-heimat-heckrinder-beziehen-bischofsaue.da43f823-1a91-4eef-93d9-d9a4caaf644c.html; NABU Thüringen, "Heckrinder weiden auf Grünem Band," November 28, 2018, https://www.ngpr-gruenes-band.de/images/presse/pressemitteilungen/181128_PM_Einweihung_Weide_Bischoftsaue.pdf.

17. Jaime Lorimer and Clemens Driessen, "From Nazi Cows to Cosmopolitan Ecological Engineers: Specifying Rewilding through a History of Heck Cattle," *Annals of the Association of American Geographers* 106, no. 3 (2016): 631–652.

18. Lorimer and Driessen, "From Nazi Cows to Cosmopolitan Ecological Engineers," 636.

19. Elizabeth Kolbert, "Recall of the Wild: The Quest to Engineer a World before Humans," *New Yorker*, December 24–31, 2012, https://www.newyorker.com/magazine/2012/12/24/recall-of-the-wild.

20. Zweckverband Grünes Band Rodachtal–Lange Berge–Steinachtal, "Anbau alter Sorten," accessed October 8, 2021, https://www.ngpr-gruenes-band.de/massnahmen/anbau-alter-sorten.

21. IUCN, "Protected Areas," accessed July 10, 2021, https://www.iucn.org/theme/protected-areas/about/protected-area-categories/category-ib-wilderness-area.

22. There is ongoing debate, often along disciplinary lines, whether wilderness exists in the world—a discussion sharpened by the introduction of the *Anthropocene* as a term invoking

the global human footprint on terrestrial, aquatic, and atmospheric systems. For an example of this controversy, see George Wuerthner, Eileen Crist, and Tum Butler, eds., *Keeping the Wild: Against the Domestication of Earth* (Washington, DC: Island Press, 2014).

23. Thomas Kirchhoff, "Wildnis," in *Naturphilosophische Grundbegriffe*, ed. Thomas Kirchhoff, accessed September 14, 2021, http://www.naturphilosophie.org/wildnis/.

24. Eva Lirsch, "Der Held in der Wildnis: Zur Darstellung des (Natur-)Raumes bei Karl May" (PhD diss., University of Vienna, 2006).

25. Thomas M. Lekan, *Our Gigantic Zoo: A German Quest to Save the Serengeti* (New York: Oxford University Press, 2020). On the problematic of Orientalizing and exoticizing Africa in conservation, see Jonathan S. Adams and Thomas O. McShane, *The Myth of Wild Africa: Conservation without Illusions* (Berkeley: University of California Press, 1996).

26. Paul Jepson and Cain Blythe, *Rewilding: The Radical New Science of Ecological Recovery* (London: Icon Books, 2020), 2–4.

27. On the push for passive management, called *Prozeßschutz* in German (as in "protecting the ecological process"), see, for instance, Knut Sturm, "Prozeßschutz—Ein Konzept für naturschutzgerechte Waldwirtschaft," *Zeitschrift für Ökologie und Naturschutz* 2 (1993): 181–192. For a more recent publication at the national level, see Peter Finck, Manfred Klein, Uwe Riecken, and Cornelia Paulsch, *Wildnis im Dialog: Wege zu mehr Wildnis* (Bonn: BfN, 2015).

28. BMUB, *Nationale Strategie zur biologischen Vielfalt* (Berlin: BMUB, 2007), 40–41.

29. Heiko Schumacher, Peter Finck, Uwe Riecken, and Manfred Klein, "More Wilderness for Germany: Implementing an Important Objective of Germany's National Strategy on Biological Diversity," *Journal for Nature Conservation* 42 (2018): 45–52.

30. Wir für Wildnis, "Wildnis in Deutschland," accessed October 19, 2021, https://wildnisin deutschland.de/.

31. Robert L. Chapman, "Ecological Restoration Restored," *Environmental Values* 15, no. 4 (2006): 468.

32. Michael Soulé and Reed Noss, "Rewilding and Biodiversity: Complementary Goals for Continental Conservation," *Wild Earth* 3 (1998): 28. On the shifts in rewilding ideas over time, see Dolly Jørgensen, "Rethinking Rewilding," *Geoforum* 65 (2014): 482–488.

33. Erick J. Lundgren, Daniel Ramp, John Rowan, Owen Middleton, Simon D. Schowanek, Oscar Sanisidro, Scott P. Carroll, et al., "Introduced Herbivores Restore Late Pleistocene Ecological Functions," *PNAS* 117, no. 14 (April 2020): 7871–7878.

34. Laetitia M. Navarro and Henrique M. Pereira, "Rewilding Abandoned Landscapes in Europe," *Ecosystems* 15 (2012): 906.

35. Koenrad van Meerbeek, Bart Buys, Simon D. Wchowanek, and Jens-Christian Svenning, "Reconciling Conflicting Paradigms of Biodiversity Conservation: Human Intervention and Rewilding," *BioScience* 69, no. 12 (2019): 998.

36. J. V. Ward, K. Tockner, and F. Schiemer, "Biodiversity of Floodplain River Ecosystems: Ecotones and Connectivity," *River Research and Applications* 15, no. 1–3 (January–June 1999): 125–139.

37. J. V. Ward, K. Tockner, D. B. Arscott, and C. Claret, "Riverine Landscape Diversity," *Freshwater Biology* 47, no. 4 (April 2002): 518.

38. Volker Lüderitz and Uta Langheinrich, "Die Elbe und ihre Altgewässer als Lebensraum," in *Natur- und Kulturraum Elbe*, ed. Thorsten Unger (Halle: Mitteldeutscher Verlag, 2014), 108–113.

39. Mathias Scholz, Sabine Stab, Frank Dziock, and Klaus Henle, eds., *Lebensräume der Elbe und ihrer Auen* (Berlin: Weissensee, 2002).

40. Johannes Prüter, "Die Elbe im Biosphärenreservat 'Niedersächsische Elbtalaue,'" *Zeitschrift für Stadt-, Regional-, und Landesentwicklung* 2 (2015): 72–87.

41. Lüderitz and Langheinrich, "Die Elbe und ihre Altgewässer," 113.

42. Center for Disaster Management and Risk Reduction Technology, *Juni-Hochwasser 2013 in Mitteleuropa: Fokus Deutschland*, accessed September 18, 2022, https://www.cedim.kit.edu/download/FDA-Juni-Hochwasser-Bericht2.1.pdf.

43. BfN, *Auenzustandsbericht: Flussauen in Deutschland* (Bonn: BfN, 2012), https://www.bfn.de/fileadmin/BfN/wasser/Dokumente/Auenzustandsbericht.pdf.

44. Even as recently as 1988, well after the start of the environmental movement in both West and East Germany, the Elbe carried staggering annual chemical loads: 160,000 tons nitrogen, 10,000 tons phosphorous, 23 tons of mercury, 124 tons of lead, 112 tons of arsenic, 13 tons of ammonia, 1,300 pounds of lindane, 1,100 pounds of PCBs, and 6,600 pounds of highly toxic pentachlorophenol (used in the production of pesticides). See Uwe Rada, *Die Elbe: Europas Geschichte im Fluss* (Munich: Siedler, 2013), 258.

45. Ernst Paul Dörfler, *Die Elbe: Vom Elbsandsteingebirge bis nach Geesthacht* (Berlin: Trescher Verlag, 2016), 111.

46. Klaus Schroeder and Jochen Staadt, *Die Todesopfer des DDR-Grenzregimes an der innerdeutschen Grenze 1949–1989: Ein biographisches Handbuch* (Berlin: Forschungsverbund SED-Staat, 2017).

47. Katja Lüdemann, "Ort des Erinnerns: Gedenken an Hans-Friedrich Franck," *Altmark Zeitung*, April 10, 2016, https://www.az-online.de/altmark/salzwedel/erinnerns-gedenken-hans-friedrich-franck-6807682.html.

48. Annette Kaminsky, ed., *Orte des Erinnerns: Gedenkzeichen, Gedenkstätten und Museen zur Diktatur in SBZ und DDR* (Berlin: Ch. Links, 2016), 306.

49. David Blackbourn, *The Conquest of Nature: Water, Landscape, and the Making of Modern Germany* (New York: W. W. Norton and Company, 2007).

50. Hansjörg Küster, *Die Elbe: Landschaft und Geschichte* (Munich: C. H. Beck, 2007), 211.

51. Christian Damm, "Deichrückverlegung Lenzen-Wustrow—Geschichte und Umsetzung im Rahmen eines Naturschutzgroßprojektes," *BAW Mitteilungen* 97 (2013), 25; Christian Damm, "Ecological Restoration and Dike Relocation on the River Elbe, Germany," *Scientific Annals of the Danube Delta Institute* 19 (2013): 80.

52. The following section draws heavily from Sonja K. Pieck, "Conserving Novel Ecosystems and Layered Landscapes along the Inter-German Border," *Landscape Research* 45, no. 3 (2020): 346–358.

53. IUCN, *Guidelines for Protected Area Management Categories* (Gland, Switzerland: IUCN, 1994), 19, https://portals.iucn.org/library/efiles/edocs/1994-007-En.pdf.

54. Eckart Krüger, "Wir brauchen Wildniszonen," *BUND Magazin* 4 (1997), https://www.bund-niedersachsen.de/service/bundmagazin/41997/wir_brauchen_wildniszonen/.

55. Oberverwaltungsgericht Lüneburg, "Urteil vom 22.2.1999–3 K 2630/98," *Natur und Recht* 8 (1999): 471.

56. Susanne Stoll-Kleemann, "Barriers to Nature Conservation in Germany: A Model Explaining Opposition to Protected Areas," *Journal of Environmental Psychology* 21 (2001): 369–385.

57. VSKE, "Unser Leitbild," accessed August 22, 2021, https://www.kulturland-elbtal.de/unser-leitbild.html.

58. Tim Ingold, *The Perception of the Environment: Essays on Livelihood, Dwelling and Skill* (New York: Routledge, 2000).

59. UNESCO, "Ecological Sciences for Sustainable Development: Biosphere Reserves—Learning Sites for Sustainable Development," accessed June 25, 2019, http://www.unesco.org/new/en/natural-sciences/environment/ecological-sciences/biosphere-reserves/.

60. Burg Lenzen, "Naturschutzgroßprojekt 'Lenzener Elbtalaue,'" accessed September 10, 2021, http://www.burg-lenzen.de/projekte/naturschutzgrossprojekt/naturschutzgrossprojekt.html.

61. BfN, *Die Lage der Natur in Deutschland* (Bonn: BfN, 2014), 14; Burg Lenzen, "Naturschutzgroßprojekt 'Lenzener Elbtalaue': Der Auwald kehrt zurück," accessed September 15, 2017, http://www.naturschutzgrossprojekt-lenzen.de/inhalte/i_set.html.

62. Christian Damm, "Naturschutzgroßprojekt Lenzener Elbtalaue: Umsetzung und Erfahrungen eines Pilotprojekts," *Natur und Landschaft* 91, no. 8 (2016): 361. Bioreserve brochures also reference Prussian maps for the historical baseline. For an impression of these, see Landesvermessung und Geobasisinformation Brandenburg, *Die Vermesser am Fluss* (Potsdam: Landesvermessung und Geobasisinformation Brandenburg, 2009).

63. Jochen Purps, Christian Damm, and Frank Neuschulz, "Naturschutzgrossprojekt Lenzener Elbtalaue, Brandenburg: Auenregenration durch Deichrückverlegung an der Elbe," *Natur und Landschaft* 79, no. 9–10 (2004): 409.

64. Köhnlein 1996, cited in Purps, Damm, and Neuschulz, "Naturschutzgrossprojekt," 409.

65. Damm, "Deichrückverlegung Lenzen-Wustrow," 25.

66. Damm, "Deichrückverlegung Lenzen-Wustrow," 24.

67. Matthias Alexey, "Numerische Modelluntersuchungen zu den Auswirkungen der Deichrück-verlegung Lenzen und von geplanten Vorlandanpflanzungen," *BAW Mitteilungen* 97 (2013): 73–98.

68. Christian Damm, "Ecological Restoration and Dike Relocation on the River Elbe, Germany," *Scientific Annals of the Danube Delta Institute* 19 (2013): 80.

69. Planland, *Alles fließt—Der Pflege- und Entwicklungsplan für das Naturschutzgroßprojekt Lenzener Elbtalaue*, accessed September 26, 2021, https://www.planland.de/alles-fliesst-i-der-pflege-und-entwicklungsplan-fuer-das-naturschutzgrossprojekt-lenzener-elbtalaue/.

70. Damm, "Ecological Restoration," 81.

71. Katrina Z. S. Schwartz, *Nature and National Identity after Communism: Globalizing the Ethnoscape* (Pittsburgh: University of Pittsburgh Press, 2006), 153. For more on the Dutch approach, see Frans Vera, *Grazing Ecology and Forest History* (Wallingford, CT: CABI, 2000).

72. Stiftung Liebenthaler Pferde, "Chronologie," accessed October 5, 2021, https://www.liebenthaler-pferdeherde.de/seite/276393/chronologie.html.

73. Interview with the author, May 30, 2016.

74. Biosphere reserve administrator for Lower-Saxony, interview with the author, May 30, 2016.

75. Biosphere reserve administrator for Lower-Saxony, interview with the author, May 30, 2016. This was also discussed by the director of the farmers' union of northeast Lower Saxony; interview with the author July 10, 2018.

76. See Biosphärenreservat Niedersächsische Elbtalaue, *Biosphärenreservatsplan mit integriertem Umweltbericht* (Hitzacker: Biosphärenreservatsverwaltung Niedersächsische Elbtalaue, 2009), section 5.1.2. (on soil and water), 81–82, and section 8.4.1., 236.

77. Damm, "Naturschutzgroßprojekt Lenzener Elbtalaue."

78. Jamie Lorimer and Clemens Driessen, "Wild Experiments at the Oostvaardersplassen: Rethinking Environmentalism in the Anthropocene," *Transactions of the Institute of British Geographers* 39, no. 2 (April 2014): 178–179.

79. Garry D. Peterson, "Contagious Disturbance, Ecological Memory, and the Emergence of Landscape Pattern," *Ecosystems* 5 (2002): 329.

80. Jill F. Johnstone, Craig D. Allen, Jerry F. Franklin, Lee E. Frelich, Brian J. Harvey, Philip E. Higuera, Michelle C. Mack, et al., "Changing Disturbance Regimes, Ecological Memory, and Forest Resilience," *Frontiers in Ecology and the Environment* 14, no. 7 (2016): 369–378.

81. Nancy Langston, *Climate Ghosts: Migratory Species in the Anthropocene* (Waltham, MA: Brandeis University Press, 2021); Paul K. Dayton, Mia J. Tegner, Peter B. Edwards, and Kristin L. Riser, "Sliding Baselines, Ghosts, and Reduced Expectations in Kelp Forest Communities," *Ecological Applications* 8, no. 2 (May 1998): 309–322. See also Adam Searle,

"Spectral Ecologies: De/extinction in the Pyrenees," *Transactions of the Institute of British Geographers* 47 (2022):167–183.

82. Naturschutzbund Schleswig-Holstein, "Fische in der Elbe und Haseldorfer Marsch," accessed September 26, 2021, https://schleswig-holstein.nabu.de/tiere-und-pflanzen/fische-und-neunaugen/03308.html.

83. Shane McCorristine and William M. Adams, "Ghost Species: Spectral Geographies of Biodiversity Conservation," *Cultural Geographies* 27, no. 1 (2020): 101–115.

84. Ben Jacob Novak, "De-Extinction," *Genes* 9, no. 11 (November 2018): 548; Beth Shapiro, "Pathways to De-Extinction: How Close Can We Get to Resurrection of an Extinct Species?," *Functional Ecology* 31, no. 5 (May 2017): 996–1002.

85. Biosphere reserve administrator for Brandenburg, interview with the author, May 30, 2016.

86. Besserwessi is a play on words. Besser*wisser* is the German word for a "know-it-all" (literally a "better knower"). Besser*wessi* merges this with *Wessi*, the colloquial term for a West German.

87. Biosphärenreservat Flusslandscahft Elbe-Brandenburg, "Neobiota in der Region," accessed September 29, 2021, https://www.elbe-brandenburg-biosphaerenreservat.de/unser-auftrag/naturschutz/neobiota/.

88. Fred Pearce, *The New Wild: Why Invasive Species Will Be Nature's Salvation* (Boston: Beacon Press, 2015).

89. Jonah H. Peretti, "Nativism and Nature," *Environmental Values* 7 (1998): 198–200.

90. Nonnative in this case appears as *gebietsfremd* or *standortsfremd* (alien to a place). The BUND's overarching position on nonnative species reads as a nuanced and measured document that treats species on a case-by-case basis. See BUND, *Neobiota: Anregungen für eine Neubewertung* (Berlin: BUND, 2015), https://www.bund.net/fileadmin/user_upload_bund/publikationen/bund/standpunkt/neobiota_standpunkt.pdf.

91. Barbara A. Misztal, *Theories of Social Remembering* (Philadelphia: Open University Press, 2003), 13.

92. For a variation on this argument, see Nils M. Franke, "Umweltschutz ist Heimatschutz? Der Zugang des rechtsextremistischen Denkens zum Thema Heimat und eine demokratische Gegenposition," in *Heimat: Ein vielfältiges Konstrukt*, ed. Martina Hülz, Olaf Kühne, and Florian Weber (Wiesbaden: Springer, 2019), 391–401.

CHAPTER 6

1. Thor Hanson, Thomas M. Brooks, Gustavo A. B. Da Fonseca, Michael Hoffmann, John F. Lamoreux, Gary Machlis, Cristina G. Mittermeier, et al., "Warfare in Biodiversity Hotspots," *Conservation Biology* 23, no. 3 (June 2009): 578–587.

2. Kaitlyn M. Gaynor, Kathryn J. Fiorella, Gillian H. Gregory, David J. Kurz, Katherine L. Seto, Lauren S. Withey, and Justin S. Brashares, "War and Wildlife: Linking Armed Conflict to Conservation," *Frontiers in Ecology and Environment* 14, no. 10 (December 2016): 533–542.

3. Owen J. Dwyer, "Symbolic Accretion and Commemoration," *Social and Cultural Geography* 5, no. 3 (September 2004): 419–435.

4. EuroNatur Foundation, *The European Green Belt Initiative: 10 Years of Challenges, Experiences and Achievements* (Radolfzell: EuroNatur Foundation and BUND Project Office Green Belt, 2014), accessed January 2, 2022, https://www.euronatur.org/fileadmin/docs/projekte/Gruenes_Band/European_Greenbelt_10_years_Brochure.pdf.

5. European Green Belt, "Structure," November 19, 2021, https://www.europeangreenbelt.org/initiative/structure/.

6. EuroNatur Foundation, *The European Green Belt Initiative*.

7. Andrew Terry, Karin Ullrich, and Uwe Riecken, *The Green Belt of Europe: From Vision to Reality* (Gland, Switzerland: IUCN, 2006), 7.

8. International Center for Transitional Justice, "Transitional Justice in the Former Yugoslavia," accessed October 16, 2021, https://www.ictj.org/sites/default/files/ICTJ-FormerYugoslavia-Justice-Facts-2009-English.pdf.

9. Euronatur Stiftung, "Balkan Green Belt: Where EuroNatur Has Particular Experience," accessed October 19, 2021, https://www.euronatur.org/en/what-we-do/project-areas/project-areas-a-z/balkan-green-belt/.

10. Jessie Fyfe and Maximilian Steinberg, "Unsettled Landscapes: Traumatic Memory in a Croatian Hinterland," *Space and Polity* 23, no. 3 (2019): 299–318.

11. A. Nußdorf-Debant, *Sava River Restoration from Brežice to Rugvica* (Radolfzell: Euronatur Stiftung, 2021), 25, https://www.balkanrivers.net/uploads/files/5/REVITAL_Sava_River.pdf.

12. Susan Neiman, *Learning from the Germans: Race and the Memory of Evil* (New York: Farrar, Straus and Giroux, 2019).

13. Karl Heinz Gaudry, Katharina Diehl, Manuel Oelke, Gunnar Finke, and Werner Konold, *Machbarkeitsstudie Welterbe Grünes Band: Schlussbericht* (Bonn: BfN, 2014), 66–67, 110, 112, https://www.bfn.de/fileadmin/BfN/internationalernaturschutz/Dokumente/BfN_Machbarkeitsstudie_Welterbe_Gruenes_Band.pdf.

14. Etienne François, "Europa als Erinnerungsgemeinschaft? Anmerkungen zur Frage nach einem europäischen Gedächtnis," in *Arbeit am europäischen Gedächtnis: Diktaturerfahrung und Demokratieentwicklung*, ed. Volkhard Knigge, Hans-Joachim Veen, Ulrich Mählert, and Franz-Josef Schlichting (Weimar: Bohlau Verlag, 2011), 13–26; Klaus Schönhoven, "Europa als Erinnerungsgemeinschaft," *Gesprächskreis Geschichte* 75 (Bonn: Friedrich Ebert Stiftung, 2007), https://library.fes.de/pdf-files/historiker/05122.pdf.

15. Suk Kyung Shim, "Governance of the German Green Belt Ecological Network: Implications for the Demilitarized Zone" (PhD diss., Humboldt-Universität zu Berlin, 2011), 43; Eric Wagner, "The DMZ's Thriving Resident: The Crane," *Smithsonian Magazine*, April

2011, https://www.smithsonianmag.com/science-nature/the-dmzs-thriving-resident-the
-crane-953694/.

16. Shim, "Governance of the German Green Belt," 45–46.

17. Lisa M. Brady, "Valuing the Wounds of War: Korea's DMZ as Nature Preserve," in *Collateral Values: The Natural Capital Created by Landscapes of War*, ed. Todd Lookingbill and Peter Smallwood (Cham, Switzerland: Springer, 2019), 157–176.

18. Shim, "Governance of the German Green Belt," 46–47.

19. Brady, "Valuing the Wounds of War," 167.

20. Wagner, "The DMZ's Thriving Resident"; Kai Frobel, "Grünes Band als Vorbild für Korea?," Grünes Band Deutschland, June 30, 2019, https://www.30-jahre-gruenes-band
.de/2019/06/30/gr%C3%BCnes-band-als-vorbild-f%C3%BCr-korea/.

21. Governments of Germany and Korea, "Joint Declaration of Intent," February 23, 2012, https://www.bfn.de/fileadmin/MDB/documents/presse/Declaration_BfNGP_23_Februar
.pdf.

22. BfN, "Die koreanische 'demilitarisierte Zone' (DMZ) und das Grüne Band," February 2, 2021, https://www.bfn.de/themen/biotop-und-landschaftsschutz/gruenes-band/korea.html; Park Kyung-man, "Germany's Green Belt Serves as Model for Korea's DMZ," *Hankyoreh*, November 4, 2019, https://english.hani.co.kr/arti/english_edition/e_northkorea/915752
.html.

23. David Havlick, *Bombs Away: Militarization, Conservation, and Ecological Restoration* (Chicago: University of Chicago Press, 2018), 94–95.

24. *The Republic of Korea's Fourth National Biodiversity Strategy, 2019–2023*, 23, https://www.cbd
.int/doc/world/kr/kr-nbsap-v4-en.pdf. A few protected areas already exist along the DMZ, mostly oriented toward the conservation of white-naped and red-crowned cranes.

25. Patrick Heuveline, "The Boundaries of Genocide: Quantifying the Uncertainty of the Death Toll during the Pol Pot Regime in Cambodia (1975–79)," *Population Studies* 69, no. 2 (2015): 201–218.

26. Ben Kiernan, *The Pol Pot Regime: Race, Power, and Genocide in Cambodia under the Khmer Rouge, 1975–79*, 3rd ed. (New Haven, CT: Yale University Press, 2008).

27. Pong-Rasy Pheng, David Chandler, Christopher Dearing, and Pheana Sopheak, *A History of Democratic Kampuchea (1975–1979)*, 2nd ed. (Phnom Penh: Documentation Center of Cambodia, 2020), 4, http://dccam.org/a-history-of-democratic-kampuchea-1975-1979.

28. BBC News, "Khmer Rouge Leaders Found Guilty of Cambodia Genocide," November 16, 2018, https://www.bbc.com/news/world-asia-46217896.

29. James A. Tyner, *Landscape, Memory, and Post-Violence in Cambodia* (London: Rowman and Littlefield, 2017), 7.

30. Fauna and Flora International, "Cambodia," accessed October 1, 2021, https://www.fauna -flora.org/countries/cambodia. For context, Cambodia is only about the size of Oklahoma, but it harbors as many as half the number of species as the entire United States.

31. Norman Myers, Russell A. Mittermeier, Cristina G. Mittermeier, Gustavo A. B. da Fonseca, and Jennifer Kent, "Biodiversity Hotspots for Conservation Priorities," *Nature* 403 (2000): 853–858; David M. Olson and Eric Dinerstein, "The Global 200: Priority Ecoregions for Global Conservation," *Annals of the Missouri Botanical Garden* 89, no. 2 (Spring 2002): 199–224.

32. Srey Chanthy and Jim Schweithelm, "Forest Resources in Cambodia's Transition to Peace: Lessons for Peacebuilding," in *Livelihood, Natural Resources, and Post-Conflict Peacebuilding*, ed. Helen Young and Lisa Goldman (New York: Routledge, 2015), 67–76.

33. Peter Potapov, Matthew C. Hansen, Lars Laestadius, Svetlana Turubanova, Alexey Yaroshenko, Christoph Thies, Wynet Smith, et al., "The Last Frontiers of Wilderness: Tracking Loss of Intact Forest Landscapes from 2000 to 2013," *Science Advances* 3, no 1 (2017): e1600821.

34. Lauren Coad, Sotheary Lim, and Lim Nuon, "Wildlife and Livelihoods in the Cardamom Mountains, Cambodia," *Frontiers in Ecology and Evolution* 7 (August 2019): 296.

35. Eve Monique Zucker, *Forest of Struggle: Moralities of Remembers in Upland Cambodia* (Honolulu: University of Hawai'i Press, 2013), 146.

36. Colby Loucks, Michael B. Mascia, Andy Maxwell, Keavuth Huy, Kong Duong, Nareth Chea, Barney Long, et al., "Wildlife Decline in Cambodia, 1953–2005: Exploring the Legacy of Armed Conflict," *Conservation Letters* 2 (2009): 89.

37. On the Colombian conflict, see Abbey Steele, *Democracy and Displacement in Colombia's Civil War* (Ithaca, NY: Cornell University Press, 2017). For a deeply moving, testimonial approach to the displaced and dead, see Alfredo Molano, *The Dispossessed: Chronicles of the Desterrados of Colombia* (Chicago: Haymarket Books, 2005).

38. Claire Felter and Danielle Renwick, "Colombia's Civil Conflict," *Council on Foreign Relations*, January 11, 2017, https://www.cfr.org/backgrounder/colombias-civil-conflict; Conflict and Environment Observatory, "Colombia Country Brief," accessed October 20, 2021, https:// ceobs.org/wp-content/uploads/2018/03/CEOBS_country_brief_Colombia_2018.pdf. The numbers are still under considerable debate. The 2022 report by Colombia's Truth Commission significantly elevated the estimate of fatalities.

39. Colombia Reports, "Civilian Casualties of Colombia's Armed Conflict," accessed July 20, 2019, https://colombiareports.com/civilians-killed-armed-conflict/.

40. Convention on Biological Diversity, "Colombia Country Profile," accessed October 20, 2021, https://www.cbd.int/countries/profile/?country=co.

41. World Wildlife Fund, *Living Colombia: A Megadiverse Country Facing the Future* (Cali: WWF-Colombia, 2017), 9, https://wwflac.awsassets.panda.org/downloads/colombia_viva ___informe_2017__resumen_en_ingles.pdf.

42. Conflict and Environment Observatory, "Colombia Country Brief."

43. Lorenzo Morales, *Peace and Environmental Protection: Proposals for Sustainable Rural Development*, Inter-American Dialogue 2017, 9, accessed October 21, 2021, https://www.thedialogue.org/wp-content/uploads/2017/01/Colombia-report-Eng_Web-Res_Final-for-web.pdf.

44. Alejandro Salazar, Adriana Sanchez, Juan Camilo Villegas, Juan F. Salazar, Daniel Ruiz Carrascal, Stephen Sitch, Juan Darío Restrepo, et al., "The Ecology of Peace: Preparing Colombia for New Political and Planetary Climates," *Frontiers in Ecology and Environment* 16, no. 9 (2018): 525–531.

45. Nicola Clerici, Dolors Armenteras, P. Kareiva, R. Botero, Juan Pablo Ramírez-Delgado, G. Forero-Medina, et al., "Deforestation in Colombian Protected Areas Increased during Post-Conflict Periods," *Scientific Reports* 10 (2020): 4971.

46. Juan Francisco Salazar, "Healing Colombia's War-Ravaged Landscapes," *Conversation*, August 25, 2017, https://theconversation.com/healing-colombias-war-ravaged-landscapes-82494.

47. Michael-Shawn Fletcher, Rebecca Hamilton, Wolfram Dressler, and Lisa Palmer, "Indigenous Knowledge and the Shackles of Wilderness," *PNAS* 118, no. 40 (October 2021): e2022218118.

48. World Wildlife Fund, *Living Planet Report 2020*, https://f.hubspotusercontent20.net/hubfs/4783129/LPR/PDFs/ENGLISH-FULL.pdf.

49. Intergovernmental Science-Policy Platform on Biodiversity and Ecosystem Services, *Global Assessment Report on Biodiversity and Ecosystem Services: Summary for Policymakers*, 2019, https://ipbes.net/sites/default/files/2020-02/ipbes_global_assessment_report_summary_for_policymakers_en.pdf.

50. Stuart L. Pimm, Gareth J. Russell, John L. Gittleman, and Thomas M. Brooks, "The Future of Biodiversity," *Science* 269, no. 5222 (1995): 347–350.

51. UNEP-WCMC and IUCN, *Protected Planet Report 2020* (Cambridge, UK: UNEP-WCMC, 2021), https://livereport.protectedplanet.net/.

52. UN Convention on Biological Diversity, "First Draft of the Post-2020 Global Biodiversity Framework," accessed November 5, 2021, https://www.cbd.int/doc/c/abb5/591f/2e46096d3f0330b08ce87a45/wg2020-03-03-en.pdf.

53. Edward O. Wilson, *Half-Earth: Our Planet's Fight for Life* (New York: Liveright Publishing, 2016).

54. High Ambition Coalition for Nature and People, https://www.hacfornatureandpeople.org/home.

55. David Stanway, "Countries Call for Urgent Action on Biodiversity with 'Kunming Declaration,'" Reuters, October 13, 2021, https://www.reuters.com/world/china/countries-adopt-kunming-declaration-boost-biodiversity-china-says-2021-10-13/.

56. Quoted in Campaign for Nature, "Economic Benefits of Protecting 30% of Planet's Land and Ocean Outweigh the Costs at Least 5-to-1," accessed November 3, 2021, https://www .campaignfornature.org/protecting-30-of-the-planet-for-nature-economic-analysis.

57. Bram Büscher, Wolfram Dressler, and Robert Fletcher, eds., *Nature, Inc.: Environmental Conservation in the Neoliberal Age* (Tucson: University of Arizona Press, 2014); Kathleen McAfee, "Selling Nature to Save It? Biodiversity and Green Developmentalism," *Environment and Planning D* 17, no. 2 (April 1999): 133–154; Morgan M. Robertson, "The Nature That Capital Can See: Science, State, and Market in the Commodification of Ecosystem Services," *Environment and Planning D* 24, no. 3 (June 2006): 367–387.

58. "NGO Concerns over the Proposed 30% Target for Protected Areas and Absence of Safeguards for Indigenous Peoples and Local Communities," accessed October 20, 2021, https:// assets.survivalinternational.org/documents/1959/final-en-ngo-concerns-over-the-proposed -30-target-for-protected-areas-and-absence-of-safeguards-for-Indigenous-people-and -local-communities-200901.pdf.

59. "Philanthropic Statement on CBD 30x30 Initiative," accessed October 20, 2021, https:// redd-monitor.org/wp-content/uploads/2021/08/Philanthropic-Statement-on-CBD -30x30-INITIATIVE-FINAL-2021.Aug_.13-submitted-to-Mr.-Francis-Ogwal-Mr.-Basile -van-Havre-Co-Chairs-of-GBF.pdf.

60. "An Open Letter to the Lead Authors of 'Protecting 30% of the Planet for Nature: Costs, Benefits and Implications,'" accessed October 20, 2021, https://openlettertowaldronetal .wordpress.com/.

61. Mark David Spence, *Dispossessing the Wilderness: Indian Removal and the Making of the National Parks* (New York: Oxford University Press, 1999); Karen Jones, "Unpacking Yellowstone: The American National Park in Global Perspective," in *Civilizing Nature: National Parks in Global Historical Perspective*, ed. Bernhard Gissibl, Sabine Höhler, and Patrick Kupper (New York: Berghahn, 2015), 31–47.

62. James Igoe, *Conservation and Globalization: A Study of National Parks and Indigenous Communities from East Africa to South Dakota* (Belmont, CA: Thomson/Wadsworth, 2004); Roderick Neumann, *Imposing Wilderness: Struggles over Livelihood and Nature Preservation in Africa* (Berkeley: University of California Press, 1998); Mark Dowie, *Conservation Refugees: The Hundred-Year Conflict between Global Conservation and Native Peoples* (Cambridge, MA: MIT Press, 2009).

63. John M. MacKenzie, *The Empire of Nature: Hunting, Conservation, and British Imperialism* (New York: Manchester University Press, 1988); William Beinart and Lotte Hughes, *Environment and Empire* (New York: Oxford University Press, 2007).

64. Marshall W. Murphree, "The Strategic Pillars of Communal Natural Resource Management: Benefit, Empowerment and Conservation," *Biodiversity and Conservation* 18 (2009): 2551–2562; Krishna Roka, "Community-Based Natural Resources Management," in *Life on Land: Encyclopedia of the UN Sustainable Development Goals*, ed. Walter Leal Filho, Anabela Marisa

Azul, Luciana Brandli, Amanda Lange Salvia, and Tony Wall (Cham, Switzerland: Springer, 2021), 1–14.

65. For a longer description of this history, see Sonja K. Pieck, "Opportunities for Transnational Indigenous Eco-Politics: The Changing Landscape in the New Millennium," *Global Networks* 6, no. 3 (July 2006): 309–329; Sonja K. Pieck and Sandra A. Moog, "Competing Entanglements in the Struggle to Save the Amazon: The Shifting Terrain of Transnational Civil Society," *Political Geography* 28, no. 7 (September 2009): 416–425.

66. Roderick Neumann, "Stories of Nature's Hybridity in Europe," in *The Social Lives of Forests: Past, Present, and Future of Woodland Resurgence*, ed. Susannah B. Hecht (Chicago: University of Chicago Press, 2014), 43.

67. Patrick Roberts, Rebecca Hamilton, and Dolores R. Piperno, "Tropical Forests as Key Sites of the 'Anthropocene': Past and Present Perspectives," *PNAS* 118, no. 40 (October 2021): e2109243118.

68. Fikret Berkes, Johan Colding, and Carl Folke, eds., *Navigating Social-Ecological Systems: Building Resilience for Complexity and Change* (Cambridge: Cambridge University Press, 2003); David O. Obura, Yemi Katerere, Mariam Mayet, Dickson Kaelo, Simangele Msweli, Khalid Mather, Jean Harris, et al., "Integrate Biodiversity Targets from Local to Global Levels," *Science* 373, no. 6556 (August 2021): 746–748; Victoria Reyes-García, Álvaro Fernández-Llamazares, Pamela McElwee, Zsolt Molnár, Kinga Öllerer, Sarah J. Wilson, and Eduardo S. Brondizio, "The Contributions of Indigenous Peoples and Local Communities to Ecological Restoration," *Restoration Ecology* 27, no. 1 (January 2019): 3–8.

69. Indigenous Circle of Experts, *We Rise Together: Achieving Pathways to Canada Target 1 through the Creation of Indigenous Protected and Conserved Areas in the Spirit and Practice of Reconciliation*, accessed September 18, 2022, https://www.iccaconsortium.org/wpcontent/uploads/2018/03/PA234-ICE_Report_2018_Mar_22_web.pdf; Tanya C. Tran, Natalie C. Ban, and Jonaki Bhattacharyya, "Indigenous Approaches to Conservation: A Review of Successes, Challenges, and Lessons from Indigenous Protected and Conserved Areas," *Biological Conservation* 241 (January 2020): 108271; Kyle A. Artelle, Melanie Zurba, Jonaki Bhattacharyya, Diana E. Chan, Kelly Brown, Jess Housty, and Faisal Moola, "Supporting Resurgent Indigenous-Led Governance: A Nascent Mechanism for Just and Effective Conservation," *Biological Conservation* 240 (December 2019): 108284.

70. Paul Nadasdy, *Hunters and Bureaucrats: Power, Knowledge, and Aboriginal-State Relations in the Southwest Yukon* (Vancouver: University of British Columbia Press, 2004); Annette Watson, "Misunderstanding the 'Nature' of Co-Management: A Geography of Regulatory Science and Indigenous Knowledges (IK)," *Environmental Management* 52 (2013): 1085–1102; Jake M. Robinson, Nick Gellie, Danielle MacCarthy, Jacob G. Mills, Kim O'Donnell, and Nicole Redvers, "Traditional Ecological Knowledge in Restoration Ecology: A Call to Listen Deeply, to Engage with, and Respect Indigenous Voices," *Restoration Ecology* 29, no. 4 (May 2021): e13381.

71. K. Whitney Mauer, "Unsettling Resilience: Colonial Ecological Violence, Indigenous Futurisms, and the Restoration of the Elwha River," *Rural Sociology* 86, no. 3 (September 2021): 611–634; Meg Parsons, Karen Fisher, and Roa Petra Crease, *Decolonising Blue Spaces in the Anthropocene* (Cham, Switzerland: Springer, 2021).

72. Jeff Corntassel, "Re-Envisioning Resurgence: Indigenous Pathways to Decolonization and Sustainable Self-Determination," *Decolonization: Indigeneity, Education and Society* 1, no. 1 (2012): 86–101.

73. Parsons, Fisher, and Crease, *Decolonising Blue Spaces*, 383. See also Priscilla M. Wehi and Janice M. Lord, "Importance of Including Cultural Practices in Ecological Restoration," *Conservation Biology* 31, no. 5 (October 2017): 1109–1118.

74. Parsons, Fisher, and Crease, *Decolonising Blue Spaces*, 382.

75. Cedric J. Robinson, *Black Marxism: The Making of the Black Radical Tradition* (Chapel Hill: University of North Carolina Press, 2000); Charles W. Mills, *The Racial Contract* (Ithaca, NY: Cornell University Press, 1997); Iris Marion Young, *Justice and the Politics of Difference* (Princeton, NJ: Princeton University Press, 1990).

76. Margaret Urban Walker, *Moral Repair: Reconstructing Moral Relations after Wrongdoing* (Cambridge: Cambridge University Press, 2012), 15.

77. Susanne Buckley-Zistel, Teresa Koloma Beck, Christian Braun, and Friederike Mieth, eds., *Transitional Justice Theories* (New York: Routledge, 2014).

78. Mark Hamilton, *Environmental Crime and Restorative Justice* (Cham, Switzerland: Palgrave Macmillan, 2021); Miranda Forsyth, Deborah Cleland, Felicity Tepper, Deborah Hollingworth, Milena Soares, Alistair Nairn, and Cathy Wilkinson, "A Future Agenda for Environmental Restorative Justice?," *International Journal of Restorative Justice* 4, no. 1 (2021): 17–40.

79. Tom Perreault, "The Meaning of Mining, the Memory of Water: Collective Experience as Environmental Justice," in *Water Justice*, ed. Rutgerd Boelens, Tom Perreault, and Jeroen Vos (New York: Cambridge University Press, 2018), 316–329.

80. River Restoration Northwest, "Biocultural Restoration," November 1, 2021, https://www.rrnw.org/biocultural/. Also see Robin Wall Kimmerer, "Restoration and Reciprocity: The Contributions of Traditional Ecological Knowledge," in *Human Dimensions of Ecological Restoration: Integrating Science, Nature, and Culture*, ed. Dave Egan, Evan E. Hjerpe, and Jesse Abrams (Washington, DC: Island Press, 2011), 257–276.

81. Melanie Barron, "Remediating a Sense of Place: Memory and Environmental Justice in Anniston, Alabama," *Southeastern Geographer* 57, no. 1 (Spring 2017): 62–79.

82. The scope of this literature is, of course, enormous. Recent examples include May-Lee Chai, *Trespass: Ecotone Essayists beyond the Boundaries of Place, Identity, and Feminism* (Wilmington, NC: Lookout Books, 2018); Camille Dungy, ed., *Black Nature: Four Centuries of African American Nature Poetry* (Athens: University of Georgia Press, 2009); Carolyn Finney, *Black Faces, White Spaces: Reimagining the Relationship of African Americans to the Great Outdoors* (Chapel Hill: University of North Carolina Press, 2014); Walter Hood and Grace Mitchell

Tada, eds., *Black Landscapes Matter* (Charlottesville: University of Virginia Press, 2020); Katherine McKittrick, *Demonic Grounds* (Minneapolis: University of Minnesota Press, 2006); Deborah McGregor, "Indigenous Environmental Justice, Knowledge, and Law," *Kalfou* 5, no. 2 (Fall 2018): 279–296; Sarah D. Wald, David J. Vázquez, Priscilla Solis Ybarra, and Sarah Jaquette Ray, eds., *Latinx Environmentalisms: Place, Justice, and the Decolonial* (Philadelphia: Temple University Press, 2019).

83. Perreault, "The Meaning of Mining," 326.

84. Indigenous Circle of Experts, *We Rise Together*, 17.

85. Documentation Center of Cambodia, "Anlong Veng Master Plan," accessed October 6, 2021, http://dccam.org/anlong-veng-master-plan; Julia Mayer, "Connecting the Past to the Future: A Vision for Reconciliation in Anlong Veng, Cambodia," *ICOMOS*, December 13–14, 2017, http://openarchive.icomos.org/id/eprint/1978.

86. Carolina Murcia, Manuel R. Guariguata, Ángela Andrade, Germán Ignacio Andrade, James Aronson, Elsa Matilde Escobar, Andrés Etter, et al., "Challenges and Prospects for Scaling-Up Ecological Restoration to Meet International Commitments: Colombia as a Case Study," *Conservation Letters* 9, no. 3 (May–June 2016): 213–220.

87. Centro Nacional de Memoria Histórica, "Mapa de acciones en territorio," accessed December 1, 2021, https://centrodememoriahistorica.gov.co/donde-lo-hacemos/.

88. Sembrando Paz, "Misión y visión," accessed December 10, 2021, https://www.sembrandopaz.org/mision-y-vision/.

89. For the latter, see for instance the Universities Studying Slavery consortium, https://slavery.virginia.edu/universities-studying-slavery/.

90. Miles A. Powell, *Vanishing America: Species Extinction, Racial Peril, and the Origins of Conservation* (Cambridge, MA: Harvard University Press, 2016); Spence, *Dispossessing the Wilderness*; Jonathan Spiro, *Defending the Master Race: Conservation, Eugenics, and the Legacy of Madison Grant* (Lebanon, NH: University of New England Press, 2009).

91. Center for Native Peoples and the Environment, "Center for Native Peoples and the Environment and the Nature Conservancy Embark on Partnership," September 22, 2021, https://cnpe.home.blog/2021/09/22/center-for-native-peoples-and-the-environment-and-the-nature-conservancy-embark-on-partnership/.

92. See The Conservation Fund, "Cultural Conservation," accessed December 1, 2022, https://www.conservationfund.org/our-work/land-conservation/cultural-conservation?xlimitstart=30.

CONCLUSION

1. William Cronon, "A Place for Stories: Nature, History, and Narrative," *Journal of American History* 78, no. 4 (March 1992): 1370.

2. Interview with the author, August 15, 2018.

3. Volkhard Knigge, "Jenseits der Erinnerung: Zu einer Zivilgeschichte der Zukunft," *Kultur-politische Mitteilungen* 128, no 1 (2010): 62–65. For another approach to the role of memory for ethics, see Avishai Margalit, *The Ethics of Memory* (Cambridge, MA: Harvard University Press, 2004).

4. Aleida Assmann, "Transformations between History and Memory," *Social Research: An International Quarterly* 75, no. 1 (Spring 2008): 63.

5. Tim Ingold, *The Perception of the Environment: Essays on Livelihood, Dwelling and Skill* (New York: Routledge, 2000), 207.

6. Eben Kirksey, *Emergent Ecologies* (Durham, NC: Duke University Press, 2015), 1.

7. Robin L. Chazdon, *Second Growth: The Promise of Tropical Forest Regeneration in an Age of Deforestation* (Chicago: University of Chicago Press, 2014).

8. Bill Cooke and Uma Kothari, eds., *Participation: The New Tyranny?* (New York: Zed Books, 2001); Samuel Hickey and Giles Mohan, eds., *Participation: From Tyranny to Transformation?* (New York: Zed Books, 2004); Chris Kelty, *The Participant: A Century of Participation in Four Stories* (Chicago: University of Chicago Press, 2020); Christine Noe and Richard Y. M. Kangalawe, "Wildlife Protection, Community Participation in Conservation, and (Dis)-Empowerment in Southern Tanzania," *Conservation and Society* 13, no. 3 (2015): 244–253; Emilio Rodríguez-Izquierdo, M. Gavin, and Miguel O. Macedo-Bravo, "Barriers and Triggers to Community Participation across Different Stages of Conservation Management," *Environmental Conservation* 37, no. 3 (2010): 239–249.

9. Lilian Pearce, "Critical Histories for Ecological Restoration" (PhD diss., Australian National University, 2019), 300.

10. Joern Fischer and Maraja Riechers, "From Grief to Hope in Conservation," *Conservation Biology* 35, no. 5 (October 2021): 1698–1700; William R. Jordan, *The Sunflower Forest: Ecological Restoration and the New Communion with Nature* (Berkeley: University of California Press, 2012).

11. *Merriam-Webster*, "Memory," accessed August 6, 2019, https://www.merriam-webster.com/dictionary/mnemonic.

12. *American Heritage Dictionary of the English Language*, "Indo-European Roots Appendix," https://www.ahdictionary.com/word/indoeurop.html#IR094600.

13. Francis Weller, *The Wild Edge of Sorrow: Rituals of Renewal and the Sacred Work of Grief* (Berkeley, CA: North Atlantic Books, 2015), 18.

14. This point has been made well by feminist theorists, including Annemarie Mol, Ingunn Moser, and Jeannette Pols, eds., *Care in Practice: On Tinkering in Clinics, Homes and Farms* (Bielefeld: Transcript Verlag, 2010); Nel Noddings, *Caring: A Relational Approach to Ethics and Moral Education*, 2nd ed. (Berkeley: University of California Press, 2013); Joan Tronto, *Moral Boundaries: A Political Argument for an Ethic of Care* (New York: Routledge, 1993). For a critical take on caring in conservation, see María Puig de la Bellacasa, *Matters of Care:*

Speculative Ethics in More Than Human Worlds (Minneapolis: University of Minnesota Press, 2017); Juno Salazar Parreñas, *Decolonizing Extinction: The Work of Care in Orangutan Rehabilitation* (Durham, NC: Duke University Press, 2018); Krithika Srinivasan, "Caring for the Collective: Biopower and Agential Subjectification in Wildlife Conservation," *Environment and Planning D: Society and Space* 32, no. 3 (June 2014): 501–517.

15. Kyle Powys Whyte and Chris Cuomo, "Ethics of Caring in Environmental Ethics: Indigenous and Feminist Philosophies," in *The Oxford Handbook of Environmental Ethics*, ed. Stephen M. Gardiner and Allen Thompson (New York: Oxford University Press, 2017), 234–235.

16. Thom van Dooren, *Flight Ways: Life and Loss at the Edge of Extinction* (New York: Columbia University Press, 2014), 140.

Bibliography

Adam, Thomas. "Die Verteidigung des Vertrauten: Zur Geschichte der Natur- und Umweltschutz-bewegung in Deutschland seit Ende des 19. Jahrhunderts." *Zeitschrift für Politik* 45, no. 1 (1998): 20–48.

Adams, Jonathan S., and Thomas O. McShane. *The Myth of Wild Africa: Conservation without Illusions*. Berkeley: University of California Press, 1996.

Ahonen, Pertti. *Death at the Berlin Wall*. Oxford: Oxford University Press, 2011.

Albrecht, Glenn, Gina-Maree Sartore, Linda Connor, Nick Higginbotham, Sonia Freeman, Brian Kelly, Helen Stain, Anne Tonna, and Georgia Pollard. "Solastalgia: The Distress Caused by Environmental Change." *Australasian Psychiatry* 15, suppl. 1 (February 2007): S95–S98.

Alexey, Matthias. "Numerische Modelluntersuchungen zu den Auswirkungen der Deichrückver-legung Lenzen und von geplanten Vorlandanpflanzungen." *BAW Mitteilungen* 97 (2013): 73–98.

Ali, Saleem H., ed. *Peace Parks: Conservation and Conflict Resolution*. Cambridge, MA: MIT Press, 2007.

Allison, Stuart K. *Ecological Restoration and Environmental Change: Renewing Damaged Ecosystems*. London: Routledge, 2012.

American Heritage Dictionary of the English Language. "Indo-European Roots Appendix." https://www.ahdictionary.com/word/indoeurop.html#IR094600.

American Psychological Association. "Trauma." Accessed July 31, 2019. https://www.apa.org/topics/trauma/.

Amos, Heike. *Die Vertriebenenpolitik der SED 1949 bis 1990*. Munich: Oldenbourg Wissenschafts-verlag, 2009.

Angé, Olivia, and David Berliner, eds. *Ecological Nostalgias: Memory, Affect and Creativity in Times of Ecological Upheavals*. New York: Berghahn Books, 2021.

Artelle, Kyle A., Melanie Zurba, Jonaki Bhattacharyya, Diana E. Chan, Kelly Brown, Jess Housty, and Faisal Moola. "Supporting Resurgent Indigenous-Led Governance: A Nascent Mechanism for Just and Effective Conservation." *Biological Conservation* 240 (December 2019): 108284.

Assmann, Aleida. *Shadows of Trauma: Memory and the Politics of Postwar Identity.* New York: Fordham University Press, 2016.

Assmann, Aleida. "Transformations between History and Memory." *Social Research: An International Quarterly* 75, no 1 (Spring 2008): 49–72.

Assmann, Jan. "Communicative and Cultural Memory." In *Cultural Memories: The Geographical Point of View,* edited by Peter Meusburger, Michael Heffernan, and Edgar Wunder, 15–27. Dordrecht: Springer, 2011.

Assmann, Jan. *Cultural Memory and Early Civilization: Writing, Remembrance, and Political Imagination.* Cambridge: Cambridge University Press, 2011.

Aßmann, Thorsten, Estève Boutaud, Peter Finck, Werner Härdtle, Diethart Matthies, Dorothea Nolte, Goddert von Oheimb, Uwe Riecken, Eliane Travers, and Karin Ullrich. *Halboffene Verbundkorridore: Ökologische Funktion, Leitbilder und Praxis-Leitfaden.* Bonn: BfN, 2016.

Aufgebauer, Peter, Dietrich Denecke, Klaus Grote, Markus Krüsemann, Eckart Schröder, and Hans-Georg Wehling. *Das Eichsfeld: Ein deutscher Grenzraum.* Duderstadt: Mecke Druck und Verlag, 2002.

Avery, Gordon F. *Ghostly Matters: Haunting and the Sociological Imagination.* Minneapolis: University of Minnesota Press, 2008.

Bargheer, Stefan. "Apocalypse Adjourned: The Rise and Decline of Cold War Environmentalism in Germany." *Environmental Politics* 27, no. 6 (2018): 973–993.

Barron, Melanie. "Remediating a Sense of Place: Memory and Environmental Justice in Anniston, Alabama." *Southeastern Geographer* 57, no. 1 (Spring 2017): 62–79.

Bauernkämper, Arnd. "The Industrialization of Agriculture and Its Consequences for the Natural Environment: An Inter-German Comparative Perspective." *Historical Social Research* 29, no. 3 (2004): 124–149.

BBC News. "Khmer Rouge Leaders Found Guilty of Cambodia Genocide." November 16, 2018. https://www.bbc.com/news/world-asia-46217896.

Beck, Ralf-Uwe. "Baumkreuz: Erinnerungsort. Denkmal. Skulptur." Accessed September 20, 2021. https://www.bund-thueringen.de/fileadmin/thueringen/Gruenes_Band/BAUMKREUZ_Info.pdf.

Beinart, William, and Lotte Hughes. *Environment and Empire.* New York: Oxford University Press, 2007.

Bennett, Jane. *Vibrant Matter: A Political Ecology of Things.* Durham, NC: Duke University Press, 2010.

Bennewitz, Inge, and Rainer Potratz. *Zwangsaussiedlungen an der innerdeutschen Grenze: Analysen und Dokumente.* Berlin: Ch. Links, 2012.

Bennhold, Katrin. "Germany Has Been Unified for 30 Years. Its Identity Still Is Not." *New York Times,* November 8, 2019. https://www.nytimes.com/2019/11/08/world/europe/germany-identity.html.

Bergmann, Martin S., and Milton E. Jucovy, eds. *Generations of the Holocaust*. New York: Columbia University Press, 1990.

Berkes, Fikret, Johan Colding, and Carl Folke, eds. *Navigating Social-Ecological Systems: Building Resilience for Complexity and Change*. Cambridge: Cambridge University Press, 2003.

Betz, Hans-Georg. "Perplexed Normalcy: German Identity after Reunification." In *Rewriting the German Past: History and Identity in the New Germany*, edited by Reinhard Alter and Peter Monteath, 40–64. Atlantic Highlands, NJ: Humanities Press, 1997.

Bille, Mikkel, Frida Hastrup, and Tim Flohr Sørensen. "Introduction: An Anthropology of Absence." In *An Anthropology of Absence: Materializations of Transcendence and Loss*, edited by Mikkel Bille, Frida Hastrup, and Tim Flohr Soerensen, 3–22. New York: Springer, 2010.

Biosphärenreservat Flusslandschaft Elbe-Brandenburg. "Neobiota in der Region." Accessed September 29, 2021. https://www.elbe-brandenburg-biosphaerenreservat.de/unser-auftrag/natur schutz/neobiota/.

Biosphärenreservat Niedersächsische Elbtalaue. *Biosphärenreservatsplan mit integriertem Umweltbericht*. Hitzacker: Biosphärenreservatsverwaltung Niedersächsische Elbtalaue, 2009.

Blackbourn, David. *The Conquest of Nature: Water, Landscape, and the Making of Modern Germany*. New York: W. W. Norton and Company, 2007.

Blickle, Peter. *Heimat: A Critical Theory of the German Idea of Homeland*. Rochester, NY: Camden House, 2002.

Bode, Sabine. *Die vergessene Generation: Die Kriegskinder brechen ihr Schweigen*. Stuttgart: Klett Cotta Verlag, 2015.

Brady, Lisa M. "Valuing the Wounds of War: Korea's DMZ as Nature Preserve." In *Collateral Values: The Natural Capital Created by Landscapes of War*, edited by Todd Lookingbill and Peter Smallwood, 157–176. Cham, Switzerland: Springer, 2019.

Breymayer, Ursula, and Bernd Ulrich. *Unter Bäumen: Die Deutschen und der Wald*. Dresden: Sandstein, 2011.

Buckley-Zistel, Susanne, Teresa Koloma Beck, Christian Braun, and Friederike Mieth, eds. *Transitional Justice Theories*. New York: Routledge, 2014.

Bund für Umwelt und Naturschutz (BUND). "Aktuelle Projekte am Grünen Band." Accessed August 27, 2019. https://www.bund.net/themen/gruenes-band/aktuelle-projekte/#c1196.

Bund für Umwelt und Naturschutz (BUND). *Biotopmanagement am Grünen Band*. Nuremberg: BUND Projektbüro Grünes Band, 2012.

Bund für Umwelt und Naturschutz (BUND). "Bundesumweltministerin Hendricks: 'Das Grüne Band kann Vorbildcharakter für gutes Zusammenwirken von der Landwirtschaft mit Naturschutz entfalten.'" August 15, 2017. https://www.bund-niedersachsen.de/fileadmin/niedersachsen/publi kationen/pressemitteilungen/2017/2017-08-15_BUND_PM_Bundesumweltministerin-Hen dricks_Gruenes_Band.pdf.

Bund für Umwelt und Naturschutz (BUND). *Das Grüne Band—Dauereinsatz für eine Vision.* Nuremberg: BUND Projektbüro Grünes Band, 2019.

Bund für Umwelt und Naturschutz (BUND). *Das Grüne Band: Ein Handlungsleitfaden.* Bonn: BfN, 2001.

Bund für Umwelt und Naturschutz (BUND). "Grünes Band: Entscheidender Meilenstein für den Naturschutz in Deutschland erreicht?" March 25, 2003. https://www.bund-naturschutz.de/pressemitteilungen/gruenes-band-8211-entscheidender-meilenstein-fuer-den-naturschutz-in-deutschland-erreicht-1.html.

Bund für Umwelt und Naturschutz (BUND). "Lenzener Erklärung zum Grünen Band." September 29, 2019. https://www.bund.net/service/publikationen/detail/publication/lenzener-erklaerung-zum-gruenen-band/.

Bund für Umwelt und Naturschutz (BUND). "Monument: Das Grüne Band auf dem Weg zum nationalen Naturmonument: Thüringen hat den Anfang gemacht." Accessed August 26, 2021. http://www.grünes-band-monumental.de.

Bund für Umwelt und Naturschutz (BUND). *Monumental: Das Grüne Band ist auf dem Weg Nationales Naturmonument zu werden.* Accessed August 15, 2021. https://www.youtube.com/watch?v=nP4YF8aYt9Q.

Bund für Umwelt und Naturschutz (BUND). *Neobiota: Anregungen für eine Neubewertung.* Berlin: BUND, 2015. https://www.bund.net/fileadmin/user_upload_bund/publikationen/bund/standpunkt/neobiota_standpunkt.pdf.

Bund für Umwelt und Naturschutz (BUND). *Spur in der Landschaft.* Erfurt: BUND Thüringen, 2012. https://www.bund.net/fileadmin/user_upload_bund/publikationen/gruenes_band/gruenes_band_spur_in_der_landschaft.pdf.

Bundesamt für Naturschutz (BfN). *Auenzustandsbericht: Flussauen in Deutschland.* Bonn: BfN, 2012. https://www.bfn.de/fileadmin/BfN/wasser/Dokumente/Auenzustandsbericht.pdf.

Bundesamt für Naturschutz (BfN). "Die koreanische 'demilitarisierte Zone' (DMZ) und das Grüne Band." February 2, 2021. https://www.bfn.de/themen/biotop-und-landschaftsschutz/gruenes-band/korea.html.

Bundesamt für Naturschutz (BfN). *Die Lage der Natur in Deutschland: Ergebnisse von EU-Vogelschutz- und FFH-Bericht.* Bonn: BfN, 2014. https://bmu.de/fileadmin/Daten_BMU/Download_PDF/Naturschutz/natur_deutschland_bericht_bf.pdf.

Bundesamt für Naturschutz (BfN). "Erlebnis Grünes Band." Accessed March 2, 2011. https://www.bfn.de/foerderung/e-e-vorhaben/liste-abgeschlossener-vorhaben/e-e-abgschl-steckbriefe-biotopschutz/erlebnis-gruenes-band.html.

Bundesamt für Naturschutz (BfN). "Lückenschluss Grünes Band: Sicherung der Biologischen Vielfalt durch Weiterentwicklung des Grünen Bandes als zentrale Achse des nationalen Biotopverbunds." Accessed July 5, 2018. https://biologischevielfalt.bfn.de/bundesprogramm/projekte/projektbeschreibungen/lueckenschluss-gruenes-band-sicherung-der-biologischen-vielfalt-durch-weiterentwicklung-des-gruenen-bandes-als-zentrale-achse-des-nationalen-biotopverbunds.html.

Bundesamt für Naturschutz (BfN). *Naturbewusstsein 2017*. Bonn: BfN, 2017.

Bundesamt für Naturschutz (BfN). *Naturbewusstseinsstudie 2019*. Bonn: BfN, 2019. https://www
.bmu.de/fileadmin/Daten_BMU/Pools/Broschueren/naturbewusstsein_2019_bf.pdf.

Bundesministerium für Umwelt, Naturschutz, Bau und Reaktorsicherheit (BMUB). *Nationale
Strategie zur biologischen Vielfalt*. Berlin: BMUB, 2007.

Bundesministerium für Umwelt, Naturschutz, nukleare Sicherheit und Verbraucherschutz
(BMUV). "Das Bundesprogramm Wiedervernetzung." Accessed January 13, 2022. https://www
.bmuv.de/download/das-bundesprogramm-wiedervernetzung.

Bundesministerium für Umwelt, Naturschutz, nukleare Sicherheit und Verbraucherschutz
(BMUV). "Kleine Nationalparks oder große Naturdenkmäler?" Accessed January 7, 2018. https://
www.bmub.bund.de/themen/natur-biologische-vielfalt-arten/naturschutz-biologische-vielfalt
/gebietsschutz-und-vernetzung/nationale-naturlandschaften/nationale-naturmonumente.

Bundeszentrale für politische Bildung. "Wer war Opfer des DDR-Grenzregimes? Ansichten zu
einem umstrittenen Thema." *Deutschland Archiv*. Accessed July 15, 2021. https://www.bpb.de
/themen/deutschlandarchiv/295078/wer-war-opfer-des-ddr-grenzregimes.

Burg Lenzen. "Naturschutzgroßprojekt 'Lenzener Elbtalaue.'" Accessed September 10, 2021.
http://www.burg-lenzen.de/projekte/naturschutzgrossprojekt/naturschutzgrossprojekt.html.

Burg Lenzen. "Naturschutzgroßprojekt 'Lenzener Elbtalaue': Der Auwald kehrt zurück." Accessed
September 15, 2017. http://www.naturschutzgrossprojekt-lenzen.de/inhalte/i_set.html.

Büscher, Bram, Wolfram Dressler, and Robert Fletcher, eds. *Nature, Inc.: Environmental Conservation in the Neoliberal Age*. Tucson: University of Arizona Press, 2014.

CABI Invasive Species Compendium. "*Chalara fraxinea*." Accessed October 16, 2021. https://
www.cabi.org/isc/datasheet/108083#tosummaryOfInvasiveness.

Campaign for Nature. "Economic Benefits of Protecting 30% of Planet's Land and Ocean Outweigh the Costs at Least 5-to-1." Accessed November 3, 2021. https://www.campaignfornature
.org/protecting-30-of-the-planet-for-nature-economic-analysis.

Carlson, Allen. *Nature and Landscape: An Introduction to Environmental Aesthetics*. New York:
Columbia University Press, 2009.

Center for Disaster Management and Risk Reduction Technology. *Juni-Hochwasser 2013 in Mitteleuropa: Fokus Deutschland*. Accessed September 18, 2022. https://www.cedim.kit.edu/down
load/FDA-Juni-Hochwasser-Bericht2.1.pdf.

Center for Native Peoples and the Environment. "Center for Native Peoples and the Environment
and the Nature Conservancy Embark on Partnership." September 22, 2021. https://cnpe.home
.blog/2021/09/22/center-for-native-peoples-and-the-environment-and-the-nature conservancy
-embark-on-partnership/.

Centro Nacional de Memoria Histórica. "Mapa de Acciones en Territorio." Accessed December 1,
2021. https://centrodememoriahistorica.gov.co/donde-lo-hacemos/.

Chai, May-Lee. *Trespass: Ecotone Essayists beyond the Boundaries of Place, Identity, and Feminism.* Wilmington, NC: Lookout Books, 2018.

Chaney, Sandra. *Nature of the Miracle Years: Conservation in West Germany 1945–1975.* New York: Berghahn, 2012.

Chaney, Sandra. "Protecting Nature in a Divided Nation: Conservation in the Two Germanys, 1945–1972." In *Germany's Nature: Cultural Landscapes and Environmental History,* edited by Thomas Lekan and Thomas Zeller, 207–243. New Brunswick, NJ: Rutgers University Press, 2005.

Chanthy, Srey, and Jim Schweithelm. "Forest Resources in Cambodia's Transition to Peace: Lessons for Peacebuilding." In *Livelihood, Natural Resources, and Post-Conflict Peacebuilding,* edited by Helen Young and Lisa Goldman, 67–76. New York: Routledge, 2015.

Chapman, Robert L. "Ecological Restoration Restored." *Environmental Values* 15, no. 4 (2006): 463–478.

Chazdon, Robin L. *Second Growth: The Promise of Tropical Forest Regeneration in an Age of Deforestation.* Chicago: University of Chicago Press, 2014.

Clerici, Nicola, Dolors Armenteras, P. Kareiva, R. Botero, Juan Pablo Ramírez-Delgado, G. Forero-Medina, J. Ochoa, Carlos Pedraza, Laura Schneider, C. Lora, C. Gómez, M. Linares, Claire Hirashiki, and D. Biggs. "Deforestation in Colombian Protected Areas Increased during Post-Conflict Periods." *Scientific Reports* 10 (2020): 4971.

Clewell, Andre F. "Restoration for Natural Authenticity." *Ecological Restoration* 18, no. 4 (Winter 2000): 216–217.

Cloke, Paul, and Owain Jones. *Tree Cultures: The Place of Trees and Trees in Their Place.* Oxford: Routledge, 2002.

Cloke, Paul, and Eric Pawson. "Memorial Trees and Treescape Memories." *Environment and Planning D* 26 (2008): 107–122.

Coad, Lauren, Sotheary Lim, and Lim Nuon. "Wildlife and Livelihoods in the Cardamom Mountains, Cambodia." *Frontiers in Ecology and Evolution* 7 (August 2019): 296.

Colombia Reports. "Civilian Casualties of Colombia's Armed Conflict." Accessed July 20, 2019. https://colombiareports.com/civilians-killed-armed-conflict.

Conflict and Environment Observatory. "Colombia Country Brief." Accessed October 20, 2021. https://ceobs.org/wp-content/uploads/2018/03/CEOBS_country_brief_Colombia_2018.pdf.

Convention on Biological Diversity. "Colombia Country Profile." Accessed October 20, 2021. https://www.cbd.int/countries/profile/?country=co.

Cooke, Bill, and Uma Kothari, eds. *Participation: The New Tyranny?* New York: Zed Books, 2001.

Corntassel, Jeff. "Re-Envisioning Resurgence: Indigenous Pathways to Decolonization and Sustainable Self-Determination." *Decolonization: Indigeneity, Education and Society* 1, no. 1 (2012): 86–101.

Cronon, William. "A Place for Stories: Nature, History, and Narrative." *Journal of American History* 78, no. 4 (March 1992): 1347–1376.

Cronon, William. "The Trouble with Wilderness, or: Getting Back to the Wrong Nature." In *Uncommon Ground: Rethinking the Human Place in Nature*, edited by William Cronon, 69–90. New York: W. W. Norton and Company, 1995.

Cunsolo, Ashlee, and Neville R. Ellis. "Ecological Grief as a Mental Health Response to Climate Change-Related Loss." *Nature Climate Change* 8 (April 2018): 275–281.

Damm, Christian. "Deichrückverlegung Lenzen-Wustrow—Geschichte und Umsetzung im Rahmen eines Naturschutzgroßprojektes." *BAW Mitteilungen* 97 (2013): 23–35.

Damm, Christian. "Ecological Restoration and Dike Relocation on the River Elbe, Germany." *Scientific Annals of the Danube Delta Institute* 19 (2013): 79–86.

Damm, Christian. "Naturschutzgroßprojekt Lenzener Elbtalaue: Umsetzung und Erfahrungen eines Pilotprojekts." *Natur und Landschaft* 91, no. 8 (2016): 359–365.

Davies, Douglas. "The Evocative Symbolism of Trees." In *The Iconography of Landscape: Essays on the Symbolic Representation, Design and Use of Past Environments*, edited by David Cosgrove and Stephen Daniels, 32–42. Cambridge: Cambridge University Press, 1989.

Dayton, Paul K., Mia J. Tegner, Peter B. Edwards, and Kristin L. Riser. "Sliding Baselines, Ghosts, and Reduced Expectations in Kelp Forest Communities." *Ecological Applications* 8, no. 2 (May 1998): 309–322.

de la Bellacasa, María Puig. *Matters of Care: Speculative Ethics in More Than Human Worlds*. Minneapolis: University of Minnesota Press, 2017.

DeSilvey, Caitlin. *Curated Decay: Heritage beyond Saving*. Minneapolis: University of Minnesota Press, 2017.

Dietrich, Christian. "Einer Ökologisierung der Zeitgeschichte muss widerstanden werden." *Thüringer Landtagskurier* 10 (2016): 8. https://www.tlfdi.de/fileadmin/tlfdi/presse/landtags kurier_10_2016_internet.pdf.

Documentation Center of Cambodia. "Anlong Veng Master Plan." Accessed October 6, 2021. http://dccam.org/anlong-veng-master-plan.

Dominick, Raymond. "Capitalism, Communism, and Environmental Protection: Lessons from the German Experience." *Environmental History* 3, no. 3 (July 1998): 311–332.

Donohue, Janet. "The Betweenness of Monuments." In *Interpreting Nature: The Emerging Field of Environmental Hermeneutics*, edited by Forrest Clingerman, Brian Treanor, Martin Drenthen, and David Utsler, 264–280. New York: Fordham University Press, 2013.

Dörfler, Ernst Paul. *Die Elbe: Vom Elbsandsteingebirge bis nach Geesthacht*. Berlin: Trescher Verlag, 2016.

Dowie, Mark. *Conservation Refugees: The Hundred-Year Conflict between Global Conservation and Native Peoples*. Cambridge, MA: MIT Press, 2009.

Drenthen, Martin. "Developing Nature along Dutch Rivers: Place or Non-Place." In *New Visions of Nature: Complexity and Authenticity*, edited by Martin Drenthen, Joseph Keulartz, and James Proctor, 205–228. Heidelberg: Springer, 2009.

Drenthen, Martin. "New Nature Narratives: Landscape Hermeneutics and Environmental Ethics." In *Interpreting Nature: The Emerging Field of Environmental Hermeneutics*, edited by Forrest Clingerman, Brian Treanor, Martin Drenthen, and David Utsler, 225–241. New York: Fordham University Press, 2013.

Dungy, Camille, ed. *Black Nature: Four Centuries of African American Nature Poetry*. Athens: University of Georgia Press, 2009.

Dwyer, Owen J. "Symbolic Accretion and Commemoration." *Social and Cultural Geography* 5, no. 3 (September 2004): 419–435.

Ebbinghaus, Ruth. "Psychische Langzeitfolgen und Probleme in der Kausalitätsbegutachtung nach politischer Verfolgung in der ehemaligen SBZ und DDR." In *Übersicht über Beratungsangebote für Opfer politischer Verfolgung in der SBZ/DDR*, 23–32. 7th ed. Berlin: Bundesstiftung zur Aufarbeitung der SED-Diktatur.

Eckert, Astrid. *West Germany's Iron Curtain: Environment, Economy, and Culture in the Borderlands*. New York: Oxford University Press, 2019.

Edensor, Tim. "National Identity and the Politics of Memory: Remembering Bruce and Wallace in Symbolic Space." *Environment and Planning D* 29 (1997): 175–194.

Eisenfeld, Bernd, and Roger Engelmann. *13.8.1961: Mauerbau—Fluchtbewegung und Machtsicherung*. Bremen: Edition Temmen, 2001.

Ellwanger, Götz, Axel Ssymank, and Mareike Vischer-Leopold. *Erhaltung von Offenlandlebensräumen auf aktiven und ehemaligen militärischen Übungsflächen*. Bonn: BfN, 2012.

Engels, Jens Ivo. *Naturpolitik in der Bundesrepublik: Ideenwelt und politische Verhaltensstile in Naturschutz und Umweltbewegung 1950–1980*. Paderborn: Ferdinand Schöningh, 2006.

Erll, Astrid. *Memory in Culture*. London: Palgrave Macmillan, 2011.

EuroNatur Foundation. "Balkan Green Belt: Where EuroNatur Has Particular Experience." Accessed October 19, 2021. https://www.euronatur.org/en/what-we-do/project-areas/project-areas-a-z/balkan-green-belt/.

EuroNatur Foundation. *The European Green Belt Initiative: 10 Years of Challenges, Experiences and Achievements*. Radolfzell: EuroNatur Foundation and BUND Project Office Green Belt, 2014. Accessed January 2, 2022. https://www.euronatur.org/fileadmin/docs/projekte/Gruenes_Band/European_Greenbelt_10_years_Brochure.pdf.

European Commission. "The Habitats Directive." Accessed September 3, 2020. http://ec.europa.eu/environment/nature/legislation/habitatsdirective/index_en.htm.

European Green Belt. "Structure." Accessed November 19, 2021. https://www.europeangreenbelt.org/initiative/structure/.

Falter, Reinhard. "Rettet die Natur vor den Umweltschützern." *Garten und Landschaft 7* (1994): 4–6.

Fauna and Flora International. "Cambodia." Accessed October 1, 2021. https://www.fauna-flora.org/countries/cambodia.

Feldman, James. *Storied Wilderness: Rewilding the Apostle Islands*. Seattle: University of Washington Press, 2013.

Felter, Claire, and Danielle Renwick. "Colombia's Civil Conflict." *Council on Foreign Relations*, January 11, 2017. https://www.cfr.org/backgrounder/colombias-civil-conflict.

Finck, Peter, Manfred Klein, Uwe Riecken, and Cornelia Paulsch. *Wildnis im Dialog: Wege zu mehr Wildnis*. Bonn: BfN, 2015.

Finney, Carolyn. *Black Faces, White Spaces: Reimagining the Relationship of African Americans to the Great Outdoors*. Chapel Hill: University of North Carolina Press, 2014.

Fischer, Joern, and Maraja Riechers. "From Grief to Hope in Conservation." *Conservation Biology* 35, no. 5 (October 2021): 1698–1700.

Fivush, Robyn, and Catherine A. Haden. *Autobiographical Memory and the Construction of a Narrative Self: Developmental and Cultural Perspectives*. Mahwah, NJ: Lawrence Erlbaum and Associates, 2003.

Fleischman, Thomas. "The Half-Life of Socialism: What Radioactive Wild Boars Tell Us about the Environmental History of Reunified Germany." In *Ecologies of Socialisms: Germany, Nature, and the Left in History, Politics, and Culture*, edited by Sabine Mödersheim, Scott Moranda, and Eli Rubin, 227–250. New York: Peter Lang, 2019.

Flesch, Aaron D., Clinton W. Epps, James W. Cain III, Matt Clark, Paul R. Krausman, and John R. Morgart. "Potential Effects of the United States–Mexico Border Fence on Wildlife." *Conservation Biology* 24, no. 1 (February 2010): 171–181.

Fletcher, Michael-Shawn, Rebecca Hamilton, Wolfram Dressler, and Lisa Palmer. "Indigenous Knowledge and the Shackles of Wilderness." *PNAS* 118, no. 40 (October 2021): e2022218118.

Foroutan, Naika, and Jana Hensel. *Die Gesellschaft der Anderen*. Berlin: Aufbau Verlag, 2020.

Forsyth, Miranda, Deborah Cleland, Felicity Tepper, Deborah Hollingworth, Milena Soares, Alistair Nairn, and Cathy Wilkinson. "A Future Agenda for Environmental Restorative Justice?" *International Journal of Restorative Justice* 4, no. 1 (2021): 17–40.

Foster, David, Frederick Swanson, John Aber, Ingrid Burke, Nicholas Brokaw, David Tilman, and Alan Knapp. "The Importance of Land-Use Legacies to Ecology and Conservation." *BioScience* 53, no. 1 (January 2003): 77–88.

François, Etienne. "Europa als Erinnerungsgemeinschaft? Anmerkungen zur Frage nach einem europäischen Gedächtnis." In *Arbeit am europäischen Gedächtnis: Diktaturerfahrung und Demokratieentwicklung*, edited by Volkhard Knigge, Hans-Joachim Veen, Ulrich Mählert, and Franz-Josef Schlichting, 13–26. Weimar: Bohlau Verlag, 2011.

Franke, Nils M. *40 Jahre BUND: Die Geschichte des Bund für Umwelt und Naturschutz Deutschland e.V. 1975–2015*. Berlin: BUND, 2015.

Franke, Nils M. *Naturschutz—Landschaft—Heimat: Romantik als eine Grundlage des Naturschutzes in Deutschland*. Wiesbaden: Springer, 2017.

Franke, Nils M. "Umweltschutz ist Heimatschutz? Der Zugang des rechtsextremistischen Denkens zum Thema Heimat und eine demokratische Gegenposition." In *Heimat: Ein vielfältiges Konstrukt*, edited by Martina Hülz, Olaf Kühne, and Florian Weber, 391–401. Wiesbaden: Springer, 2019.

Frobel, Kai. "Grünes Band als Vorbild für Korea?" Grünes Band Deutschland, June 30, 2019. https://www.30-jahre-gruenes-band.de/2019/06/30/gr%C3%BCnes-band-als-vorbild-f%C3%BCr-korea/.

Frohn, Hans-Werner. "Naturschutz und Staat 1880–1976: Von naturalen Memorialinseln zur Landschaftsökologie." In *Jetzt ist die Landschaft ein Katalog voller Wörter: Beiträge zur Sprache der Ökologie*, edited by Bernd Busch, 35–41. Göttingen: Wallstein, 2007.

Fromm, Erich. *The Anatomy of Human Destructiveness*. New York: Holt, Rinehart and Winston, 1973.

Fulbrook, Mary. "The Limits of Totalitarianism: God, State and Society in the GDR." *Transactions of the Royal Historical Society* 7, no. 43 (1997): 25–52.

Füßer, Klaus, and Katharina Nowak. "Rechtsprobleme bei der Unterschutzstellung des Grünen Bandes Thüringen." *Thüringer Verwaltungsblätter* 3 (2018).

Fyfe, Jessie, and Maximilian Steinberg. "Unsettled Landscapes: Traumatic Memory in a Croatian Hinterland." *Space and Polity* 23, no. 3 (2019): 299–318.

Gagliano, Monica, Michael Renton, Martial Depczynski, and Stefano Mancuso. "Experience Teaches Plants to Learn Faster and Forget Slower in Environments Where It Matters." *Oecologia* 175, no. 1 (May 2014): 63–72.

Gann, George D., Tein McDonald, Bethanie Walder, James Aronson, Cara R. Nelson, Justin Jonson, James G. Hallett, Cristina Eisenberg, Manuel R. Guariguata, Junguo Liu, Fangyuan Hua, Cristian Echeverría, Emily Gonzales, Nancy Shaw, Kris Decleer, and Kingsley W. Dixon. "International Principles and Standards for the Practice of Ecological Restoration." *Restoration Ecology* 27, no. S1 (September 2019): S1–S46S3.

Gaudry, Karl Heinz, Katharina Diehl, Manuel Oelke, Gunnar Finke, and Werner Konold. *Machbarkeitsstudie Welterbe Grünes Band: Schlussbericht*. Bonn: BfN, 2014. https://www.bfn.de/fileadmin/BfN/internationalernaturschutz/Dokumente/BfN_Machbarkeitsstudie_Welterbe_Gruenes_Band.pdf.

Gaynor, Kaitlyn M., Kathryn J. Fiorella, Gillian H. Gregory, David J. Kurz, Katherine L. Seto, Lauren S. Withey, and Justin S. Brashares. "War and Wildlife: Linking Armed Conflict to Conservation." *Frontiers in Ecology and Environment* 14, no. 10 (December 2016): 533–542.

Geidezis, Liana, Thomas Bausch, and Helmut Schlumprecht. "Erlebnis Grünes Band: Entwicklung und Nutzung von Synergien zwischen Naturschutz und Tourismus." *Natur und Landschaft* 86, no. 12 (2011): 539–542.

Geidezis, Liana, Daniela Leitzbach, and Helmut Schlumprecht. *Aktualisierung der Bestandsaufnahme Grünes Band mit Schwerpunkt auf den Veränderungen in den Offenlandbereichen*. Bonn: BfN, 2015.

Geilhufe, Martin. "Ökologische Erinnerungsorte: Das Grüne Band." Accessed October 2012. http://www.umweltunderinnerung.de/index.php/kapitelseiten/oekologische-zeiten/96-das -gruene-band.

Ginsberg, Robert. *The Aesthetics of Ruins*. Amsterdam: Rodopi, 2004.

Goldstein, Mario. *Abenteuer Grünes Band: 100 Tage zu Fuss entlang der ehemaligen deutsch-deutschen Grenze*. Munich: Knesebeck, 2019.

Governments of Germany and Korea. "Joint Declaration of Intent." February 23, 2012. https:// www.bfn.de/fileadmin/MDB/documents/presse/Declaration_BfNGP_23_Februar.pdf.

Grass, Ingo, Péter Batáry, and Teja Tscharntke. "Combining Land-Sparing and Land-Sharing in European Landscapes." *Advances in Ecological Research* 64 (2021): 251–303.

Grenzstreifenkartierung, 234. Copy with Zweckverband Grünes Band Rodachtal—Lange Berge— Steinachtal, Coburg.

Grohmann, Andreas, W. Winter, and H. Ottenwälder. "Kurzbericht der Fachkommission Soforthilfe Trinkwasser (FKST) über mögliche Beeinträchtigungen des Trinkwassers durch Pestizide aus dem ehemaligen Grenzstreifen." *NNA Mitteilungen* 5, no. 3 (1994): 30–33.

Grünes Band Deutschland. "Durch eine Errinerungslandsch aft in der Altmark." October 28, 2019. https://www.30-jahre-gruenes-band.de/2019/10/28/durch-eine-erinnerungslandschaft-in-der-alt mark/.

Haber, Wolfgang. *Landwirtschaft und Naturschutz*. Weinheim: Wiley-VCH, 2014.

Hallmann, Caspar A., Martin Sorg, Eelke Jongejans, Henk Siepel, Nick Hofland, Heinz Schwan, Werner Stenmans, Andreas Müller, Hubert Sumser, Thomas Hörren, Dave Goulson, and Hans de Kroon. "More Than 75 Percent Decline over 27 Years in Total Flying Insect Biomass in Protected Areas." *PLoS ONE* 12, no. 10 (October 2017): e0185809.

Hamilton, Mark. *Environmental Crime and Restorative Justice*. Cham, Switzerland: Palgrave Macmillan, 2021.

Hänel, Kersten, and Heinrich Reck. *Nationwide Priorities for Re-Linking Ecosystems*. Bonn: BfN, 2010.

Hanson, Thor, Thomas M. Brooks, Gustavo A. B. Da Fonseca, Michael Hoffmann, John F. Lamoreux, Gary Machlis, Cristina G. Mittermeier, Russell A Mittermeier, and John D Pilgrim. "Warfare in Biodiversity Hotspots." *Conservation Biology* 23, no. 3 (June 2009): 578–587.

Harteisen, Ulrich, Silke Neumeyer, Susanne Schlagbauer, Kilian Bizer, Stephan Hensel, and Lukas Krüger. *Grünes Band: Modellregion für Nachhaltigkeit*. Göttingen: Universitätsverlag, 2010.

Hartmann, Andreas, and Sabine Künsting. *Grenzgeschichten: Berichte aus dem deutschen Niemandsland*. Frankfurt am Main: Fischer, 1990.

Harvey, David. "Monument and Myth." *Annals of the Association of American Geographers* 69, no. 3 (September 1979): 362–381.

Hasenöhrl, Ute. *Zivilgesellschaft und Protest: Eine Geschichte der Naturschutz- und Umweltbewegung in Bayern 1945–1980.* Göttingen: Vandenhoeck und Ruprecht, 2011.

Havlick, David G. *Bombs Away: Militarization, Conservation, and Ecological Restoration.* Chicago: University of Chicago Press, 2018.

He, Yuehui, and Zicong Li. "Epigenetic Environmental Memories in Plants: Establishment, Maintenance, and Reprogramming." *Trends in Genetics* 34, no. 11 (November 2018): 856–866.

Heinz Sielmann Stiftung. "Übersichts- und Detailkarten." Accessed December 9, 2022. https://naturschutzgrossprojekt-eichsfeld-werratal.de/de/service/projektinfos/Detailkarten/index.php.

Henkel, Martin, mayor of Geisa. Position statement. March 6, 2018. http://forum-landtag.thueringen.de/sites/default/files/downloads/Zuschrift%20Stadt%20Geisa.pdf.

Hermann, Julia-Maria, Kathrin Kiehl, Anita Kirmer, Sabine Tischew, and Johannes Kollmann. "Renaturierungsökologie im Spannungsfeld zwischen Naturschutz und neuartigen Ökosystemen." *Natur und Landschaft* 88, no 4. (2013): 149–154.

Heuveline, Patrick. "The Boundaries of Genocide: Quantifying the Uncertainty of the Death Toll during the Pol Pot Regime in Cambodia (1975–79)." *Population Studies* 69, no. 2 (2015): 201–218.

Hickey, Samuel, and Giles Mohan, eds. *Participation: From Tyranny to Transformation?* New York: Zed Books, 2004.

Higgs, Eric. *Nature by Design: People, Natural Process, and Ecological Restoration.* Cambridge, MA: MIT Press, 2003.

Higgs, Eric, Donald A. Falk, Anita Guerrini, Marcus Hall, Jim Harris, Richard J. Hobbs, Stephen T. Jackson, Jeanine M. Rhemtulla, and William Throop. "The Changing Role of History in Restoration Ecology." *Frontiers in Ecology and the Environment* 12, no. 9 (November 2014): 499–506.

Hobbs, Richard J., Salvatore Arico, James Aronson, Jill S. Baron, Peter Bridgewater, Viki A. Cramer, Paul R. Epstein, John J. Ewel, Carlos A. Klink, Ariel E. Lugo, David Norton, Dennis Ojima, David M. Richardson, Eric W. Sanderson, Fernando Valladares, Montserrat Vilà, Regino Zamora, and Martin Zobel. "Novel Ecosystems: Theoretical and Management Aspects of the New Ecological World Order." *Global Ecology and Biogeography* 15, no. 1 (January 2006): 1–7.

Hobbs, Richard J., Eric S. Higgs, and Carol M. Hall. "Defining Novel Ecosystems." In *Novel Ecosystems: Intervening in the New Ecological World Order*, edited by Richard J. Hobbs, Eric S. Higgs, and Carol M. Hall, 58–60. New York: John Wiley and Sons, 2013.

Hobbs, Richard J., Eric Higgs, Carol M. Hall, Peter Bridgewater, F. Stuart Chapin III, Erle C. Ellis, John J. Ewel, Lauren M. Hallett, James Harris, Kristen B. Hulvey, Stephen T. Jackson, Patricia L. Kennedy, Christoph Kueffer, Lori Lach, Trevor C. Lantz, Ariel E. Lugo, Joseph Mascaro, Stephen D. Murphy, Cara R. Nelson, Michael P. Perring, David M. Richardson, Timothy R. Seastedt, Rachel J. Standish, Brian M. Starzomski, Katherine N. Suding, Pedro M. Tognetti, Laith Yakob, and Laurie Yung. "Managing the Whole Landscape: Historical, Hybrid, and Novel Ecosystems." *Frontiers in Ecology and the Environment* 121, no. 10 (December 2014): 557–564.

Hood, Walter, and Grace Mitchell Tada, eds. *Black Landscapes Matter*. Charlottesville: University of Virginia Press, 2020.

Hoondert, Martin, Paul Mutsaers, and William Arfman, eds. *Cultural Practices of Victimhood*. New York: Routledge, 2019.

Hourdequin, Marion. "Ecological Restoration, Continuity and Change: Negotiating History and Meaning in Layered Landscapes." In *Restoring Layered Landscapes*, edited by Marion Hourdequin and David Havlick, 13–33. New York: Oxford University Press, 2016.

Hourdequin, Marion, and David Havlick, eds. *Restoring Layered Landscapes*. New York: Oxford University Press, 2016.

Huck, Stefan. *Artensteckbrief: Keulen-Bärlapp (Lycopodium clavatum)*. Giessen: Hessen Forst, 2009.

Huff, Tobias. "Environmental Policy in the GDR: Principles, Restrictions Failure, and Legacy." In *Ecologies of Socialisms: Germany, Nature, and the Left in History, Politics, and Culture*, edited by Sabine Mödersheim, Scott Moranda, and Eli Rubin, 53–80. New York: Peter Lang, 2019.

Igoe, James. *Conservation and Globalization: A Study of National Parks and Indigenous Communities from East Africa to South Dakota*. Belmont, CA: Thomson/Wadsworth, 2004.

Indigenous Circle of Experts. *We Rise Together: Achieving Pathways to Canada Target 1 through the Creation of Indigenous Protected and Conserved Areas in the Spirit and Practice of Reconciliation*. Accessed September 18, 2022. https://www.iccaconsortium.org/wpcontent/uploads/2018/03 /PA234-ICE_Report_2018_Mar_22_web.pdf.

Ingold, Tim. *The Perception of the Environment: Essays on Livelihood, Dwelling and Skill*. New York: Routledge, 2000.

Intergovernmental Science-Policy Platform on Biodiversity and Ecosystem Services. *Global Assessment Report on Biodiversity and Ecosystem Services: Summary for Policymakers*. 2019. https:// ipbes.net/sites/default/files/2020-02/ipbes_global_assessment_report_summary_for_policymak ers_en.pdf.

International Center for Transitional Justice. "Transitional Justice in the Former Yugoslavia." Accessed October 16, 2021. https://www.ictj.org/sites/default/files/ICTJ-FormerYugoslavia-Jus tice-Facts-2009-English.pdf.

International Union for Conservation of Nature (IUCN). "Category III: Natural Monument or Feature." Accessed July 10, 2021. https://www.iucn.org/theme/protected-areas/about/protected -areas-categories/category-iii-natural-monument-or-feature.

International Union for Conservation of Nature (IUCN). *Guidelines for Protected Area Management Categories*. Gland, Switzerland: IUCN, 1994. https://portals.iucn.org/library/efiles/edocs/1994 -007-En.pdf.

International Union for Conservation of Nature (IUCN). "Protected Areas." Accessed July 10, 2021. https://www.iucn.org/theme/protected-areas/about/protected-area-categories/category -ib-wilderness-area.

International Union for Conservation of Nature (IUCN). "Thick Shelled River Mussel (*Unio crassus*)." Accessed June 5, 2020. https://www.iucnredlist.org/species/22736/42465628#habitat -ecology.

Jähner, Harald. *Aftermath: Life in the Fallout of the Third Reich, 1945–1955*. New York: Alfred Knopf, 2022.

Jepson, Paul, and Cain Blythe. *Rewilding: The Radical New Science of Ecological Recovery*. London: Icon Books, 2020.

Johnstone, Jill F., Craig D. Allen, Jerry F. Franklin, Lee E. Frelich, Brian J. Harvey, Philip E. Higuera, Michelle C. Mack, Ross K. Meentemeyer, Margaret R. Metz, George L. W. Perry, Tania Schoennagel, and Monica G. Turner. "Changing Disturbance Regimes, Ecological Memory, and Forest Resilience." *Frontiers in Ecology and the Environment* 14, no. 7 (2016): 369–378.

Jones, Karen. "Unpacking Yellowstone: The American National Park in Global Perspective." In *Civilizing Nature: National Parks in Global Historical Perspective*, edited by Bernhard Gissibl, Sabine Höhler, and Patrick Kupper, 31–47. New York: Berghahn, 2015.

Jones, Merrill E. "Origins of the East German Environmental Movement." *German Studies Review* 16, no. 2 (May 1993): 235–264.

Jones, Owain, and Paul Cloke. *Tree Cultures: The Place of Trees and Trees in Their Place*. London: Berg, 2002.

Jongman, Rob H. G., and Gloria Pungetti, eds. *Ecological Networks and Greenways: Concept, Design, Implementation*. Cambridge: University of Cambridge, 2009.

Jordan, William R. *The Sunflower Forest: Ecological Restoration and the New Communion with Nature*. Berkeley: University of California Press, 2012.

Jørgensen, Dolly. "Rethinking Rewilding." *Geoforum* 65 (2014): 482–488.

Kaminsky, Annette, ed. *Orte des Erinnerns: Gedenkzeichen, Gedenkstätten und Museen zur Diktatur in SBZ und DDR*. Berlin: Ch. Links, 2016.

Katz, Eric. "The Big Lie: Human Restoration of Nature." In *Environmental Ethics: An Anthology*, edited by Andrew Light and Holmes Rolston, 390–397. Malden, MA: Blackwell, 2003.

Katz, Eric. "Further Adventures in the Case against Restoration." *Environmental Ethics* 34 (March 2012): 67–97.

Keenleyside, Karen, Nigel Dudley, Stephanie Cairns, Carol Hall, and Sue Stolton. *Ecological Restoration for Protected Areas*. Gland, Switzerland: IUCN, 2012.

Kelty, Chris. *The Participant: A Century of Participation in Four Stories*. Chicago: University of Chicago Press, 2020.

Kiernan, Ben. *The Pol Pot Regime: Race, Power, and Genocide in Cambodia under the Khmer Rouge, 1975–79*. 3rd ed. New Haven, CT: Yale University Press, 2008.

Kimmerer, Robin Wall. "Restoration and Reciprocity: The Contributions of Traditional Ecological Knowledge." In *Human Dimensions of Ecological Restoration: Integrating Science, Nature, and*

Culture, edited by Dave Egan, Evan E. Hjerpe, and Jesse Abrams, 257–276. Washington, DC: Island Press, 2011.

Kirchhoff, Thomas. "Wildnis." In *Naturphilosophische Grundbegriffe*, edited by Thomas Kirchhoff. Accessed September 14, 2021. http://www.naturphilosophie.org/wildnis/.

Kirchhoff, Thomas, and Ludwig Trepl, eds. *Vieldeutige Natur: Landschaft, Wildnis und Ökosystem als kulturgeschichtliche Phänomene*. Bielefeld: Transcript, 2009.

Kirksey, Eben. *Emergent Ecologies*. Durham, NC: Duke University Press, 2015.

Kirschke, Dieter, Astrid Häger, and Julia Christiane Schmid. "New Trends and Drivers for Agricultural Land Use in Germany." In *Sustainable Land Management in a European Context: A Co-Design Approach*, edited by Thomas Weith, Tim Barkmann, Nadin Gaasch, Sebastian Rogga, Christian Strauß, and Jana Zscheischler, 39–61. Cham, Switzerland: Springer 2021.

Knauer, Sebastian. "Die Endlos-Debatte über den Todesstreifen." *Der Spiegel*, November 4, 2005. https://www.spiegel.de/wissenschaft/natur/gruenes-band-die-endlos-debatte-ueber-den-todes streifen-a-383228.html.

Knigge, Volkhard. "Jenseits der Erinnerung: Zu einer Zivilgeschichte der Zukunft." *Kulturpolitische Mitteilungen* 128, no 1 (2010): 62–65.

Kolbert, Elizabeth. "Recall of the Wild: The Quest to Engineer a World before Humans." *New Yorker*, December 24–31, 2012. https://www.newyorker.com/magazine/2012/12/24/recall-of -the-wild.

Köpper, Jürgen, mayor of Frankenblick. Position statement. February 13, 2018. http://forum-land tag.thueringen.de/sites/default/files/downloads/Gemeinde%20Frankenblick.pdf.

Koshar, Rudy J. *Germany's Transient Pasts: Preservation and National Memory in the Twentieth Century*. Chapel Hill: University of North Carolina Press, 1998.

Kowol, Karin. "Grenzen trennen—Natur verbindet: Jugendbegegnungen am Grünen Band." 2020. https://www.bund-thueringen.de/service/presse/detail/news/grenzen-trennen-natur-verbin det-jugendbegegnungen-am-gruenen-band/.

Kreutz, Melanie. "Ein lebendiges Denkmal für Freiheit und Demokratie." *Politik und Kultur* 6, no. 20 (2020): 23. https://www.kulturrat.de/wp-content/uploads/2020/05/puk06-20.pdf.

Krüger, Eckart. "Wir brauchen Wildniszonen." *BUND Magazin* 4 (1997). https://www.bund-nie dersachsen.de/service/bundmagazin/41997/wir_brauchen_wildniszonen.

Küster, Hansjörg. *Die Elbe: Landschaft und Geschichte*. Munich: C. H. Beck, 2007.

LaCapra, Dominick. *Writing History, Writing Trauma*. Baltimore: Johns Hopkins University Press, 2014.

Ladd, Brian. *The Ghosts of Berlin: Confronting German History in the Urban Landscape*. Chicago: University of Chicago Press, 2008.

Landesvermessung und Geobasisinformation Brandenburg. *Die Vermesser am Fluss*. Potsdam: Landesvermessung und Geobasisinformation Brandenburg, 2009.

Langston, Nancy. *Climate Ghosts: Migratory Species in Anthropocene*. Waltham, MA: Brandeis University Press, 2021.

Lapp, Peter Joachim. *Grenzregime der DDR*. Aachen: Helios, 2013.

Leibenath, Markus. "Biotopverbund und räumliche Koordination: Chancen, Risiken und Nebenwirkungen des Metaphernpaares 'Fragmentierung—Biotopverbund.'" *Raumforschung und Raumordnung* 68 (2010): 91–101.

Lekan, Thomas. "A 'Noble Prospect': Tourism, Heimat, and Conservation on the Rhine, 1880–1914." *Journal of Modern History* 81, no. 4 (December 2009): 824–858.

Lekan, Thomas M. *Our Gigantic Zoo: A German Quest to Save the Serengeti*. New York: Oxford University Press, 2020.

Lekan, Thomas M., and Thomas M. Zeller, eds. *Imagining the Nation in Nature: Landscape Preservation and German Identity, 1885–1945*. Cambridge, MA: Harvard University Press, 2009.

Lekan, Thomas M., and Thomas M. Zeller. Introduction to *Imagining the Nation in Nature: Landscape Preservation and German Identity, 1885–1945*, edited by Thomas M. Lekan and Thomas M. Zeller, 1–18. Cambridge, MA: Harvard University Press, 2009.

Lekan, Thomas M., and Thomas Zeller. "The Landscape of German Environmental History." In *Germany's Nature: Cultural Landscapes and Environmental History*, edited by Thomas Zeller and Thomas Lekan, 1–17. New Brunswick, NJ: Rutgers University Press, 2005.

Lirsch, Eva. "Der Held in der Wildnis: Zur Darstellung des (Natur-)Raumes bei Karl May." PhD diss., University of Vienna, 2006.

Litz, Norbert. "Zur Kenntnis der Belastungssituation durch Herbizide im Bereich ehemaliger Grenzstreifen." *Nachrichtenblatt des Deutschen Pflanzenschutzdienstes* 43, no. 12 (1991): 257–261.

Lorimer, Jaime, and Clemens Driessen. "From Nazi Cows to Cosmopolitan Ecological Engineers: Specifying Rewilding through a History of Heck Cattle." *Annals of the Association of American Geographers* 106, no. 3 (2016): 631–652.

Lorimer, Jamie, and Clemens Driessen. "Wild Experiments at the Oostvaardersplassen: Rethinking Environmentalism in the Anthropocene." *Transactions of the Institute of British Geographers* 39, no. 2 (April 2014): 169–181.

Loucks, Colby, Michael B. Mascia, Andy Maxwell, Keavuth Huy, Kong Duong, Nareth Chea, Barney Long, Nick Cox, and Teak Seng. "Wildlife Decline in Cambodia, 1953–2005: Exploring the Legacy of Armed Conflict." *Conservation Letters* 2 (2009): 82–92.

Lüdemann, Katja. "Ort des Erinnerns: Gedenken an Hans-Friedrich Franck." *Altmark Zeitung*, April 10, 2016. https://www.az-online.de/altmark/salzwedel/erinnerns-gedenken-hans-friedrich-franck-6807682.html.

Lüderitz, Volker, and Uta Langheinrich. "Die Elbe und ihre Altgewässer als Lebensraum." In *Natur- und Kulturraum Elbe*, edited by Thorsten Unger, 108–113. Halle: Mitteldeutscher Verlag, 2014.

Lukas, Andreas, Thomas Jäger, and Franziska Heß. *Rechtsgutachten zur Unterschutzstellung des Grünen Bandes Thüringen als Nationales Naturmonument*. June 10, 2018. https://www.bund-thueringen.de/fileadmin/thueringen/Verfahrensbeteiligung/Baumann_Rechtsanwaelte_-__Rechtsgutachten_Gruenes_Band_Thueringen_fuer_BUND_2018.pdf.

Lundgren, Erick J., Daniel Ramp, John Rowan, Owen Middleton, Simon D. Schowanek, Oscar Sanisidro, Scott P. Carroll, Matt Davis, Christopher J. Sandom, Jens-Christian Svenning, and Arian D. Wallach. "Introduced Herbivores Restore Late Pleistocene Ecological Functions." *PNAS* 117, no. 14 (April 2020): 7871–7878.

MacKenzie, John M. *The Empire of Nature: Hunting, Conservation, and British Imperialism*. New York: Manchester University Press, 1988.

Maercker, Andreas, Ira Gäbler, and Matthias Schützwohl. "Verläufe von Traumafolgen bei ehemaligen politisch Inhaftierten der DDR." *Nervenarzt* 84, no. 1 (2013): 72–78.

Mahlzahn, Claus Christian. "Der Traum vom Leben in der Provinz." *Die Welt*, July 20, 2014. https://www.welt.de/print/wams/politik/article130348888/Der-Traum-vom-Leben-in-der-Provinz.html.

Mahnkopf, Kuno. "Grünes Band Eichsfeld-Werratal: Landvolk bekräftigt Protest." *Göttinger Tageblatt*, April 14, 2014. http://www.goettinger-tageblatt.de/Duderstadt/Uebersicht/Gruenes-Band-Eichsfeld-Werratal-Landvolk-bekraeftigt-Protest.

Margalit, Avishai. *The Ethics of Memory*. Cambridge, MA: Harvard University Press, 2004.

Markham, William T. *Environmental Organizations in Modern Germany: Hardy Survivors in the Twentieth Century and Beyond*. New York: Berghahn Books, 2008.

Mascaro, Joseph, James A. Harris, Lori Lach, Allen Thompson, Michael P. Perring, David M. Richardson, and Erle C. Ellis. "Origins of the Novel Ecosystem Concept." In *Novel Ecosystems: Intervening in the New Ecological World Order*, edited by Richard J. Hobbs, Eric S. Higgs, and Carol M. Hall, 45–57. New York: John Wiley and Sons, 2013.

Mauer, K. Whitney. "Unsettling Resilience: Colonial Ecological Violence, Indigenous Futurisms, and the Restoration of the Elwha River." *Rural Sociology* 86, no. 3 (September 2021): 611–634.

Mayer, Julia. "Connecting the Past to the Future: A Vision for Reconciliation in Anlong Veng, Cambodia." *ICOMOS*, December 13–14, 2017. http://openarchive.icomos.org/id/eprint/1978.

McAfee, Kathleen. "Selling Nature to Save It? Biodiversity and Green Developmentalism." *Environment and Planning D* 17, no. 2 (April 1999): 133–154.

McCorristine, Shane, and William M Adams. "Ghost Species: Spectral Geographies of Biodiversity Conservation." *Cultural Geographies* 27, no. 1 (2020): 101–115.

McGaugh, James. *Memory and Emotion: The Making of Lasting Memories*. New York: Columbia University Press, 2006.

McGregor, Deborah. "Indigenous Environmental Justice, Knowledge, and Law." *Kalfou* 5, no. 2 (Fall 2018): 279–296.

McKenna, Phil. "The Boys Who Loved Birds." Medium, February 16, 2015. https://medium.com/thebigroundtable/the-boys-who-loved-birds-cd6e117a608.

McKittrick, Katherine. *Demonic Grounds*. Minneapolis: University of Minnesota Press, 2006.

Meißner, Norman. "Grünes Band: Protest gegen Fällarbeiten bei Dippach." *Thüringische Landeszeitung*, February 22, 2015. https://www.tlz.de/leben/natur-umwelt/gruenes-band-protest-gegen-faellarbeiten-bei-dippach-id220729703.html.

Meißner, Norman. "Ifta: Neue Bäume am früheren Todesstreifen." *Thüringer Allgemeine Zeitung*, November 4, 2019. https://www.thueringer-allgemeine.de/regionen/eisenach/ifta-neue-baeume-am-frueheren-todesstreifen-id227541765.html.

Merriam-Webster. "Memory." Accessed August 6, 2019. https://www.merriam-webster.com/dictionary/mnemonic.

Meskell, Lynn. "An Anthropology of Absence: Commentary." In *An Anthropology of Absence: Materializations of Transcendence and Loss*, edited by Bille Mikkel, Frida Hastrup, and Tim Flohr Soerensen, 207–213. New York: Springer, 2010.

Mills, Charles W. *The Racial Contract*. Ithaca, NY: Cornell University Press, 1997.

Milton, Kay. *Loving Nature: Towards an Ecology of Emotion*. New York: Routledge, 2003.

Misztal, Barbara A. *Theories of Social Remembering*. Philadelphia: Open University Press, 2003.

Mol, Annemarie, Ingunn Moser, and Jeannette Pols, eds. *Care in Practice: On Tinkering in Clinics, Homes and Farms*. Bielefeld: Transcript Verlag, 2010.

Molano, Alfredo. *The Dispossessed: Chronicles of the Desterrados of Colombia*. Chicago: Haymarket Books, 2005.

Morales, Lorenzo. "Peace and Environmental Protection: Proposals for Sustainable Rural Development." *Inter-American Dialogue*. Accessed October 21, 2021. https://www.thedialogue.org/wp-content/uploads/2017/01/Colombia-report-Eng_Web-Res_Final-for-web.pdf.

Morley, David, and Kevin Robins. *Spaces of Identity*. London: Routledge, 1995.

Mühlhausen, Christian. "Gegen 'Grünes Band': Landwirte demonstrierten in Duderstadt." *HNA*, April 9, 2013. https://www.hna.de/lokales/goettingen/goettingen-ort28741/landwirte-demonstrieren-duderstadt-gegen-naturschutzgebiet-2842066.html.

Müller, Martin. "How Natural Disturbance Triggers Political Conflict: Bark Beetles and the Meaning of Landscape in the Bavarian Forest." *Global Environmental Change* 21, no. 3 (August 2011): 935–946.

Müller, Monika C. M., ed. *Viele Vögel sind schon weg: Vogelsterben und Biodiversität—Ursachen und Gegenmassnahmen*. Rudolstadt: Harfe Verlag, 2018.

Murcia, Carolina, James Aronson, Gustavo H. Kattan, David Moreno-Mateos, Kingsley Dixon, and Daniel Simberloff. "A Critique of the 'Novel Ecosystem' Concept." *Trends in Ecology and Evolution* 29, no. 10 (October 2014): 548–553.

Murcia, Carolina, Manuel R. Guariguata, Ángela Andrade, Germán Ignacio Andrade, James Aronson, Elsa Matilde Escobar, Andrés Etter, Flavio H. Moreno, Wilson Ramírez, and Elena Montes. "Challenges and Prospects for Scaling-Up Ecological Restoration to Meet International Commitments: Colombia as a Case Study." *Conservation Letters* 9, no. 3 (May–June 2016): 213–220.

Murphree, Marshall W. "The Strategic Pillars of Communal Natural Resource Management: Benefit, Empowerment and Conservation." *Biodiversity and Conservation* 18 (2009): 2551–2562.

Muzaini, Hamzah. "On the Matter of Forgetting and 'Memory Returns.'" *Transactions of the Institute of British Geographers* 40, no. 1 (January 2015): 102–112.

Myers, Norman, Russell A. Mittermeier, Cristina G. Mittermeier, Gustavo A. B. da Fonseca, and Jennifer Kent. "Biodiversity Hotspots for Conservation Priorities." *Nature* 403 (2000): 853–858.

"NABU bestätigt Vogelsterben in der Agrarlandschaft." *Deutschlandfunk*, May 9, 2019. https://www.deutschlandfunk.de/artenschwund-nabu-bestaetigt-vogelsterben-in-der.697.de.html?dram:article_id=448355.

NABU Thüringen. "Heckrinder weiden auf Grünem Band." November 28, 2018. https://www.ngpr-gruenes-band.de/images/presse/pressemitteilungen/181128_PM_Einweihung_Weide_Bischoftsaue.pdf.

Nadasdy, Paul. *Hunters and Bureaucrats: Power, Knowledge, and Aboriginal-State Relations in the Southwest Yukon.* Vancouver: University of British Columbia Press, 2004.

Nash, Roderick. *Wilderness and the American Mind.* New Haven, CT: Yale University Press, 2001.

National Parks Service. "American Antiquities Act of 1906." Accessed February 5, 2021. https://www.nps.gov/subjects/legal/the-antiquities-act-of-1906.htm.

Naturschutzbund Schleswig-Holstein. "Fische in der Elbe und Haseldorfer Marsch." Accessed September 26, 2021. https://schleswig-holstein.nabu.de/tiere-und-pflanzen/fische-und-neunaugen/03308.html.

Naujoks, Friedhelm. *Ökologische Erneuerung der ehemaligen DDR: Begrenzungsfaktor oder Impulsgeber für eine gesamtdeutsche Entwicklung?* Bonn: JHW Dietz, 1991.

Navarro, Laetitia M., and Henrique M. Pereira. "Rewilding Abandoned Landscapes in Europe." *Ecosystems* 15 (2012): 906.

Neiman, Susan. *Learning from the Germans: Race and the Memory of Evil.* New York: Farrar, Straus and Giroux, 2019.

Nelson, Arvid. *Cold War Ecology: Forests, Farms, and People in the East German Landscape, 1945–1989.* New Haven, CT: Yale University Press, 2005.

Neumann, Roderick. *Imposing Wilderness: Struggles over Livelihood and Nature Preservation in Africa.* Berkeley: University of California Press, 1998.

Neumann, Roderick. "Stories of Nature's Hybridity in Europe." In *The Social Lives of Forests: Past, Present, and Future of Woodland Resurgence*, edited by Susannah B. Hecht, 31–44. Chicago: University of Chicago Press, 2014.

"NGO Concerns over the Proposed 30% Target for Protected Areas and Absence of Safeguards for Indigenous Peoples and Local Communities." Accessed October 20, 2021. https://assets.sur vivalinternational.org/documents/1959/final-en-ngo-concerns-over-the-proposed-30-target-for -protected-areas-and-absence-of-safeguards-for-Indigenous-people-and-local-communities-200 901.pdf.

Noddings, Nel. *Caring: A Relational Approach to Ethics and Moral Education.* 2nd ed. Berkeley: University of California Press, 2013.

Noe, Christine, and Richard Y. M. Kangalawe. "Wildlife Protection, Community Participation in Conservation, and (Dis)Empowerment in Southern Tanzania." *Conservation and Society* 13, no. 3 (2015): 244–253.

Novak, Ben Jacob. "De-Extinction." *Genes* 9, no. 11 (November 2018): 548.

Nußdorf-Debant, A. *Sava River Restoration from Brežice to Rugvica.* Radolfzell: Euronatur Stiftung, 2021. https://www.balkanrivers.net/uploads/files/5/REVITAL_Sava_River.pdf.

Oberverwaltungsgericht Lüneburg. "Urteil vom 22.2.1999–3 K 2630/98." *Natur und Recht* 8 (1999): 471.

Obura, David O., Yemi Katerere, Mariam Mayet, Dickson Kaelo, Simangele Msweli, Khalid Mather, Jean Harris, Maxi Louis, Rachel Kramer, Taye Teferi, Melita Samoilys, Linzi Lewis, Andrew Bennie, Frederick Kumah, Moenieba Isaacs, and Pauline Nantongo. "Integrate Biodiversity Targets from Local to Global Levels." *Science* 373, no. 6556 (August 2021): 746–748.

Oelschlaeger, Max. *The Idea of Wilderness: From Prehistory to the Age of Ecology.* New Haven, CT: Yale University Press, 1993.

Ogden, Lesley Evans. "Border Walls and Biodiversity: New Barriers, New Horizons." *BioScience* 67, no. 6 (June 2017): 498–505.

Olson, David M., and Eric Dinerstein. "The Global 200: Priority Ecoregions for Global Conservation." *Annals of the Missouri Botanical Garden* 89, no. 2 (Spring 2002): 199–224.

Omnibus für Direkte Demokratie. "30 Jahre friedliche Revolution: Baumkreuz—Ein Ort, an dem die Seele nachkommen kann." Accessed September 19, 2021. https://www.youtube.com /watch?v=w30ZlZAKB7I.

"An Open Letter to the Lead Authors of 'Protecting 30% of the Planet for Nature: Costs, Benefits and Implications.'" Accessed October 20, 2021. https://openlettertowaldronetal.wordpress.com/.

Palmer, Margaret A., Joy B. Zedler, and Donald A. Falk. "Ecological Theory and Restoration Ecology." In *Foundations of Restoration Ecology*, edited by Margaret A. Palmer, Joy B. Zedler, and Donald A. Falk, 3–26. Washington, DC: Island Press, 2016.

Pan-European Common Bird Monitoring Scheme (PECBMS). "The State of Common European Birds." Accessed July 15, 2019. https://pecbms.info/wp-content/uploads/2019/03/sate-of-com mon-european-birds-2018-download.pdf.

Park, Kyung-man. "Germany's Green Belt Serves as Model for Korea's DMZ." *Hankyoreh*, November 4, 2019. https://english.hani.co.kr/arti/english_edition/e_northkorea/915752.html.

Parreñas, Juno Salazar. *Decolonizing Extinction: The Work of Care in Orangutan Rehabilitation.* Durham, NC: Duke University Press, 2018.

Parsons, Meg, Karen Fisher, and Roa Petra Crease. *Decolonising Blue Spaces in the Anthropocene.* Cham, Switzerland: Springer, 2021.

Pearce, Fred. *The New Wild: Why Invasive Species Will Be Nature's Salvation.* Boston: Beacon Press, 2015.

Pearce, Lilian. "Critical Histories for Ecological Restoration." PhD diss., Australian National University, 2019.

Pearson, Chris. "Remembering Resistance: The 'More-Than-Human' Memorial Landscapes at the Vercors and Larzac, France." *Cultural History* 2, no. 2 (2013): 199–212.

Pearson, Chris, Peter Coates, and Tim Cole. "Introduction: Beneath the Camouflage: Revealing Militarized Landscapes." In *Militarized Landscapes: From Gettysburg to Salisbury Plain*, edited by Chris Pearson, Peter Coates, and Tim Cole, 1–18. London: Bloomsbury, 2010.

Pennebaker, James W., and Becky L. Banasik. "On the Creation and Maintenance of Collective Memories: History as Social Psychology." In *Collective Memory of Political Events: Social Psychological Perspectives*, edited by James W. Pennebaker, Dario Paez, and Bernard Rimé, 3–20. Mahwah, NJ: Lawrence Erlbaum Associates, 1997.

Perazio, Vincent, dir. *Die Wildnis meldet sich zurück.* ARTE, 2019. Streaming. https://www.arte.tv/de/videos/079386-003-A/die-wildnis-meldet-sich-zurueck.

Peretti, Jonah H. "Nativism and Nature." *Environmental Values* 7 (1998): 198–200.

Perlman, Michael. *The Power of Trees: The Reforesting of the Soul.* Woodstock, CT: Spring Publications, 1994.

Perreault, Tom. "The Meaning of Mining, the Memory of Water: Collective Experience as Environmental Justice." In *Water Justice*, edited by Rutgerd Boelens, Tom Perreault, and Jeroen Vos, 316–329. New York: Cambridge University Press, 2018.

Peterson, Garry D. "Contagious Disturbance, Ecological Memory, and the Emergence of Landscape Pattern." *Ecosystems* 5 (2002): 329–338.

Pheng, Pong-Rasy, David Chandler, Christopher Dearing, and Pheana Sopheak. *A History of Democratic Kampuchea (1975–1979).* 2nd ed. Phnom Penh: Documentation Center of Cambodia, 2020. http://dccam.org/a-history-of-democratic-kampuchea-1975-1979.

"Philanthropic Statement on CBD 30x30 Initiative." Accessed October 20, 2021. https://redd-monitor.org/wp-content/uploads/2021/08/Philanthropic-Statement-on-CBD-30x30-INITIATIVE-FINAL-2021.Aug_.13-submitted-to-Mr.-Francis-Ogwal-Mr.-Basile-van-Havre-Co-Chairs-of-GBF.pdf.

Picchocki, Reinhard. *Landschaft, Heimat, Wildnis: Schutz der Natur—aber welcher und warum?* Munich: C. H. Beck, 2010.

Piechocki, Reinhard, Konrad Ott, Thomas Potthast, and Norbert Wiersbinski, eds. *Vilmer Thesen zu Grundsatzfragen des Naturschutzes*. Bonn: BfN, 2010.

Pieck, Sonja K. "Conserving Novel Ecosystems and Layered Landscapes along the Inter-German Border." *Landscape Research* 45, no. 3 (2020): 346–358.

Pieck, Sonja K. "Opportunities for Transnational Indigenous Eco-Politics: The Changing Landscape in the New Millennium." *Global Networks* 6, no. 3 (July 2006): 309–329.

Pieck, Sonja K. "What Stories Should a National Nature Monument Tell? Lessons from the German Green Belt." *Cultural Geographies* 26, no. 2 (2018): 195–210.

Pieck, Sonja K., and David G. Havlick. "From Iron Curtain to Green Belt: Considering Central Europe as a Mnemonic Ecosystem." *Society and Natural Resources* 32, no. 11 (2019): 1312–1329.

Pieck, Sonja K., and Sandra A. Moog. "Competing Entanglements in the Struggle to Save the Amazon: The Shifting Terrain of Transnational Civil Society." *Political Geography* 28, no. 7 (September 2009): 416–425.

Pimm, Stuart L., Gareth J. Russell, John L. Gittleman, and Thomas M. Brooks. "The Future of Biodiversity." *Science* 269, no. 5222 (1995): 347–350.

Planland. *Alles fließt—Der Pflege- und Entwicklungsplan für das Naturschutzgroßprojekt Lenzener Elbtalaue*. Accessed September 26, 2021. https://www.planland.de/alles-fliesst-i-der-pflege-und-entwicklungsplan-fuer-das-naturschutzgrossprojekt-lenzener-elbtalaue/.

Potapov, Peter, Matthew C. Hansen, Lars Laestadius, Svetlana Turubanova, Alexey Yaroshenko, Christoph Thies, Wynet Smith, Ilona Zhuravleva, Anna Komarova, Susan Minnemeyer, and Elena Esipova. "The Last Frontiers of Wilderness: Tracking Loss of Intact Forest Landscapes from 2000 to 2013." *Science Advances* 3, no 1 (2017): e1600821.

Powell, Miles A. *Vanishing America: Species Extinction, Racial Peril, and the Origins of Conservation*. Cambridge, MA: Harvard University Press, 2016.

Prominski, Martin. "Dilemma Landschaft?" *Stadt + Grün* 3 (2004): 34–39.

Prüter, Johannes. "Die Elbe im Biosphärenreservat 'Niedersächsische Elbtalaue.'" *Zeitschrift für Stadt-, Regional-, und Landesentwicklung* 2 (2015): 72–87.

Purps, Jochen, Christian Damm, and Frank Neuschulz. "Naturschutzgrossprojekt Lenzener Elbtalaue, Brandenburg: Auenregenration durch Deichrückverlegung an der Elbe." *Natur und Landschaft* 79, no. 9–10 (2004): 408–415.

Pyne, Stephen. *Fire: A Brief History*. Seattle: University of Washington Press, 2019.

Rada, Uwe. *Die Elbe: Europas Geschichte im Fluss*. Munich: Siedler, 2013.

Radkau, Joachim. *The Age of Ecology*. Malden, MA: Polity Press, 2013.

Rekow, Alexander. "Ein Dorf als stummer Zeuge." *Volksstimme*, January 25, 2018. https://www.volksstimme.de/lokal/salzwedel/ein-dorf-als-stummer-zeuge-872962.

Republic of Korea. *Fourth National Biodiversity Strategy, 2019–2023*. https://www.cbd.int/doc/world/kr/kr-nbsap-v4-en.pdf.

"Resolution." Bund Naturschutz in Bayern, December 9, 1989. Copy with BUND Green Belt office.

Reusswig, Fritz. "Heimat und politische Parteien." In *Heimat: Ein vielfältiges Konstrukt*, edited by Martina Hülz, Olaf Kühne, and Florian Weber, 371–390. Wiesbaden: Springer, 2019.

Reusswig, Fritz. "Lebensstile und Naturorientierungen: Gesellschaftliche Naturbilder und Einstellungen zum Naturschutz." In *Lebensstile und Nachhaltigkeit: Konzepte, Befunde und Potentiale*, edited by Dieter Rink, 156–180. Wiesbaden: Springer, 2002.

Reyes-García, Victoria, Álvaro Fernández-Llamazares, Pamela McElwee, Zsolt Molnár, Kinga Öllerer, Sarah J. Wilson, and Eduardo S. Brondizio. "The Contributions of Indigenous Peoples and Local Communities to Ecological Restoration." *Restoration Ecology* 27, no. 1 (January 2019): 3–8.

River Restoration Northwest. "Biocultural Restoration." Accessed November 1, 2021. https://www.rrnw.org/biocultural/.

Roberts, Patrick, Rebecca Hamilton, and Dolores R. Piperno. "Tropical Forests as Key Sites of the 'Anthropocene': Past and Present Perspectives." *PNAS* 118, no. 40 (October 2021): e2109243118.

Robertson, Morgan M. "The Nature That Capital Can See: Science, State, and Market in the Commodification of Ecosystem Services." *Environment and Planning D* 24, no. 3 (June 2006): 367–387.

Robinson, Cedric J. *Black Marxism: The Making of the Black Radical Tradition*. Chapel Hill: University of North Carolina Press, 2000.

Robinson, Jake M., Nick Gellie, Danielle MacCarthy, Jacob G. Mills, Kim O'Donnell, and Nicole Redvers. "Traditional Ecological Knowledge in Restoration Ecology: A Call to Listen Deeply, to Engage with, and Respect Indigenous Voices." *Restoration Ecology* 29, no. 4 (May 2021): e13381.

Rodríguez-Izquierdo, Emilio, M. Gavin, and Miguel O. Macedo-Bravo. "Barriers and Triggers to Community Participation across Different Stages of Conservation Management." *Environmental Conservation* 37, no. 3 (2010): 239–249.

Rogers, Alisdair, Noel Castree, and Rob Kitchin. *A Dictionary of Human Geography*. Oxford: Oxford University Press, 2013.

Rohwedder, Cecile. "Deep in the Forest, Bambi Remains the Cold War's Last Prisoner." *Wall Street Journal*, November 4, 2009. https://www.wsj.com/articles/SB125729481234926717.

Rohwer, Yasha, and Emma Marris. "Renaming Restoration: Conceptualizing and Justifying the Activity as a Restoration of Lost Moral Value rather than a Return to a Previous State." *Restoration Ecology* 24, no. 5 (September 2016): 674–679.

Roka, Krishna. "Community-Based Natural Resources Management." In *Life on Land: Encyclopedia of the UN Sustainable Development Goals*, edited by Walter Leal Filho, Anabela Marisa Azul, Luciana Brandli, Amanda Lange Salvia, and Tony Wall, 1–14. Cham, Switzerland: Springer, 2021.

Roth, Roland, and Dieter Rucht, eds. *Die sozialen Bewegungen in Deutschland seit 1945: Ein Handbuch*. Frankfurt am Main: Campus, 2008.

Rubin, Eli. "The Greens, the Left, and the GDR: A Critical Reassessment." In *Ecologies of Socialisms: Germany, Nature, and the Left in History, Politics, and Culture*, edited by Sabine Mödersheim, Scott Moranda, and Eli Rubin, 167–200. New York: Peter Lang, 2019.

Rucht, Dieter, and Jochen Roose. "Zur Institutionalisierung von Bewegungen: Umweltverbände und Umweltprotest in der Bundesrepublik." In *Verbände und Demokratie in Deutschland*, edited by Annette Zimmer and Bernhard Weßels, 261–290. Opladen: Leske+Budrich, 2001.

Rudnick, Carola. *Die andere Hälfte der Erinnerung: Die DDR in der deutschen Geschichtspolitik nach 1989*. Bielefeld: Transcript, 2011.

Salazar, Alejandro, Adriana Sanchez, Juan Camilo Villegas, Juan F. Salazar, Daniel Ruiz Carrascal, Stephen Sitch, Juan Darío Restrepo, Germán Poveda, Kenneth J. Feeley, Lina M. Mercado, Paola A. Arias, Carlos A. Sierra, Maria del Rosario Uribe, Angela M. Rendón, Juan Carlos Pérez, Guillermo Murray Tortarolo, Daniel Mercado-Bettin, José A. Posada, Qianlai Zhuang, and Jeffrey S. Dukes. "The Ecology of Peace: Preparing Colombia for New Political and Planetary Climates." *Frontiers in Ecology and Environment* 16, no. 9 (2018): 525–531.

Salazar, Juan Francisco. "Healing Colombia's War-Ravaged Landscapes." *Conversation*, August 25, 2017. https://theconversation.com/healing-colombias-war-ravaged-landscapes-82494.

Schaefer, Sagi. *States of Division: Borders and Boundary Formation in Cold War Rural Germany*. New York: Oxford University Press, 2014.

Schama, Simon. *Landscape and Memory*. New York: Alfred Knopf, 1995.

Scharnowski, Susanne. *Heimat: Geschichte eines Missverständnisses*. Darmstadt: WBG, 2019.

Scholz, Mathias, Sabine Stab, Frank Dziock, and Klaus Henle, eds. *Lebensräume der Elbe und ihrer Auen*. Berlin: Weissensee, 2002.

Schönhoven, Klaus. "Europa als Erinnerungsgemeinschaft." *Gesprächskreis Geschichte* 75, 5–31. Bonn: Friedrich Ebert Stiftung, 2007. https://library.fes.de/pdf-files/historiker/05122.pdf.

Schroeder, Klaus, and Jochen Staadt. *Die Todesopfer des DDR-Grenzregimes an der innerdeutschen Grenze 1949–1989: Ein biographisches Handbuch*. Berlin: Forschungsverbund SED-Staat, 2017.

Schumacher, Heiko, Peter Finck, Uwe Riecken, and Manfred Klein. "More Wilderness for Germany: Implementing an Important Objective of Germany's National Strategy on Biological Diversity." *Journal for Nature Conservation* 42 (2018): 45–52.

Schwartz, Katrina Z. S. *Nature and National Identity after Communism: Globalizing the Ethnoscape*. Pittsburgh: University of Pittsburgh Press, 2006.

Sembrando Paz. "Misión y Visión." Accessed December 10, 2021. https://www.sembrandopaz.org/mision-y-vision.

Shapiro, Beth. "Pathways to De-Extinction: How Close Can We Get to Resurrection of an Extinct Species?" *Functional Ecology* 31, no. 5 (May 2017): 996–1002.

Sheffer, Edith. *Burned Bridge: How East and West Germans Made the Iron Curtain*. New York: Oxford University Press, 2011.

Shim, Suk Kyung. "Governance of the German Green Belt Ecological Network: Implications for the Demilitarized Zone." PhD diss., Humboldt-Universität zu Berlin, 2011.

Sielmann, Heinz, dir. *Expeditionen ins Tierreich: Tiere im Schatten der Grenze*, 1988. https://www.ndr.de/fernsehen/sendungen/expeditionen_ins_tierreich/expeditionen249.html.

Singh, Neera M. "Introduction: Affective Ecologies and Conservation." *Conservation and Society* 16, no. 1 (2018): 1–7.

Society for Ecological Restoration. *The SER International Primer on Ecological Restoration*. Tucson: Society for Ecological Restoration International, 2004.

Soulé, Michael, and Reed Noss. "Rewilding and Biodiversity: Complementary Goals for Continental Conservation." *Wild Earth* 3 (1998): 18–28.

Spence, Mark David. *Dispossessing the Wilderness: Indian Removal and the Making of the National Parks*. New York: Oxford University Press, 1999.

Spiro, Jonathan. *Defending the Master Race: Conservation, Eugenics, and the Legacy of Madison Grant*. Lebanon, NH: University of New England Press, 2009.

Spundflasch, Frank. "Renaturierung des Fließgewässers Föritz: Ein Beitrag zur Umsetzung der Europäischen Wasserrahmenrichtlinie." In *Bericht zur Landentwicklung 2005*, 45–49. Erfurt: Thüringer Ministerium für Landwirtschaft, Naturschutz und Umwelt, 2005.

Srinivasan, Krithika. "Caring for the Collective: Biopower and Agential Subjectification in Wildlife Conservation." *Environment and Planning D* 32, no. 3 (June 2014): 501–517.

Stacy, William E. *US Army Border Operations in Germany, 1945–1983*. Heidelberg: Military History Office, 1984. https://history.army.mil/documents/BorderOps/content.htm.

Standish, Rachel J., Allen Thompson, Eric S. Higgs, and Stephen Murphy. "Concerns about Novel Ecosystems." In *Novel Ecosystems: Intervening in the New Ecological World Order*, edited by Richard J. Hobbs, Eric S. Higgs, and Carol M. Hall, 296–309. New York: John Wiley and Sons, 2013.

Stanway, David. "Countries Call for Urgent Action on Biodiversity with 'Kunming Declaration.'" Reuters, October 13, 2021. https://www.reuters.com/world/china/countries-adopt-kunming-declaration-boost-biodiversity-china-says-2021-10-13/.

Steele, Abbey. *Democracy and Displacement in Colombia's Civil War*. Ithaca, NY: Cornell University Press, 2017.

"Stellungnahme des Landesbeauftragen zur Aufarbeitung der SED-Diktatur zum Gesetzesentwurf Nationales Naturmonument Grünes Band Thüringen." June 13, 2018. http://www.thla-thueringen.de/images/Stellungnahme_Umweltausschuss.pdf.

Stiftung Liebenthaler Pferde. "Chronologie." Accessed October 5, 2021. https://www.liebenthaler-pferdeherde.de/seite/276393/chronologie.html.

Stoll-Kleemann, Susanne. "Barriers to Nature Conservation in Germany: A Model Explaining Opposition to Protected Areas." *Journal of Environmental Psychology* 21 (2001): 369–385.

Strauss, H. "Zur Diskussion über Biotopverbundsysteme: Versuch einer kritischen Bestandsauf-nahme." *Natur und Landschaft* 63, no. 9 (1988): 374–378.

Sturm, Knut. "Prozeßschutz—Ein Konzept für naturschutzgerechte Waldwirtschaft." *Zeitschrift für Ökologie und Naturschutz* 2 (1993): 181–192.

Succow, Michael, Lebrecht Jeschke, and Hans Dieter Knapp. *Naturschutz in Deutschland: Rückblicke—Einblicke—Ausblicke*. Munich: Ch. Links, 2013.

Sustr, Pavel. "For Red Deer, Iron Curtain Habits Die Hard." NPR, March 1, 2014. https://www.npr.org/2014/05/01/308737872/for-red-deer-iron-curtain-habits-die-hard.

Sweatt, J. David. *Mechanisms of Memory*. London: Elsevier, 2010.

Terry, Andrew, Karin Ullrich, and Uwe Riecken. *The Green Belt of Europe: From Vision to Reality*. Gland, Switzerland: IUCN, 2006.

Theiss, Norbert. "Lebensraum Grenzstreifen." *Ornithologischer Anzeiger* 32 (1993): 1–9.

Thomas, Julia Adeney. "The Exquisite Corpses of Nature and History: The Case of the Korean DMZ." In *Militarized Landscapes: From Gettysburg to Salisbury Plain*, edited by Chris Pearson, Peter Coates, and Tim Cole, 151–170. London: Bloomsbury, 2010.

Thönges-Stringaris, Rhea. "Joseph Beuys: 7000 Eichen—Eine unsichtbare Skulptur." Stiftung 7000 Eichen. Accessed October 14, 2021. http://www.7000eichen.de/?id=32.

Thüringer Landesanstalt für Umwelt und Geologie. "Landkreis Eichsfeld: Landwirtschaftliche Standortbedingungen." Accessed October 27, 2020. http://www.tlug-jena.de/uw_raum/umwelt regional/eic/eic06.html.

Thüringer Landtag. "Diskussionsforum: Nationales Naturmonument und Grünes Band Thürin-gen." Accessed October 22, 2021. http://forum-landtag.thueringen.de/dokument/nationales -naturmonument-und-gruenes-band-thueringen.

Thüringer Landtag. "Gesetzentwurf der Landesregierung: Thüringer Gesetz über das Nationale Naturmonument Grünes Band Thüringen." September 13, 2017. https://parldok.thueringer -landtag.de/ParlDok/dokument/64115/thueringer_gesetz_ueber_das_nationale_naturmonu ment_gruenes_band_thueringen_thueringer_gruenes_band_gesetz_thuergbg.pdf.

Thüringer Landtag. "Thüringer Gesetz über das Nationale Naturmonument Grünes Band Thürin-gen." December 18, 2018. https://umwelt.thueringen.de/fileadmin/001_TMUEN/Unsere_The men/Natur_Artenschutz/Gruenes_Band/thueringer_Gesetz_12.18_thurgbg.pdf.

Till, Karen. *The New Berlin: Memory, Politics, Place*. Minneapolis: University of Minnesota Press, 2005.

Tran, Tanya C., Natalie C. Ban, and Jonaki Bhattacharyya. "Indigenous Approaches to Conserva-tion; A Review of Successes, Challenges, and Lessons from Indigenous Protected and Conserved Areas." *Biological Conservation* 241 (January 2020): 108271.

Tronto, Joan. *Moral Boundaries: A Political Argument for an Ethic of Care*. New York: Routledge, 1993.

Tyner, James A. *Landscape, Memory, and Post-Violence in Cambodia.* London: Rowman and Littlefield, 2017.

Uekötter, Frank. *Die Wahrheit ist auf dem Feld: Eine Wissensgeschichte der deutschen Landwirtschaft.* Göttingen: Vandenhoeck und Ruprecht, 2012.

Uekötter, Frank. *The Green and the Brown: A History of Conservation in Nazi Germany.* New York: Cambridge University Press, 2006.

Uekötter, Frank. *The Greenest Nation? A New History of German Environmentalism.* Cambridge, MA: MIT Press, 2015.

Ullrich, Maren. *Geteilte Ansichten: Erinnerungslandschaft deutsch-deutsche Grenze.* Berlin: Aufbau, 2006.

UN Convention on Biological Diversity. "First Draft of the Post-2020 Global Biodiversity Framework." Accessed November 5, 2021. https://www.cbd.int/doc/c/abb5/591f/2e46096d3f0330b 08ce87a45/wg2020-03-03-en.pdf.

UNEP-WCMC and IUCN. *Protected Planet Report 2020.* Cambridge, UK: UNEP-WCMC, 2021. https://livereport.protectedplanet.net/.

Union der Opferverbände kommunistischer Gewaltherrschaft. "Mahnmal gegen das Vergessen: Am Grünen Band zwischen Mechau und Bockleben wird an getöteten Grenzflüchtling erinnert." August 2018. https://www.uokg.de/2018/08/rainer-burgis-wird-mit-mahnmal-geehrt.

United Nations Educational, Scientific, and Cultural Organization (UNESCO). "Ecological Sciences for Sustainable Development: Biosphere Reserves—Learning Sites for Sustainable Development." Accessed June 25, 2019. http://www.unesco.org/new/en/natural-sciences/environment /ecological-sciences/biosphere-reserves/.

van der Kolk, Bessel. *The Body Keeps the Score: Brain, Mind, and Body in the Healing of Trauma.* New York: Viking, 2014.

van der Windt, Henny, and J. A. A. Swart. "Ecological Corridors, Connecting Science and Politics: The Case of the Green River in the Netherlands." *Journal of Applied Ecology* 45 (2008): 124–132.

van Dooren, Thom. *Flight Ways: Life and Loss at the Edge of Extinction.* New York: Columbia University Press, 2014.

van Meerbeek, Koenrad, Bart Buys, Simon D. Wchowanek, and Jens-Christian Svenning. "Reconciling Conflicting Paradigms of Biodiversity Conservation: Human Intervention and Rewilding." *BioScience* 69, no. 12 (2019): 997–1007.

Vera, Frans. *Grazing Ecology and Forest History.* Wallingford, UK: CABI, 2000.

Verein zum Schutz der Kulturlandschaft und des Eigentums im Elbtal (VSKE). "Unser Leitbild." Accessed August 22, 2021. https://www.kulturland-elbtal.de/unser-leitbild.html.

Wagner, Eric. "The DMZ's Thriving Resident: The Crane." *Smithsonian Magazine*, April 2011. https://www.smithsonianmag.com/science-nature/the-dmzs-thriving-resident-the-crane-953694/.

Wald, Sarah D., David J. Vázquez, Priscilla Solis Ybarra, and Sarah Jaquette Ray, eds. *Latinx Environmentalisms: Place, Justice, and the Decolonial.* Philadelphia: Temple University Press, 2019.

Walker, Margaret Urban. *Moral Repair: Reconstructing Moral Relations after Wrongdoing.* Cambridge: Cambridge University Press, 2012.

Wallington, Tabatha J., Richard J. Hobbs, and Susan A. Moore. "Implications of Current Ecological Thinking for Biodiversity Conservation: A Review of the Salient Issues." *Ecology and Society* 10, no. 1 (June 2005): 15.

Ward, J. V., K. Tockner, D. B. Arscott, and C. Claret. "Riverine Landscape Diversity." *Freshwater Biology* 47, no. 4 (April 2002): 517–539.

Ward, J. V., K. Tockner, and F. Schiemer. "Biodiversity of Floodplain River Ecosystems: Ecotones and Connectivity." *River Research and Applications* 15, no. 1–3 (January–June 1999): 125–139.

Watson, Annette. "Misunderstanding the 'Nature' of Co-Management: A Geography of Regulatory Science and Indigenous Knowledges (IK)." *Environmental Management* 52 (2013): 1085–1102.

Watt, Laura Alice. *The Paradox of Preservation: Wilderness and Working Landscapes at Point Reyes National Seashore.* Oakland: University of California Press, 2016.

Wehi, Priscilla M., and Janice M. Lord. "Importance of Including Cultural Practices in Ecological Restoration." *Conservation Biology* 31, no. 5 (October 2017): 1109–1118.

Weiger, Hubert. Letter, November 30, 1989. Copy with BUND Green Belt office in Nuremberg.

Weller, Francis. *The Wild Edge of Sorrow: Rituals of Renewal and the Sacred Work of Grief.* Berkeley, CA: North Atlantic Books, 2015.

Wensierski, Peter. *Von oben nach unten wächts gar nichts: Umweltzerstörung und Protest in der DDR.* Reinbek: Fischer Verlag, 1986.

Wensierski, Peter. "Wir haben Angst um unsere Kinder." *Der Spiegel* 29 (1985): 62–68.

Whyte, Kyle Powys, and Chris Cuomo. "Ethics of Caring in Environmental Ethics: Indigenous and Feminist Philosophies." In *The Oxford Handbook of Environmental Ethics,* edited by Stephen M. Gardiner and Allen Thompson, 234–235. New York: Oxford University Press, 2017.

Wild, Trevor, and Philip Jones. "From Peripherality to New Centrality? Transformation of Germany's Zonenrandgebiet." *Geography* 78, no. 3 (1993): 281–294.

Wilke, Christiane. "Recognizing Victimhood: Politics and Narratives of Rehabilitation in Germany." *Journal of Human Rights* 6, no. 4 (2007): 479–496.

Williams, Florence. *The Nature Fix: Why Nature Makes Us Happier, Healthier, and More Creative.* New York: W. W. Norton and Company, 2017.

Willis, Katherine J., and Harry John Birks. "What Is Natural? The Need for a Long-Term Perspective in Biodiversity Conservation." *Science* 314, no. 5803 (November 2006): 1261–1265.

Wilson, Anne, and Michael Ross. "The Identity Function of Autobiographical Memory: Time Is on Our Side." *Memory* 11, no. 2 (March 2003): 137–149.

Wilson, Edward O. *Biophilia*. Cambridge, MA: Harvard University Press, 1984.

Wilson, Edward O. *Half-Earth: Our Planet's Fight for Life*. New York: Liveright Publishing, 2016.

Windle, Phyllis. "The Ecology of Grief." *BioScience* 42, no. 5 (May 1992): 363–366.

Wir für Wildnis. "Wildnis in Deutschland." Accessed October 19, 2021. https://wildnisindeutsch land.de/.

Wiseman, Hadas, and Jacques P. Barber. *Echoes of the Trauma: Relational Themes and Emotions in Children of Holocaust Survivors*. Cambridge: Cambridge University Press, 2008.

Wollschläger, Katja. "Neue Heimat: Heckrinder beziehen Bischofsaue." *Südthüringen*, November 28, 2018. https://www.insuedthueringen.de/inhalt.hildburghausen-neue-heimat-heckrinder -beziehen-bischofsaue.da43f823-1a91-4eef-93d9-d9a4caaf644c.html.

World Wildlife Fund. *Living Colombia: A Megadiverse Country Facing the Future*. Cali: WWF-Colombia, 2017. https://wwflac.awsassets.panda.org/downloads/colombia_viva___informe _2017__resumen_en_ingles.pdf.

World Wildlife Fund. *Living Planet Report 2020*. https://f.hubspotusercontent20.net/hubfs /4783129/LPR/PDFs/ENGLISH-FULL.pdf.

Worster, Donald. *Nature's Economy: A History of Ecological Ideas*. New York: Cambridge University Press, 1994.

Wuerthner, George, Eileen Crist, and Tom Butler, eds. *Keeping the Wild: Against the Domestication of Earth*. Washington, DC: Island Press, 2014.

Yehuda, Rachel. "Post-Traumatic Stress Disorder." *New England Journal of Medicine* 346 (January 2002): 108–114.

Young, Iris Marion. *Justice and the Politics of Difference*. Princeton, NJ: Princeton University Press, 1990.

Zerbe, Stefan. *Renaturierung von Ökosystemen im Spannungsfeld von Mensch und Umwelt*. Berlin: Springer, 2019.

Zimmerer, Karl, ed. *Globalization and New Geographies of Conservation*. Chicago: University of Chicago Press, 2006.

Zucker, Eve Monique. *Forest of Struggle: Moralities of Remembrance in Upland Cambodia*. Honolulu: University Hawai'i Press, 2013.

Zweckverband Grünes Band Rodachtal–Lange Berge–Steinachtal. "Anbau alter Sorten." Accessed October 8, 2021. https://www.ngpr-gruenes-band.de/massnahmen/anbau-alter-sorten.

Index

Note: page numbers in italics refer to figures.

Agriculture in Germany. *See also* Farmers
  conservationists' idealized view of, 68
  damage to biodiversity, 62–63
  declining employment and outmigration,
    109
  effect of inter-German border on, 37–38
  as greatest threat to Green Belt, 49
  huge tracts as norm in, 109
Animals. *See also* Birds; De-extinction; Eco-
    logical ghosts
  as cocreators of landscape, 128–129, 142–
    144
  current endangered status, 61–64
  loss of due to border, 40–43
  as memorial devices, 30, 146–147
  and mnemonic ecologies, 32
  native (*beheimatet*) vs. invasive (*gebiets-
    fremd*), 149
Arbeitskreis Ökologie Coburg. *See* Ecological
    Working Group Coburg
Art. *See* Ecological art along border
Association for Homeland Preservation, 70
Association for the Protection of the Cultural
    Landscape and Property in the Elbe Valley
    (VSKE), 139, 148
Aufarbeitung (reckoning with the past)
  Korean DMZ and, 161
  restoration and conservation as type of, 191

  as term, 203n12
  US and, 178

Baumkreuz von Ifta. See *Tree Cross of Ifta*
    (*Baumkreuz von Ifta*)
Bavarian Association for Nature Conservation
    (BN), 48
  criticisms of, 71
  and founding of BUND, 73
  influence of German conservationist tradi-
    tion on, 71
Bavarian Environmental Ministry, and Green
    Belt, 49
Beavers, reintroduction of, 7
Beuys, Joseph, 87
BfN. *See* Federal Agency for Nature Conser-
    vation
Biocultural restoration, 175–176, 179
Biodiversity
  global, rapid decline in, 167
  high, percentage of wars fought in regions
    with, 153
  as term, and *Naturschutz* vs. *Umweltschutz*,
    79
Biodiversity, global conservation efforts
  burden on local people and, 169–170
  and community-based conservation, 170,
    181

Biodiversity, global conservation efforts (cont.)
  and cultural landscapes concept, 171, 188
  divergent viewpoints in, 171
  in economic terms, 168–169
  efforts toward post-2020 policy on, 168–171, 181
  "half-earth" proposal, 168
  and neocolonialism, 169–170
  science-based approach separate from social concerns, 170
  and sustainable development, 170
  30x30 proposal, 168–169
Biophilia, 33
Birds
  in Cambodia, 163, 165
  declining numbers in Germany, 62–63
  in Korea's DMZ, 160
  nonnative, concerns about, 149
  species thriving in Green Belt, 6, 41, 43, 44, 49
BN. See Bavarian Association for Nature Conservation
Border fortifications, East German, 37
  deforestation and flattening of border zone, 1, 40
  development over time, 36–38
  on Elbe River, 136–137
  and herbicide drift into West, 38, 40
  local people's dismantling of, after reunification, 59
  mines and spring guns in, 2, 37, 40, 106
  number of GDR guards along, 106
  physical remnants of, 2, 59–60
Borderlands, definition of, 197n1 (intro)
Border zone between East and West. See also Green Belt (Grünes Band)
  animal deaths from land mines, 40
  critics of West German perspective on, 107
  discovery of novel ecologies in, 64
  disruption of migration patterns, 40
  ecological effects, 40–43
  effect on agriculture, 37–38

establishment of, 35
fatalities in, 35, 106, 137, 202n2
grasslands on Western side of fence, 41
injury to residents' sense of belonging, 122
land and property seized to create, 1, 2, 10, 36–37
land ownership as ongoing issue in, 39
as layered landscape, 15, 34, 53
maintaining trace of, in Green Belt open land, 57–58, 58
memorials to local tragedies in, 5
preservation of river environments in, 43, 204n25
rare and endangered species in, 1, 6, 40–42, 43–45, 44, 49
residents displaced to create, 36, 38
return of wetlands, 6–7, 42
suffering caused by, 35
uses of, immediately after reunification, 49–50
Brandt, Willy, 72
BUND (Bund für Umwelt und Naturschutz Deutschland)
  absorption of East German environmental groups, 78
  and activism for Green Belt creation, 64–65
  and Elbe River national park designation, 138–140
  founding and growth of, 73–74, 209n19
  and gaps in Green Belt, 54–55
  and Green Belt Experience, 52–54
  Green Belt project office, founding of, 50
  and initial meeting on Green Belt, 47
  layered landscape concept of, as model, 161–162
  Lenzen Declaration (2019), 61, 152
  and management of Green Belt, 8, 56–58
  as NGO spearheading Green Belt, 8
  purchase of border zone lands, 50–51
  sale of "shares" to fund Green Belt land purchases, 51

turn to environmental protection (*Umwelt-schutz*), 75

work with South Koreans on DMZ conservation plans, 160–161

BUND, and Green Belt as memorial landscape

BUND programs emphasizing, 60–61

and ecological art along border, 86, 88

and Lenzen Declaration, 61, 186

and ruins as memorial sites, 94

and storytelling as memorial, 95, 96, 99, 100

turn to focus on, 65, 184

youth camps to train volunteers, 60–61

BUND campaign to make Green Belt a nature monument, 100, 101–108. *See also* Nature Monument Law, in Thuringia

avoidance of criticism of GDR, 107

broad themes of, 104–105

BUND website on, 103–105, *104*, 106–107, *107*, 108

complexity of, 101

debate in Thuringian parliament on, 114–115

focus on *Erinnerungsarbeit* (memory work) as response to, 116

and *Heimatschutz*, connection to, 107–108

laws on nature monuments, 102

legal challenge to, 116

opposition to, 109–113, 114–116

story of border fortifications and GDR oppression in, 106–107

story of ecological resurgence in, 105–106

strategies for overcoming opposition, 113–114

Thuringia and, 102–103

values revealed by narratives of, 101

Bundesamt für Naturschutz (BfN). *See* Federal Agency for Nature Conservation (BfN)

Bundesnaturschutzgesetz (BNatSchG). *See* Federal Conservation Law of 2009

Bundesstiftung zur Aufarbeitung der SED-Diktatur. *See* Federal Foundation for the Study of the Communist Dictatorship in Eastern Germany

Bund für Heimatschutz. *See* Association for Homeland Preservation

Bund für Umwelt und Naturschutz Deutschland. *See* BUND

Bund Naturschutz Bayern (BN). *See* Bavarian Association for Nature Conservation (BN)

Calcareous grasslands, 124, 128, 145, 146, 217n4

Cambodia, 162–164

deforestation in, 163

ecological diversity at risk in, 163

inevitability of mnemonic ecology in, 163–164

mnemonic ecologies and social justice in, 176–177

Cambodia, Khmer Rouge regime in

death and destruction under, 162

memorialization of sites of violence, 162–163

ongoing trauma from, 163–164

Campaign for Nature, 168, 169

Carson, Rachel, 72

Castle Lenzen Association, 141

Center for Native American Peoples and the Environment, 175, 178

Climate change, and ecological instability, 172

Club of Rome, 72, 76

Colombia, 164–167

civil war in, 164–165

ecological diversity at risk in, 165–166

inevitability of mnemonic ecology in, 166

local remembrance of violence in, 166, 189

mnemonic ecologies and social justice in, 177–178

National Center for Historic Memory (CNMH), 165, 177

post–civil war economic development, 166

Colonialism, identity-crushing effects of, 173
  as inherent in conservation, 131, 169–171,
    188
Commemorative practices, and mnemonic
  ecologies, 30–31
Conservation
  cultural, 179
  decolonized, 172–173
  importance of emotions to, 100–101
  issues of power, space, and national identity
    in, 117
  new nonequilibrium paradigm in, 16–17,
    19
  and novel ecosystems, 19
  political, economic, and cultural factors in,
    126
  vs. restoration, 16, 17, 19, 180
Conservation Fund, 178–179
Conservation in East Germany, 75–77
  coal use and, 75–76, 210n26
  and concern about Western opinion,
    210n27
  focus on homeland protection (*Heimatsch-
    utz*), 77
  government suppression of environmental-
    ism, 76
  pre-reunification creation of nature reserves,
    77–78
  West German absorption of environmental
    groups, 78
Conservation in Germany. *See also* Environ-
    mentalism in Germany
  blending of conservation and restoration,
    19
  cultural landscape as focus of, 20, 68, 70, 71
  and emotional ties to environment, 79–81,
    82
  and local and national identity, 80–81
  and natural monuments preservation
    (*Denkmalschutz*), 68–69, 71, 82
  nature preservation (*Naturschutz*) as one
    thread in, 71, 82

postwar empiricism of, 72
  as reaction to industrialization, 67–68, 70,
    71–72
  and rise of scientific environmentalism,
    72–74
  space limitations and, 183
  state jurisdiction over, 214n35
  vs. US version, 70, 125
Conservation International, 163
Conwentz, Hugo, 69
Cultural conservation, 179. *See also* Biocul-
    tural restoration
Cultural functions of landscape, importance
    to environmental action, 151
Cultural landscape. *See also* Homeland protec-
    tion (*Heimatschutz*); Nostalgia
  and decolonization, 188
  different historical reference points for, 130
  Elbe River restoration and, 138, 139–140,
    148
  European Green Belt and, 158
  farmers and, 110
  as focus of conservation in Germany, 20,
    68, 70, 71
  general applicability of concept, 188
  German romantic movement and, 67–69,
    70
  and global biodiversity efforts, 171, 188
  Green Belt as, 9–10, 108, 150
  homeland protection (*Heimatschutz*) and,
    82
  and mnemonic ecologies, 183
  preindustrial, public's nostalgia for, 126
  preindustrial, restoration of, 123–126
Cultural memory, 23, 24–25
  adherence in landscape, 26–28
  control by powerful people, 26
  German restoration projects focused on,
    123
  incorporation of constructed past in, 150
  and resentment of drastic environmental
    intervention, 121–122, 127

Decolonization
  cultural landscape concept and, 188
  decolonized conservation, 172–173
  Indigenous-led conservation, 172–174
  as inseparable from conservation work,
    173–174
De-extinction, 26
  of Heck cattle, 128–129
  as impossibility, 146–147
  of Liebenthaler horses, 143, 146
  and spectral ecologies, 26
Demming, Gunter, 207n71
Documentation Center of Cambodia, 162,
  176–177

East Germany. *See* German Democratic
  Republic (GDR)
Ecological art along border
  decay as thematic element in, 91–92
  Tree Cross of Ifta (*Baumkreuz von Ifta*), 85–
    88, *86*, 91–92
  and trees, cultural meaning of, 90–91
  West-East Gate (*West-Östliches Tor*), 88–92,
    89, 156
Ecological communities, traces of past human
  lives in, 15, 31
Ecological corridors and networks
  and closing gaps in Green Belt, 54–55
  Green Belt and, 45, 56
  as new conservation geographies, 16
  political meaning of, 56
  uncertain effectiveness of, 206n55
Ecological ghosts, 146–147
Ecological grief, 33
Ecological instability, climate change and, 172
Ecological memory, 32, 145–146, 147
Ecological work
  conflicts over meaning of a place, 33
  expressions of homeland (*Heimat*) in,
    148–150
  and grief at loss of species or ecosystems, 33
  as necessarily multidisciplinary, 22

Ecological Working Group Coburg, 43
Ecological work in places of traumatic memory
  and choice of historical layers to restore, 29
  emotions stirred up in, 27
  as opportunity for remembrance and
    healing, 27
"Ecologizing of History Must Be Resisted,
  An" (Dietrich), 115
Ecology, as term, and *Naturschutz* vs. *Umweltschutz*, 79
Eco-nostalgia, 33, 124
Ecosystems. *See also* Mnemonic ecologies'
    guidelines for ecosystem restoration;
    Novel ecosystems
  as heterogeneous and permeable, 16
  resilience, ecological memory and, 145
  types of memory in, 122
  use of ecological elements in memorializa-
    tion, 15, 28
Eichsfeld region Green Belt
  as evocative of preindustrial cultural land-
    scape, 123–124
  opposition to, 109–110, 111
  Sielmann Foundation as BUND partner in,
    108–109
Elbe River
  containment in artificial channel, effects of,
    135–136
  East German border fortifications along,
    136–137
  in East Germany, as relatively free from
    modification, 137
  effort to designate as national park, 138–
    140
  fatalities along, 137
  fish stocks, destruction of, 136
  locals' resentment of outside environmental-
    ists, 139–140
  path of flow, 137
  postreunification clean-up of, 136
  restoration of alluvial forests along, as goal,
    139, 141

Elbe River (cont.)

sections designated as UNESCO biosphere reserve, 135, 137–138, 140, 143, 144, 149

segment inside Green Belt, 136, 138

wide natural floodplain and related ecosystems, 134–135

Elbe River rewilding, 138, 141–145

dike relocation and floodplain restoration, 138, 141–144, *142*

ecological past, influence on, 148

environmental toxins and, 144, 145, 220n44

fish species unlikely to return, 146

goals of, 138–139, 141, 144

as *Heimatschutz* (homeland protection), 148

mixed opinion on success of, 143–144

and restoration of alluvial forests, 139, 141, 142–144

size of project, 141

state socialism's influence on environment and, 147

wild horses introduced to maintain meadows, 143, 144, 148

Emotions. *See also* Places, emotions and meanings carried by

importance to conservation, 100–101

patterning of mnemonic ecologies by, 33

taking seriously, in ecosystem restoration, 190–192

Environmental crime, and restorative and transitional justice, 174–176

Environmental ethics of care, 191–192

Environmentalism, scientific

BUND and, 72–73

focus on environmental protection (*Umweltschutz*), 72–73, 74–75, 82

public resentment of, 112

rise of, 72–74

Environmentalism in Germany, 61–64. *See also* Wilderness

conflict with environment's meaning to local people, 151

and multiple threats to biodiversity, 62–64

as part of national identity, 61

and tension between *Naturschutz* and *Umweltschutz*, 78–79

Environmental justice movement, 174

Environmental protection (*Umweltschutz*)

conflict with *Naturschutz* in modern movement, 78–79

deemphasis of *Naturschutz* and *Heimatschutz*, and loss of public's emotional connection, 79–81, 82

turn of German environmentalism toward, 72–73, 74–75, 82

Erlebnis Grünes Band. *See* Green Belt Experience

European Green Belt, 154–161

administrative sections of, *155*, 156

concerns about dehistoricization of border, 158–159

establishment of, 156

and European identity, questions raised about, 159

expected benefits of, 157, 158

former war zones along, 156

hope for tourism in, 157

meaning of, as issue, 158–159

as memorial landscape, gradual turn to, 156–158

path of, along former Iron Curtain, 154–155, *155*

push for UNESCO world heritage site status, 158, 159

Sava River restoration, 157–158

size of, and range of habitats, 156

website for, 157–158

and Yugoslav Wars, 157–158

European Green Belt Association, 156

European Union environmental laws, local resentment of, 110

Expeditionen ins Tierreich (TV show), 45

Extinct species, replacement with engineered organisms. *See* De-extinction

Faraway places (*Fernweh*), German yearning for, 95–96, 131–132

Farmers
opposition to Green Belt land seizures, 109–111, 112–113
resentment of urban control over policy, 110–111

Federal Agency for Nature Conservation (BfN)
on destruction of German floodplains, 135
on Rodachtal-Lange Berge-Steinachtal project, 128
support for Green Belt creation, 52, 54

Federal Conservation Law of 2009, 52

Federal Foundation for the Study of the Communist Dictatorship in Eastern Germany, 39–40

Federal Research Agency for Conservation and Landscape Ecology (BEANL), 48

Federation for Environment and Nature Conservation Germany. *See* BUND (Bund für Umwelt und Naturschutz Deutschland)

Föritz River, restoration of, 43

Franz, Dieter, 5–7, 49

Frobel, Kai, *47*
as acting director of BUND's Nuremberg office, 45
and activism for creation of Green Belt, 64
early studies on Green Belt wildlife, 43–45, *44*, 49
Goldstein and, 96
on memorial function of Green Belt, 59
on postreunification road construction, 64
work on creating Green Belt, 43, 45, 46–48, 49

Fromm, Erich, 33

Gartenschläger, Michael, 96–97, 100

GDR. *See* German Democratic Republic

Generational memory, 24

German conservationism
homeland protection (*Heimatschutz*) in, 69–71, 82
monument protection (*Denkmalschutz*) in, 68–69
romantic movement and, 67–69, 70

German Democratic Republic (GDR). *See also* Border fortifications, East German; Conservation in East Germany
agrarian reform, and farmland confiscation, 38–39
and Christianity, 76, 210n28
coal use, environmental damage from, 75–76, 210n26
flight of farmers, 39
inadequate natural resources, 75
psychic scars left on citizens of, 39–40, 203n13
and redefinition of homeland (*Heimat*), 77, 211n34
West Germans' takeover of management positions, postreunification, 147

Germany, damage to biodiversity from road construction after reunification, 63–64. *See also* Agriculture in Germany; Reunification

Gesellschaft für Ökologie, 19

Ghosts and hauntings. *See also* Ecological ghosts
memories' adherence to landscape and, 26

Goldstein, Mario
career of, 95–96
Green Belt Adventure book and lectures, 96–100, 105, 116

Gorbachev, Mikhail, 51, 89, 156

Green Belt (Grünes Band), *3*. *See also* Open land in Green Belt
activism for creation of, 64–65
ad hoc memorial to murdered GDR border guards, 2–5, *4*
aerial views, *55*, *58*, 118
agencies working on, 7–8

Green Belt (cont.)

agriculture as greatest threat to, 49

as aid to healing in German reunification, 117–118, 125, 152

attraction of rare bird species requiring open land, 6

bird species in, 6, 7

border history for restoration projects, importance of, 147–148

border zone creation, scars of, 123

complex conservation issues in, 8

conservation plans' variation with specific habitat, 65

as conservation/restoration project, in original plan, 15–16

consideration of local needs in planning of, 48

contradictions to be managed in, 7

distinctiveness from surrounding land, *55*

ecological management plan, 56–59

ecological past, influence on, 146

ecological value of, 55–56

environmentalism, composite of old and new, 72

former GDR surveillance tower in, *185*

gaps in corridor, efforts to close, 54–55, 65

gaps in corridor, postreunification road construction and, 63–64

GDR's creation of nature reserves and, 77–78

German conservation traditions, influence on, 67, 69, 70–71, 82

goal for management of, 57–58

and healing needed for full reunification, 8, 13, 117–118, 125, 152

and homeland protection (*Heimatschutz*), 81, 107–108, 118–119, 149–150

inseparability of ecology and memory in, 186–187

linking of biodiversity islands, 56, 57

local residents, importance to, 99–100

local support, aesthetic, emotional, and cultural dimensions of, 126

maintaining as unforested land, ecological benefits of, 6

maintaining Cold War ecological regime as goal of, 65

maintenance required for, 6

management of, as issue, 7

as model for ecological work in war zones, 154

as model for similar projects, 160–162

and nonequilibrium paradigm, landscape-level focus of, 16–17

as novel ecosystem, 34

number of endangered species in, 2

number of habitats in, 2, 7–8, 56

ongoing effect of herbicide use in, 146

postreunification road construction and, 63–64

potential unification of environmental protection and conservation in, 82–83

preference for native species, 149

raising awareness of, with Green Belt Experience, 52–54

as repurposing of border zone, 1

size of, 2, 34

social value of working together on, 56

species dependent on, 46

and tension between *Naturschutz* and *Umweltschutz*, 78

threats to biodiversity in, 62

wetlands in, 6–7, 42

Green Belt, movement to create, 43–52

and competition from other potential land uses, 48, 49–51

development of concept before reunification, 43–46

East Germans' engagement with, 46–48

and ecological corridors concept, 45

emblematic photograph, *42*, 150

federal donation of its Green Belt lands for state government conservation, 51

federal support of, 52

Green Belt Experience tourism and, 52–54

initial meeting of ecologists, 46–48

media campaign, 49, 103–108

report on biotopes and species, 48–49

role of government, initial ambiguity of, 50–51

studies supporting, 43–45, *44*

support from former East German states, 52

Green Belt, opposition to, 109–113

addressing local concerns as strategy to overcome, 113–114

as artificial, not natural, landscape, 112

for de-historicizing the border zone, 115

East Germans' dislike of government compulsion and, 111–112

and emotions in conservation, importance of, 100–101

farmers' resentment of urban control over farm policies, 110–111

homeland protection (*Heimatschutz*) emphasis, lack of, and, 111–112

land seizures, 109–111, 115, 116, 147

local input, lack of, 8, 116

local maintenance costs, and opposition, 115, 121–122, 127

residents' desire to erase traces of border, 49–50

transparency in decisions on, lack of, 115

Green Belt Adventure book and lectures (Goldstein), 96–100, 105, 116

Green Belt as memorial landscape

and "absencing," power of, 92–93

and ad hoc memorials, 6

BUND programs for, 60–61

BUND's emphasis on *Heimat* in, 118–119

decay and "absencing" as thematic element in, 91–93, 95

and ecological art along border, 85–93

emerging memorial sites, 184

and ethicohistorical meaning, sites of, 186

Green Belt Adventure book and lectures (Goldstein), 96–100, 105, 116

increased focus on, as response to opposition, 116–117

and Lenzen Declaration call for projects with historians, 61, 186

meaning, debate over, 184–187

and memory, physical experience of, 187

and nature as healer in German reunification, 117–118

need for curation, 60

open land as most conducive to, 122

physical remnants of border fortifications, 59–60

and remembrance, vehicles of, 150

and remembrance of those killed at border, 96–97, 100

ruin sites as memorials, 93–95

turn to focus on, 15–16, 59–60, 61, 65, 85, 184–186

and visible traces of border zone, 92–93

Green Belt Experience, 52–54

Green Belt maintenance

as assault on homeland (*Heimat*), 126–127

constant work required, 125

local residents' opposition to, 121–122, 126–127

modification of, to assuage local concerns, 127

Green Belt management

areas managed against natural dynamics, 124

creation of wilderness areas (rewilding), 124, 130

human connection with landscape as goal in, 123–126

influences on, past and present, 122

local residents angered by, 127

novel ecosystems in, 123–126

open land (*Offenland*) as priority, 6, 57–58, 122, 124, 126–128

paid and volunteer work on, 126–127

and preservation/restoration of areas evocative of preindustrial cultural landscape, 123–126

Green Belt management (cont.)
  and restoration of areas evocative of ancient
    landscape, 127–130
  variations in, due to differences in ecosys-
    tems, 122–123
*Green Belt: On the Path to a National Nature
  Monument* (BUND video), 104–105
Grief. *See also* Trauma
  acknowledging, in Colombian restoration,
    177
  acknowledgment of, in Green Belt, 8, 82
  attachment to places, 1, 12
  border zone memories and, 1, 7, 35
  ecological, 33
  of Indigenous people, addressing in resto-
    ration, 173
  memory and, 191
  taking seriously, in restoration, 190–191
Große, Heinz-Josef, 96–97, 100
Grzimek, Bernard, 131–132

Harriet Tubman Rural Legacy Area, 179
Heck cattle, *129*
  de-extincting of, 128–129
  as ghost species, 146
  use in restoration projects, 129
Henning, Walter, 111–112
Holocaust memorials, *Stolpersteine* as,
  207n71
Homeland (*Heimat*)
  ecological expressions of, 148–150
  emotional freight of, 70, 80–81, 111–112
  inclusivity of, possibility of broadening, 152
  and nationalism, connection to, 81, 152
  as nostalgia, form of, 148
  VSKE views on, 148
Homeland protection (*Heimatschutz*)
  as desire for return to simpler past, 151–152
  in East German conservationism, 77
  as effective tool for conservationists, 151–
    152
  Elbe River rewilding and, 148
  in German conservationism, 69–71, 82

and German national identity, troubled
    relationship between, 119
  Green Belt's deployment of concept, 81,
    107–108, 118–119, 149–150
  Green Belt's lack of, as source of opposition,
    111–112
  as model for German nation-building, 70
  potential for negative political effects of, 81,
    151–152
  and public's emotional connection to envi-
    ronmentalism, 80–81, 151
  and restoration of areas evocative of ancient
    landscape, 129–130
  taint of National Socialism on, 71, 80
  as unifying concept, 149–150
Human lives, mnemonic ecologies as acciden-
    tal effects of past, 31
Hybrid ecosystems, vs. novel ecosystems, 19, 20

Indigenous and local communities. *See also*
    Decolonization
  recognition and inclusion in conservation,
    171–173
  socioecological memory in, 172
Industrialization, and German romantic
    movement, 67–68, 70, 71–72
Insects, declining numbers in Germany, 62–63
International Union for Conservation of
    Nature (IUCN), 18, 130, 156, 167
Invasive species, debate on, 149
IUCN. *See* International Union for Conserva-
    tion of Nature

Jahrsau village
  BUND's photographs of, emphasizing
    homeland (*Heimat*), 118–119
  East German razing of, 93
  ruins of, as memorial site, 93–95

Kimmerer, Robin Wall, 175
Korean demilitarized zone (DMZ), 159–161
  ecological importance of, 160
  fortifications, described, 159

land use patterns in North vs. South, 160
South Koreans postreunification plans for,
    160–161

Landesbeauftrager zur Aufarbeitung der SED-
    Diktatur, 115
Landscape. *See also* Layered landscapes;
    Traumatic memories adhering to places of
    violence
    ecological history's influence on, 145
    ecological memory and, 145–146
    in Germany, as highly domesticated, 61
    humans as cocreators of, 15, 31, 188
    memories' adherence to, 25–28
    of postviolence, 161–167
    as term, evocation of idyllic cultural land-
        scape, 126
Land use by previous generations, traces of
    mnemonic ecologies resulting from, 31–32
    responsibility to respond to, 32
Layered landscapes
    biological and cultural history in, 28–29
    Green Belt as, 15, 34
    militarized landscapes and, 29
    mnemonic ecologies in investigation of, 183
    as model for other war-zone conservation
        projects, 161–162
    and restoration choices, 29
Left, German, and rise of environmentalism,
    72–73
Lenzen Declaration (2019), 61, 152, 186
Liebenthaler horses, 143, 146
Limits to Growth (Club of Rome), 72, 76
Living Planet Report (World Wildlife Fund),
    167
Local people and realities
    burden of biodiversity conservation on,
        169–170
    damage to sense of belonging from radical
        ecological intervention, 121–122
    diversity and complexity of, 189
    recognition and inclusion of, 171–173,
        188–190

resentment of outside environmentalists,
    110, 139–140, 151
Local people and realities, and Green Belt
    addressing local concerns to overcome
        opposition, 113–114
    aesthetic, emotional, and cultural dimen-
        sions of local views, 126
    consideration of local needs in planning
        of, 48
    disruptive maintenance, opposition to,
        121–122, 126–127
    importance to local residents, 99–100
    lack of local input, opposition to, 8, 116
    maintenance costs, opposition to, 115
    modification of maintenance, in response to
        local concern, 127
Loss of species or ecosystems, and grief, 33
Lovejoy, Thomas, 169

Māori in New Zealand, and decolonized
    conservation, 172–173
Mauergrundstückgesetz (MauerG). *See* Wall
    Property Law of 1996
May, Karl, 131
Meanings carried by places. *See* Places, emo-
    tions and meanings carried by
Media, and Green Belt as aid to healing,
    117–118
Memorialization. *See also* Green Belt as
    memorial landscape
    and healing of traumatic memories adhering
        to places of violence, 28
    state-sponsored, reevaluation of, in light of
        local realities, 189
    tensions between past and present in, 28
    use of ecological elements for, 15, 28
    vernacular forms of, 5, 12, 164, 189
Memory. *See also* Places, emotions and
    meanings carried by; Traumatic memories
    adhering to places of violence
    as carried by images, rituals, and monu-
        ments, 25
    collective, types of, 23–25

Memory (cont.)
    decolonized conservation as act of, 173
    and ecological memorialization, 15, 28,
        150–152
    and *Erinnerungsarbeit* (memory work) in
        Green Belt, 116–117
    Green Belt as embodiment of, 150
    and grief, 191
    individual characteristics of, 23
    individual interaction with collective mem-
        ory, 23–24
    structuring of human identity and interac-
        tions, 23
Memory work (*Erinnerungsarbeit*)
    connection to *Aufarbeitung* (reckoning with
        the past), 178
    in Green Belt, 116–117
    nature of, 117–119
    US and, 178
Merkel, Angela, 81
Militarized land, conversion to wild lands,
    and layered landscape, 29
Mnemonic ecologies. *See also* BUND, and
        Green Belt as memorial landscape; Green
        Belt as memorial landscape
    in animals and plants, 32
    creation by ruin and decay, 31
    as entire field of inquiry, 30
    and Indigenous and local communities,
        recognition and inclusion of, 171–173
    inevitability of, in war-ravaged areas, 163–
        164, 166–167
    as inter- and multidisciplinary pursuit, 10,
        22, 34, 180
    and legacy of former land use, 31–32
    and legacy of prior human lives, 31
    local need for healing preempting, 191
    meaning in, collapse and reinterpretation
        of, 30–31
    and memories' adherence to place, 25–28, 30
    and memory as foundational human expe-
        rience, 23

    as new field, 183
    as patterned by emotions, 33
    as product of human and more-than-human
        agency, 122
    as result of explicit commemorative prac-
        tices, 30–31
    and ties between ecological communities
        and memory, 30
    urgency and importance of insights, 183
Mnemonic ecologies and social justice, 173–
        179
    in Cambodia, 176–177
    in Colombia, 177–178
    conservation work and social justice as
        inseparable, 173–174, 191
    contingent, open-ended relationship
        between, 176
    and differences in experience and memory,
        180
    environmental justice movement and, 174
    and justice as affective and embodied, 176
    life- and landscape-altering potential of,
        179–180
    and memory's entanglement with other
        human domains, 180
    and restoration's greater focus on human-
        environment interaction, 180–181
    and restorative and transitional justice,
        174–176
    in United States, 178–179
Mnemonic ecologies' guidelines for ecosystem
        restoration, 187–192
    broad coalitions needed in, 190–191
    and environmental ethics of care, 191–192
    planetary future of life, joy, and love as goal
        of, 192
Mnemonic ecologies in former war zones.
        See also Cambodia; Colombia; European
        Green Belt; Korean demilitarized zone
        (DMZ)
    German Green Belt as model for, 154
    need for, 153–154

Murdered border-crossers, remembrance of, in Green Belt, 96–97, 100

National Geographic, 168
National identity, German, and homeland (*Heimat*) concept, 119
National parks, US
  implication in US genocide and land theft, 169–170, 178
  as model for global conservation, 169–170
National Strategy for Biodiversity, 132
Natura 2000, 110
Natural landscapes, layers of biological and cultural history in, 28–29
Natural monuments preservation (*Denkmalschutz*), in German conservationism, 68–69, 71, 82
Nature, different types of, produced by emotions and meanings of places, 183. *See also* Ecosystems; Wilderness
Nature Conservancy, 178
Nature Conservation Law (2010), 102
Nature monument. *See* BUND campaign to make Green Belt a nature monument
Nature Monument Law, in Thuringia
  debate in Thuringian parliament on, 114–115
  legal challenge to, 116
  modification in response to criticisms, 116–117
  passage of, 117
Nature preservation (*Naturschutz*)
  environmental protection (*Umweltschutz*) and, 74–75, 78–79
  and German conservationism, 71, 82
  and public's emotional connection to environmentalism, 79–80
Nostalgia. *See also* Homeland protection (*Heimatschutz*)
  eco-nostalgia, 33, 124
  German romantic movement and, 67–69, 70

Green Belt and, 72, 119, 124
  homeland (*Heimat*) concept as form of, 148
  for preindustrial cultural landscape, 126
Novel ecosystems, 19–22
  criticisms of, 199n24
  definition of, 19–21, 25
  development in border zone, 40–43
  German version of concept, 20
  German wilderness and, 132–134
  historical reference conditions as issue in, 20, 21
  human agency as operating factor in, 20, 21–22
  vs. hybrid ecosystems, 19, 20
  target state for, as issue, 21
Novel ecosystems in Green Belt
  creation by violence, 123
  maintaining of, 123–127
  as refuge for rare and endangered species, 123
Nuclear war threat, and rise of German environmentalism, 72, 73

Omnibus for Direct Democracy, 87
Oostvaardersplassen project (Netherlands), 144–145
Open land in Green Belt
  as assault on homeland (*Heimat*), 126–127
  constant work required to maintain, 125
  definition of, 57
  local residents' resentment of measures to maintain, 121–122, 127
  modification of maintenance to assuage local concerns, 127
  as most conducive to memorial functions, 122
  as most significant characteristic of Green Belt, 57
  and preservation of border zone traces, 57–58, *58*
  and shortage of open land in Germany, 57
  use of animals to maintain, 128–129, *129*

Pan-European Bird Monitoring Scheme, 63
Places, emotions and meanings carried by.
   See also Mnemonic ecologies; Traumatic
   memories adhering to places of violence
   different kinds of nature produced by, 183
   and identity, 127
   and mnemonic ecologies, 25–28, 30
Plants
   ancient, in restorations of ancient landscape,
   130
   and mnemonic ecologies, 32
   native (*beheimatet*) vs. invasive (*gebietsfremd*), 149
Prussian State Office for Natural Monument
   Care, 69

Ramsar Wetlands Convention of 1976, 135
Refugee influx in Germany, and homeland
   (*Heimat*) concept, 81
Reissenweber, Frank, 49
Restoration, biocultural, 175–176, 179
Restoration ecology. *See also* Mnemonic ecologies' guidelines for ecosystem restoration
   vs. conservation, 16, 17, 19, 180
   criticisms of, 199n24
   definition of, 17–18, 25
   disciplines used by, 17
   ecological and social history's influence on,
   145
   historical fidelity as issue in, 21
   history of, 198n4
   human-environment interaction, focus on,
   180–181
   integration of human practices into, 17,
   21, 22
   moral component of, 22
   recovery of past ecosystems, focus on,
   17–18
   and sense of history, importance of, 21–22
   and separation of supportive and controlling
   kinds of care, 191–192
   standards for, 18

taking emotions seriously in, 190–192
as type of reckoning with the past (*Aufarbeitung*), 191
Restoration ecology in Germany
   history of, 19
   and homeland protection (*Heimatschutz*),
   129–130
   as part of broader "conservationist" concept,
   19
   as *Renaturierung* ("renaturing"), 19
   US scholarship driving, 19
Restorative and transitional justice, 174–176
Restored ecosystem, definition and characteristics of, 18
Reunification
   and damage to biodiversity from new road
   construction, 63–64
   demolition of border, 59
   East German creation of nature reserves
   prior to, 77–78
   Elbe River clean-up after, 136
   environmentalism after, 77–78, 82
   Green Belt as aid to healing in, 8, 13, 117–
   118, 125, 152
   Green Belt meaning in context of, 45, 56,
   88–92, 117–119
   Green Belt planning prior to, 43–46
   and lingering tensions, 99, 147
   local people's dismantling of border fortifications after, 59
   uses of border zone immediately after, 49–50
   West Germans' takeover of East German
   management positions after, 147
Road construction after reunification, damage
   to biodiversity, 63–64
Rodach river, renaturing of, 7
Rodachtal-Lange Berge-Steinachtal project,
   127–130
   mosaic of habitats in, 128
   number of endangered species in, 128
   use of animals to maintain open land,
   128–129

Romantic movement, German conservation-
ism and, 67–69, 70
Rudorff, Ernst, 70
Ruin and decay, mnemonic ecologies created
by, 31
Ruin sites as Green Belt memorials, 93–95

Sembrando Paz, 177
Serengeti Shall Not Die (Grzimek), 131–132
7000 Oaks (Beuys), 87
Sielmann, Heinz, 45
Sielmann Foundation
as BUND Green Belt partner in Eichsfield
region, 108–109
and opposition to Green Belt, 109–110
Silent Spring (Carson), 72
Social justice. *See* Mnemonic ecologies and
social justice
Society for Ecological Restoration, 17–18,
19, 21
Solastalgia, 33
Species
Indigenous perspective on losses of, 173
native (*beheimatet*) vs. invasive (*gebiets-
fremd*), 149
Stasi (*Ministerium für Staatssicherheit*; GDR
Ministry for State Security)
border facilities, still-visible ruins of, 60
interrogation of attempted escapees, 96
role of, 206n63
suppression of environmentalism, 76–77
targeting of border critics, 97
Stiftung Naturschutz Thüringen. *See*
Thuringia Foundation for Conservation
Stolpersteine memorials, 207n71
potential use in Green Belt, 61
Succow, Michael, 77

30x30 biodiversity conservation movement,
168–169
Thüringer Landgesellschaft (ThLG), 113–
114, 216n57

Thuringia. *See also* Nature Monument Law,
in Thuringia; Rodachtal-Lange Berge-
Steinachtal project
and border zone establishment, 35, 36
conservation groups in, 102–103
leadership in Green Belt creation, 51–52
as state with largest amount of Green Belt
lands, 51, 52
Thuringia, Green Belt in
addressing local concerns to overcome
opposition, 113–114
author's visit to, 1–8
and BUND's campaign to gain nature
monument status, 102–103
BUND's effort to win support for, 99–
100
opposition to, 109–113
residents' opposition to aggressive maintenance, 121
and tourism, 52
Thuringia Foundation for Conservation, 51,
103
Töpfer, Klaus, 49
Trace in the Landscape (*Spur in der Landschaft*)
(BUND booklet), 105, 106
Trägerverbund Burg Lenzen. *See* Castle Lenzen Association
Trauma
attached to places, 28–29, 157, 163–164,
166–167
collective/cultural, 27, 201n40
memory as key to resolution of, 27
psychic scars left on GDR citizens, 39–40,
203n13
somatic experience and resolution of, 98
typical reactions to, 27
Traumatic memories adhering to places of
violence, 1. *See also* Ecological work in
places of traumatic memory; Grief
and ghosts and hauntings, 26–27
and layered landscapes, 28–29
memory as key to resolution of, 27–28

Tree Cross of Ifta (Baumkreuz von Ifta), 85–88, 86, 91–92

Truth and reconciliation commissions, 175

Umweltschutz. See Environmental protection

Union der Opferverbände kommunistischer Gewaltherrschaft. *See* Union of Victims' Associations of Communist Tyranny

Union of Victims' Associations of Communist Tyranny, 60

United Nations
  biodiversity assessment, 167
  Conference on the Human Environment (Stockholm, 1972), 72
  Convention on Biological Diversity, 161, 168–169
  Decade on Ecosystem Restoration, 187
  UNESCO biosphere reserve status, Elbe River and, 135, 137–138, 140, 143, 144, 149
  UNESCO biosphere reserve status for European Green Belt, 158, 159

United States
  and cultural conservation, 179
  Harriet Tubman Rural Legacy Area, 179
  mnemonic ecologies and social justice in, 178–179
  National Park Service, 178
  reckoning with racist origins, as just begun, 178
  and remaking of rememberable past, 178

Urban growth in Germany, damage to biodiversity, 63

Verein zum Schutz der Kulturlandschaft und des Eigentums im Elbtal (VSKE). *See* Association for the Protection of the Cultural Landscape and Property in the Elbe Valley (VSKE)

Wall Property Law of 1996, 50

Wars. *See also* Mnemonic ecologies in former war zones

in high-biodiversity areas, 153
  need for conservation/restoration in regions ravaged by, 153

We for Wildness (Wir für Wildnis), 132–133

Weiger, Hubert, 46–48, *47*, 204n29

Weinzierl, Hubert, 73, 79

West-East Gate (West-Östliches Tor), 88–92, *89*, 156

Wiedervernetzung program, 64

Wilderness
  appeal as escape from modern life, 130–131, 132
  definitions of, 130–131

Wilderness creation (rewilding). *See also* Elbe River rewilding
  definition of *wilderness* in, 133–134, 144–145
  ecological and social history's influence on, 145
  in Germany, 132–134
  in Green Belt, 320
  Oostvaardersplassen project (Netherlands), 144–145
  organizations spearheading, 132–133

Wildlife Conservation Society, 163

Wilson, Edward O., 33, 168

Wir für Wildnis. *See* We for Wildness

Woodley, Stephen, 169

World Commission on Protected Areas, 18

World Conservation Strategy, 170

World Wildlife Fund, 163, 167, 170

Wyss Foundation, 168

Yugoslav Wars
  European Green Belt and, 157–158
  and local remembrance, 189